Making Peace

with Being

on Earth

Kim Michaels

The Avatar Revelations, vol 5

Making Peace with Being on Earth

Kim Michaels
More to Life

Making Peace with Being on Earth

Copyright © 2019 Kim Michaels. All rights reserved. No part of this book may be used, reproduced, translated, electronically stored or transmitted by any means except by written permission from the publisher. A reviewer may quote brief passages in a review.

MORE TO LIFE PUBLISHING

www.morepublish.com

For foreign and translation rights,
contact: info@ morepublish.com

ISBN: 978-87-93297-57-9

The information and insights in this book should not be considered as a form of therapy, advice, direction, diagnosis, and/or treatment of any kind. This information is not a substitute for medical, psychological, or other professional advice, counseling and care. All matters pertaining to your individual health should be supervised by a physician or appropriate health-care practitioner. No guarantee is made by the author or the publisher that the practices described in this book will yield successful results for anyone at any time. They are presented for informational purposes only, as the practice and proof rests with the individual.

Content

Introduction   7
1 | Living with what you cannot live with   9
2 | Invoking freedom from adaptation   19
3 | Experiencing yourself on earth   35
4 | Invoking the memory of why I came here   49
5 | Claiming your God-given right to forget   79
6 | Invoking my God-given right to forget   91
7 | Being creative in a quantum world   111
8 | Invoking quantum creativity   127
9 | Teaching yourself to erase memories   151
10 | Invoking the erasing of memories   167
11 | Speaking out from a state of peace   193
12 | Invoking peace with Speaking out   205
13 | Grasping the radical nature of mercy   221
14 | Invoking radical forgiveness   241
15 | Invoking freedom from taking life personally   261
16 | You are not a slave of time   285
17 | Invoking an experience of ongoingness   309
18 | Invoking freedom from the slavery of time   329
19 | A question about time   355

INTRODUCTION

This book is one of the workbooks building on the novel *My Lives with Lucifer, Satan, Hitler and Jesus*. The novel introduces the idea that many spiritual people have come to earth as volunteers or "avatars." We have then received deep spiritual traumas as a result of what we have experienced here. Many of us still carry these traumas with us, and it can explain why we sometimes can feel as if we are not making progress on the spiritual path or why there are certain issues we cannot overcome. How to overcome these traumas is explained (along with practical exercises) in the book *Healing Your Spiritual Traumas*.

This book contains further teachings on these concepts, but it also explains how to make a number of shifts so you can uncover your original purpose for coming to earth and make peace with being here.

Please note that it is recommended that you read the novel and work through *Healing Your Spiritual Traumas* before using this book. The reason is that these books contain many important teachings that can help you make use of this book

This book contains a number of invocations that you are meant to give aloud. If you are not familiar with giving such invocations, you can find further teachings and instructions on the website *www.transcendencetoolbox.com*. You can also give the invocations along with a recording and you can purchase recordings of the invocations in this book on the website *www.morepublish.com*.

1 | LIVING WITH WHAT YOU CANNOT LIVE WITH

I AM the Ascended Master Mother Mary, and it is my great joy and my great privilege to open this conference and welcome you, those who are here physically; those who are connected via the internet. The topic that was originally proposed for this conference was: "How to help people in Eastern Europe be at peace," but we felt that it was not just a matter of people here in Eastern Europe who could benefit from the teachings we wanted to give. Surely, people everywhere have trouble being at peace with being on earth. My beloved, what we desire to accomplish with this conference is to give you some teachings that are not just for avatars, not just for ascended master students, but in the long run can be for all people on earth, even the original inhabitants of the earth or those who have come here from other planets that have fallen below their natural level.

Rethinking what is normal

Naturally my beloved, you have grown up on earth and most of you have grown up with an image that perhaps earth is the only planet in the universe that has any form of life. Perhaps it is a very important planet for God—if you grew up in a Christian environment. Perhaps you have grown up thinking that you are an evolved ape and the chances of life occurring are so small that they probably only happen on very few planets. Because you have grown up with this view that earth might be the only planet, you have, without realizing it, come to accept a lot of the conditions that you see on earth. This does not mean that you have accepted them as good but you might have accepted them as normal, as natural or as inevitable, as unavoidable. "This is just the way things are."

This, of course, relates to the teachings we have given you over the years that once you are trapped in a dualistic state of consciousness, you cannot get out of it unless you have a frame of reference that shows you that there is something outside of that state of consciousness, there is a different way to look at life. My beloved, it is natural, when you have grown up in the current environment on earth, that you have not been given such a frame of reference. You have not been told, for example, that there are natural planets where many of the phenomena you see on earth are not manifest, are not occurring. You have grown up feeling that there is no point in even questioning what is going on, on earth because that is obviously the way things are. What you have to do is just find a way to live with it.

Adaptability is a blessing and a curse

You see my beloved, here we are touching upon a topic that is, in a sense, both a blessing and a curse. It is, of course, something that relates to some degree to what the evolutionists talk about, how a species adapts to its environment. Even though there are many evolutionists who always champion the credo of the survival of the fittest, if you actually look at evolutionary history, you will see that the fittest are actually not the strongest, not the most aggressive, as some of these evolutionists want you to think. No my beloved, the fittest are the most *adaptable.* The reason human beings have spread to all corners of the earth and have, at least from an evolutionary standpoint, been the most successful species on earth is that human beings are more adaptable than any other species that you see on earth. Now, why are human beings more adaptable than any animal species? Because humans are not animals. You are not actually one step up from the apes, as the evolutionists want you to think. You are a quantum leap above the apes because you have self-awareness, and it is precisely this self-awareness that makes it possible for human beings to adapt to so many different conditions.

1 | Living with what you cannot live with

An animal species is largely programmed to behave a certain way. This means that the animal, if it finds itself in a hostile environment, cannot step back and say: "How do I need to change my behavior in order to survive in this environment?" Nor can it, for that matter, step back and say: "How can I change the environment so I can survive in that environment?" An animal species does not have this ability. Human beings do, which demonstrates to anyone who is willing to look at facts that human beings are not animals. You are not further evolved animals because you cannot find an animal that has this ability to a lower degree than humans. I know some will come up with examples but the reality is that you cannot find an animal species that has a lower degree of self-awareness than humans so that from the level of awareness that the animal has, you can gradually evolve to the human level. In order to get from even the highest animal species to humans, you have to make a quantum leap because you have to be given that self awareness from a higher source—it cannot evolve.

The adaptability of human beings is a *blessing* in the sense that you can adapt to many different environments. It is also a *curse* in a sense that it is this ability that makes it possible to look at the current conditions of earth and decide: "Oh, I just have to live with it. I can't possibly change it. There's no point in even questioning it. I just have to make the best of it." Therefore, human beings have, over the course of history, adapted to many conditions that they actually could have changed if they had the awareness that this was possible, the vision of how things could be changed and the willingness to implement it. It is precisely this ability that the fallen beings have used to control the population over and over again, in civilization after civilization, even going far beyond current history. What you currently see as history is, of course, a manipulation of the fallen beings where they do not want you to know the past history of civilizations that have disappeared and that were more highly evolved than the present one.

The reason for this is, again, they do not want you to have the frame of reference that there have been civilizations in the past who were far more evolved than the current civilization but they collapsed because of the influence of the fallen beings. Therefore, it is also possible for your civilization, not only to evolve further but it is also possible for your civilization to decline—if you do allow the fallen beings to continue to run everything. They do not want you to have that frame of reference, which could actually be given to you if you knew the history of past civilizations. They want you to believe that you are a species with a very short lifespan, whether it be the few million years recognized by science, or the 6,000 years recognized by fundamentalist Christians or the also very short lifespan recognized by most religious people who believe in the Old Testament and think that God created the earth not so long ago in its present form. Naturally, God (as the highest being in the universe, what we call the Creator) did not create the earth in its present form because God surely could have envisioned a planet where war, mayhem, torture and all of these other things do not occur.

My beloved, what I am telling you here as spiritual people – as avatars, as those who are the original inhabitants of the earth who have started raising your awareness – is very simple. You have inherited from your species, from the collective consciousness, from your parents, from previous generations, this ability to adapt to material conditions, to accept conditions for what they are and find a way to live with them. This is an ability that in some ways has served humankind, but for you who are spiritual people, there comes that point in your growth where you have to take a look at this and decide: "I am going to raise myself above this collective momentum of adapting to physical conditions." What is it we have been telling you throughout the years in our teachings? You are not here to accept current conditions and adapt to them. You are here to raise current conditions, to raise the collective and even to raise the physical conditions. You cannot do that if you are an adaptive animal. You can do it only when you recognize you are a spiritual being and you decide: "I am going to raise myself above this ability to accept current conditions and adapt to them."

The condition you cannot live with

In order to fully understand this, in order to implement what I am telling you, you need to have the background that we have so carefully given you, starting even before but certainly at the conference here in Estonia last year with the teachings on the birth trauma and the primal self [In the book *Healing Your Spiritual Traumas*]. Whether you are an avatar or whether you are one of the original inhabitants of the earth, there came that point where you were exposed to such severe conditions that you had that birth trauma, or earth trauma, as we have called it for the original inhabitants of the earth. Then, you created that primal self that is a reactionary self. What you need to begin to contemplate here is that whether you are an original inhabitant or an avatar, once you come to a certain awareness, you know within you that things do not have to be the way they are on earth. There

1 | Living with what you cannot live with

is an alternative; things could be better. You may not be able to formulate this in words, you may not have even a clear conscious awareness of it but you have some frame of reference that the things that are going on here on earth are not the highest possible.

Now, the curious thing about this is – and it is most clear in an avatar so I will use this as an example – that as an avatar you come into your first embodiment on earth, and even though you do not retain the conscious memory of what it was like to be on a natural planet, you still have a strong sense that many of the things you encounter on earth are not the highest possible, that there is an alternative. Things do not have to be that way. Here you are, you are now, so to speak (because that is how most of us feel), trapped in this dense physical body in this dense physical world. You are surrounded by other people who also have physical bodies and who, regardless of how you feel, regardless of what you think, have the ability to hurt you, to use *their* physical bodies to harm *your* physical body.

There is nothing you can do about this once you are in the physical body. No matter what was done to you, even being in the physical body and looking at, experiencing, what is happening on earth, there is nothing you can do about that. We have said before that you can be an avatar who is looking down on earth and you decide that you want to take embodiment here and you can, of course, see that there are many conditions that are not right but you cannot experience those conditions from a distance. You will not truly experience what the earth is like until you are trapped, stuck in a physical body. Once you are here, once you are in that physical body, you suddenly experience what the earth is like. You even experience the energies that are here that are so dense, the collective consciousness is so dense, there is so much aggression, so much hatred, so much fear. You experience this in a way you could never even imagine as an avatar. The reality of it is that part of the shock that you experience is that there is a certain condition that most likely was one of the conditions, or maybe the primary condition, you looked at before you came to earth and you decided you wanted to help remove that condition from the earth. You now are in the body, you are experiencing this condition and when you experience how intense it is (how heavy it is, how difficult it is), then the reaction that you have is: "I can't live with this. I can't live with this condition being present on earth."

It may not be as described in the *My Lives* book that you are personally tortured. Not all of you were exposed to this kind of radical personal attack. Some of you experienced a shock just by seeing how other people are living and how they are suffering. As an avatar you have never encountered this on a natural planet and you do not feel that anyone should ever be exposed to this kind of condition. Therefore, your reaction is: "I can't live with this condition existing on this planet, I can't live with being in an environment where this condition is existing."

This is your reaction. You literally withdraw into yourself. You are so shocked that it is almost like you tried to pull your entire aura back inside to some safe spot where you can forget that this condition exists. Yet, you cannot do this because you are (as I said) stuck in the physical body. There is no way out of the physical body. As this initial shock begins to dissipate a little bit, you are faced with this very stark reality. Everything in your emotional body, your mental body and your identity body tells you: "I can't live on this planet when this condition is here. I can't live with this." Yet, your physical body, when it gets hungry enough, tells you that you *have* to live on this planet and you have to do what it takes to keep the physical body alive.

Seeing the body as an enemy

This is where many of you experience a certain split between the physical body and the three higher bodies. It is almost as if you have to create some kind of barrier between the physical and the three higher bodies in order to protect the higher bodies from what is going on in the physical realm, maybe even what your physical body experiences. If you were exposed to torture, for example, you would have to create this barrier so that the pain of the physical body did not have quite as dramatic of an impact on the three other bodies. Most of you created this division that you are still carrying around. You can see how, throughout the ages, spiritual people have looked at the body as an enemy of their spiritual growth. They have talked about the lusts of the body, the lust for food, the lust for sex, the lust for whatever, and they have seen that as an enemy of their spiritual growth.

This is based on this initial shock where you, as a defense mechanism, attempt to create this barrier. You realized, of course, to some degree that your physical body is in the physical realm and other people have their physical bodies. They can come and hurt your physical body but they cannot quite as easily hurt your three higher bodies. If you can project or create a barrier, you can protect yourself to some degree. What I am telling you is that you have all been exposed to this very mechanism and you have felt: "I can't live with this condition on earth." The stark reality is you *have* to live here on earth. What do you do? How do you respond to this? As I said, you often do it by tying in to the collective adaptation mechanism that has been created by other people in your family, in your nation, in your culture, in your civilization—even in the species as a whole, as we might say, in the collective consciousness as a whole. You tie in to this and you realize that when you are on a planet like this, you just have to adapt. You just have to accept conditions for what they are and make the best of it. Somehow, deep within your subconscious, you made a decision: "I can't live with this but I *have* to live with this and in order to live with it, I have to accept this or that belief."

You might have accepted that it is inevitable, that there is no way around it, that if you do certain things, you can avoid the condition that you cannot live with. You can avoid experiencing it yourself, you can insulate yourself from the condition. You see many people in the more developed nations who have insulated themselves from the very fact that there are many conditions taking place in third-world countries. You see, for example, many people in the developed nations who, if their own children were starving or malnourished, they could not live with that, but they *can* live with the fact that millions of children in the third-world countries are starving and malnourished. I am not, again, blaming people. I am just saying there is an example of the mechanism where you can insulate yourself from the condition so that you can still live on this planet, you can still function on the planet.

The survival mechanism

What we get to here is that this is simply a survival mechanism. It can even be a physical survival mechanism where you try to insulate yourself so that you are not taking embodiment in an area of the earth where there is more war, where there are certain diseases, where there is starvation and this and that. For most of you, it is primarily an emotional, mental, identity level survival mechanism so that you can exist on a planet where the condition exists that you cannot live with. Because you are somewhat insulated from it and not directly exposed to it personally, then you can live with it being on the planet—just somewhere else, not where *you* are.

Now, again, my beloved, we are not saying this to blame you in any way. We have all been in embodiment on earth and we all did exactly the same thing in order to be able to live here. What we are saying is that those of you who have followed these teachings up until this point, you are ready to take a look at this. You are ready to take a look at these survival mechanisms and you are ready to begin to raise yourself above it so that you can live on earth without just surviving. You are actually at peace with being on earth and you can, because you are at peace, enjoy life on earth. You can even enjoy expressing yourself, your real self, here on earth.

Naturally my beloved, when you came here, if you are an avatar (but even an original inhabitant) you all had a desire to express your real being, your real creativity on earth and you know that this is the only way the earth will improve. The only way you can help advance the earth is by expressing who you really are, expressing the creativity of your I AM Presence.

When you created this survival mechanism, you basically said: "As long as this condition, that I cannot live with, exists on earth, I can't express myself freely, I can't be creative." Many of you have even felt a certain, we might call it, solidarity with the people on earth who are suffering. Many of you have created a mechanism very, very deep in your subconscious where you have compassion for a particular group of people that are suffering from a particular condition. You have basically decided at some point: "I can't be at peace, I can't be happy, I can't be creative, I can't express myself as long as these people are suffering from this condition."

Shutting off creativity is not the solution

My beloved, it is a very understandable reaction. As I said, we have all gone into it. Those of us who ascended have also come to a point where we have realized that, even though it is *understandable*, it is not a *constructive* reaction because why did you come to earth as an avatar? Oh, you want to remove the condition of, for example, war. How could you possibly make a contribution to removing war? Well, only by expressing the creativity of your higher being. If you shut off that creativity (out of some feeling of solidarity with people who are suffering), you are also shutting off the possibility that you can do what you came for. You are not going to help remove war by suffering like other people are suffering, nor are you going to help remove war by cutting off your creativity and going into a state where you live a basically joyless existence because you feel you cannot be happy when other people are suffering. This is not the way that you remove the condition that you came here to help remove.

You see my beloved, again, if you are to have a positive impact on earth, you cannot do it by thinking about or by looking at the problem the same way everybody else looks at the problem. You cannot help overcome a problem, a condition, by adapting to that condition, as everybody else is doing. We need you to start pondering this and start looking at, as I have said before: "What are the conditions that disturb me the most on earth? What are the conditions that disturb me the most?" Nada said this in her book [*The Mystical Initiations of Peace*] where she had you go through this exercise but we have also in a greater context asked you to look at this. I am asking you again. I am asking you even as a group here to go through this, have a discussion about this. What are the conditions here on earth that you feel deep within your being that you cannot live with? Then, perhaps even discuss how you have found a way to still live on earth while this condition exists and what you have to do to get to that point. Then, you can begin to consider how can you free yourself from that condition.

You see my beloved, again, it is very, very important for you to recognize what we have said here. When you came to earth (whether you are an avatar or whether you were an original inhabitant who was exposed to the fallen beings for the first time), you had a certain level of consciousness. This was a long time ago and by being on earth (even though you may have, as I said, adapted to certain conditions, even though you may have seemingly gone into a negative spiral), you have still gained a different perspective and greater maturity by living on a planet like this. That means you can now look at your original decision for how you decided to adapt to conditions on earth. You can look at it from a greater perspective. You can see how it is limiting you, and therefore you can come to that point where you can identity this as a self. You created a self that enabled you to live on earth when this condition was here, but this self also has the function of cutting off your creativity. You can come to identify that self, look at it from the outside, realize it is not you and therefore you can make the decision to just let it die.

Being free of the problem without solving the problem

Take note of everything we have said. This self may think that you cannot be at peace on earth as long as a certain condition exists. Therefore, the self might project at you that you have to solve the condition before you can be at peace, but, as we have said, this is not the case. You – the

Conscious You – can come to see that this is just a self that is projecting this illogical decision at you, and you can decide: "This is not the decision that I want to define me, define my life on earth, anymore." You can decide to just let the self die without having to solve the problem that the self projects you have to solve.

Therefore my beloved, my first task, my first assignment to you for this conference, is to have a discussion about these topics. First of all, identify the conditions you cannot live with. Be aware, my beloved, that as part of this adaptation mechanism, many of you, who are spiritual people, you have come to feel that you need to be positive, you need to have a positive outlook on life on earth. Therefore, you tend to deny sometimes your negative feelings. You go into denial about it, you push them under the rug, so to speak, and you do not recognize that you have it. It is perfectly acceptable, as even Gautama Buddha said, for you to acknowledge that you have certain very intense feelings about certain conditions on earth. It is perfectly acceptable to bring this to your conscious awareness so you can make the calls on the energy, dissipate the energy. Therefore, you come to see the self that is creating these feelings and just let the self die—eventually.

You cannot do this if you always want to maintain in the extreme sense of some New Age people: "It's all good." As we have said before, you cannot be a thinking person, look at conditions on earth and say it is all good because it clearly is not. You know this as ascended master students but you still have, sometimes, unrecognized feelings that you are not really willing to acknowledge because it scares you a little bit. You do not know what to do with it but what I am telling you is this: Recognize the feelings; it is part of your assignment for this conference. We will help you, as we move along, to deal with it, overcome it and be free of it so that you can be at peace with being on this earth. Therefore, by being at peace, you can actually make a contribution to removing a certain condition.

Therefore, I thank you for this opening dictation, for being here, for being at the conference, being willing to be part of this Mandala. You can do something for the collective consciousness that really has never been done in this way before by a group of people, who are willing to do this consciously in the physical octave. For this, I thank you.

2 | INVOKING FREEDOM FROM ADAPTATION

In the name I AM THAT I AM, Jesus Christ, I call to all representatives of the Divine Mother, especially Mother Mary, to help me overcome all conditions in my psychology that cause me to adapt to circumstances and shut off my creativity, including…

[Make personal calls.]

Part 1

1. As I grew up, I came to accept a lot of the conditions on earth as normal, as natural or as inevitable. I took on some sense that: "This is just the way things are."

> O Blessed Mary's Song of Life,
> consuming every form of strife.
> As I attune to sound so fair,
> each cell is healthy, I declare.

**O Mother Mary, generate,
the song that does accelerate,
my mind into a peaceful state,
God's perfect love I radiate.**

2. As I grew up in the current environment on earth, I was not given a frame of reference, showing me that there are other planets where many of the phenomena on earth are not manifest.

As life's own song I ever hear,
it does consume all sense of fear.
In tune with Mother's symphony,
from all diseases I AM free.

**O Mother Mary, generate,
the song that does accelerate,
my mind into a peaceful state,
God's perfect love I radiate.**

3. As I grew up, I was given the feeling that there is no point in questioning what is going on, because that is obviously the way things are and I simply had to find a way to live with it.

In Mother's love I do transcend,
and all my struggles hereby end.
For when with Mother's eye I see,
no imperfection touches me.

**O Mother Mary, generate,
the song that does accelerate,
my mind into a peaceful state,
God's perfect love I radiate.**

4. The adaptability of human beings is a *blessing* in the sense that I can adapt to many different environments. It is also a *curse* in a sense that it is this ability that makes it possible to look at the current conditions of earth and decide: "Oh, I just have to live with it. I can't possibly change it. There's no point in even questioning it. I just have to make the best of it."

I see that healing must begin
by finding Living Christ within.
For as I see with single eye,
each cell the light does amplify.

**O Mother Mary, generate,
the song that does accelerate,
my mind into a peaceful state,
God's perfect love I radiate.**

5. I do not want to adapt to conditions that I can change. I accept the awareness that change is possible. I reach for the vision of how things can be changed and I am willing to implement it.

In Mother's music I am free,
from memories of a lesser me.
My vision in a perfect state,
that all my cells regenerate.

**O Mother Mary, generate,
the song that does accelerate,
my mind into a peaceful state,
God's perfect love I radiate.**

6. Even though I am a spiritual person, I have inherited from my species, from the collective consciousness, from my parents, from previous generations, this ability to adapt to material conditions, to accept conditions for what they are and find a way to live with them.

O Mother's Love, sweet melody,
from imperfections I AM free.
O Mother Mary, sound of sounds,
within my heart your love abounds.

**O Mother Mary, generate,
the song that does accelerate,
my mind into a peaceful state,
God's perfect love I radiate.**

7. This is the point in my growth where I am willing to take a look at this and decide: "I am going to raise myself above this collective momentum of adapting to physical conditions."

> Through Mother's beauty so sublime,
> transcending bounds of space and time.
> All cells beyond the mortal tomb,
> as they are whole in Mother's womb.
>
> **O Mother Mary, generate,**
> **the song that does accelerate,**
> **my mind into a peaceful state,**
> **God's perfect love I radiate.**

8. I am not here to accept current conditions and adapt to them. I am here to raise current conditions, to raise the collective and even to raise the physical conditions.

> In resonance with life's own song,
> in life's harmonics I belong.
> The blueprint of my perfect state
> does every cell reconsecrate.
>
> **O Mother Mary, generate,**
> **the song that does accelerate,**
> **my mind into a peaceful state,**
> **God's perfect love I radiate.**

9. I cannot do that if I am an adaptive animal. I recognize that I am a spiritual being and I decide: "I am going to raise myself above this ability to accept current conditions and adapt to them."

> The tuning fork in every cell
> is now attuned to Mother's bell.
> From curse of death I AM now free,
> I claim my immortality.
>
> **O Mother Mary, generate,**
> **the song that does accelerate,**

my mind into a peaceful state,
God's perfect love I radiate.

Part 2

1. I know within me that things do not have to be the way they are on earth. There is an alternative; things could be better. I have a frame of reference that the things that are happening on earth are not the highest possible.

> O Blessed Mary's Song of Life,
> consuming every form of strife.
> As I attune to sound so fair,
> each cell is healthy, I declare.
>
> **O Mother Mary, generate,**
> **the song that does accelerate,**
> **my mind into a peaceful state,**
> **God's perfect love I radiate.**

2. I have felt trapped in this dense physical body in this dense physical world. I have been surrounded by other people who also have physical bodies and who, regardless of how I feel, regardless of what I think, have the ability to hurt me, to use *their* physical bodies to harm *my* physical body.

> As life's own song I ever hear,
> it does consume all sense of fear.
> In tune with Mother's symphony,
> from all diseases I AM free.
>
> **O Mother Mary, generate,**
> **the song that does accelerate,**
> **my mind into a peaceful state,**
> **God's perfect love I radiate.**

3. There is nothing I can do about this once I am in the physical body. Even being in the physical body and experiencing what is happening on earth, there is nothing I can do about that.

> In Mother's love I do transcend,
> and all my struggles hereby end.
> For when with Mother's eye I see,
> no imperfection touches me.
>
> **O Mother Mary, generate,**
> **the song that does accelerate,**
> **my mind into a peaceful state,**
> **God's perfect love I radiate.**

4. Once I was in a physical body, I experienced the energies that were here that are so dense, the collective consciousness is so dense, there is so much aggression, so much hatred, so much fear.

> I see that healing must begin
> by finding Living Christ within.
> For as I see with single eye,
> each cell the light does amplify.
>
> **O Mother Mary, generate,**
> **the song that does accelerate,**
> **my mind into a peaceful state,**
> **God's perfect love I radiate.**

5. Part of the shock that I experienced was that there was a certain condition that was the primary condition I would like to see removed from the earth.

> In Mother's music I am free,
> from memories of a lesser me.
> My vision in a perfect state,
> that all my cells regenerate.
>
> **O Mother Mary, generate,**
> **the song that does accelerate,**

**my mind into a peaceful state,
God's perfect love I radiate.**

6. When I experienced how intense it was, the reaction I had was: "I can't live with this. I can't live with this condition being present on earth."

> O Mother's Love, sweet melody,
> from imperfections I AM free.
> O Mother Mary, sound of sounds,
> within my heart your love abounds.

> **O Mother Mary, generate,
> the song that does accelerate,
> my mind into a peaceful state,
> God's perfect love I radiate.**

7. I literally withdrew into myself. I was so shocked that I tried to pull my entire aura back inside to some safe spot where I could forget that this condition exists. Yet, I cannot do this because I am stuck in the physical body. There is no way out of the physical body.

> Through Mother's beauty so sublime,
> transcending bounds of space and time.
> All cells beyond the mortal tomb,
> as they are whole in Mother's womb.

> **O Mother Mary, generate,
> the song that does accelerate,
> my mind into a peaceful state,
> God's perfect love I radiate.**

8. After my initial shock, I was faced with the stark reality. Everything in my emotional body, my mental body and my identity body told me: "I can't live on this planet when this condition is here. I can't live with this." Yet, my physical body told me that I *have* to live on this planet and I have to do what it takes to survive.

> In resonance with life's own song,
> in life's harmonics I belong.

The blueprint of my perfect state
does every cell reconsecrate.

**O Mother Mary, generate,
the song that does accelerate,
my mind into a peaceful state,
God's perfect love I radiate.**

9. I experienced a split between the physical body and the three higher bodies. I had to create a barrier between the physical and the three higher bodies in order to protect the higher bodies from what is going on in the physical realm.

The tuning fork in every cell
is now attuned to Mother's bell.
From curse of death I AM now free,
I claim my immortality.

**O Mother Mary, generate,
the song that does accelerate,
my mind into a peaceful state,
God's perfect love I radiate.**

Part 3

1. I am willing to overcome this division and transcend the tendency for spiritual people to look at the body as an enemy of their spiritual growth.

O Blessed Mary's Song of Life,
consuming every form of strife.
As I attune to sound so fair,
each cell is healthy, I declare.

**O Mother Mary, generate,
the song that does accelerate,
my mind into a peaceful state,
God's perfect love I radiate.**

2 | Invoking freedom from adaptation

2. I was exposed to the mechanism where I felt: "I can't live with this condition on earth." Yet I had to live on earth so I tied in to the collective adaptation mechanism that has been created by other people in my family, in my nation, in my culture, in my civilization, in the collective consciousness.

> As life's own song I ever hear,
> it does consume all sense of fear.
> In tune with Mother's symphony,
> from all diseases I AM free.
>
> **O Mother Mary, generate,**
> **the song that does accelerate,**
> **my mind into a peaceful state,**
> **God's perfect love I radiate.**

3. I tied in to this and I realized that when I am on a planet like this, I just have to adapt. I have to accept conditions for what they are and make the best of it. Deep within my subconscious, I made a decision: "I can't live with this but I *have* to live with this, and in order to live with it, I have to accept this or that belief."

> In Mother's love I do transcend,
> and all my struggles hereby end.
> For when with Mother's eye I see,
> no imperfection touches me.
>
> **O Mother Mary, generate,**
> **the song that does accelerate,**
> **my mind into a peaceful state,**
> **God's perfect love I radiate.**

4. I accepted that certain conditions are inevitable, and I attempted to insulate myself from the condition so I did not experience it and so I could still live on this planet, I could still function on the planet.

> I see that healing must begin
> by finding Living Christ within.

For as I see with single eye,
each cell the light does amplify.

**O Mother Mary, generate,
the song that does accelerate,
my mind into a peaceful state,
God's perfect love I radiate.**

5. This is simply a survival mechanism. It can be a physical survival mechanism, but it is primarily an emotional, mental, identity level survival mechanism, so that I can live on a planet where the condition exists that I cannot live with.

In Mother's music I am free,
from memories of a lesser me.
My vision in a perfect state,
that all my cells regenerate.

**O Mother Mary, generate,
the song that does accelerate,
my mind into a peaceful state,
God's perfect love I radiate.**

6. I am ready to take a look at this. I am ready to take a look at these survival mechanisms and I am ready to begin to raise myself above it so that I can live on earth without just surviving.

O Mother's Love, sweet melody,
from imperfections I AM free.
O Mother Mary, sound of sounds,
within my heart your love abounds.

**O Mother Mary, generate,
the song that does accelerate,
my mind into a peaceful state,
God's perfect love I radiate.**

7. I want to be at peace with being on earth so I can enjoy life on earth. I want to be able to enjoy expressing myself, my real self, here on earth.

Through Mother's beauty so sublime,
transcending bounds of space and time.
All cells beyond the mortal tomb,
as they are whole in Mother's womb.

**O Mother Mary, generate,
the song that does accelerate,
my mind into a peaceful state,
God's perfect love I radiate.**

8. I have a desire to express my real being, my real creativity, on earth and I know that this is the only way the earth will improve. The only way I can help advance the earth is by expressing who I really am, expressing the creativity of my I AM Presence.

In resonance with life's own song,
in life's harmonics I belong.
The blueprint of my perfect state
does every cell reconsecrate.

**O Mother Mary, generate,
the song that does accelerate,
my mind into a peaceful state,
God's perfect love I radiate.**

9. When I created this survival mechanism, I basically said: "As long as this condition, that I cannot live with, exists on earth, I can't express myself freely, I can't be creative." I created a mechanism deep in my subconscious where I decided: "I can't be at peace, I can't be happy, I can't be creative, I can't express myself as long as these people are suffering from this condition."

The tuning fork in every cell
is now attuned to Mother's bell.
From curse of death I AM now free,
I claim my immortality.

**O Mother Mary, generate,
the song that does accelerate,**

my mind into a peaceful state,
God's perfect love I radiate.

Part 4

1. This is a very understandable reaction. Yet, even though it is *understandable,* it is not a *constructive* reaction because I want to remove the condition. I can make a contribution to removing the condition only by expressing the creativity of my higher being.

O Blessed Mary's Song of Life,
consuming every form of strife.
As I attune to sound so fair,
each cell is healthy, I declare.

**O Mother Mary, generate,
the song that does accelerate,
my mind into a peaceful state,
God's perfect love I radiate.**

2. If I shut off that creativity, I am also shutting off the possibility that I can fulfill my reason for being on earth. I am not going to help remove any limitation by suffering like other people are suffering, nor am I going to do so by cutting off my creativity and going into a state where I live a joyless existence because I feel I cannot be happy when other people are suffering. This is not the way that I remove the condition that I am here to help remove.

As life's own song I ever hear,
it does consume all sense of fear.
In tune with Mother's symphony,
from all diseases I AM free.

**O Mother Mary, generate,
the song that does accelerate,
my mind into a peaceful state,
God's perfect love I radiate.**

3. If I am to have a positive impact on earth, I cannot do it by looking at the problem the same way everybody else looks at the problem. I cannot help overcome a condition by adapting to that condition, as everybody else is doing.

> In Mother's love I do transcend,
> and all my struggles hereby end.
> For when with Mother's eye I see,
> no imperfection touches me.
>
> **O Mother Mary, generate,**
> **the song that does accelerate,**
> **my mind into a peaceful state,**
> **God's perfect love I radiate.**

4. I am willing to look at what is the condition that disturbs me the most on earth, what is the condition that I feel I cannot live with. I am willing to see how I found a way to still live on earth while this condition exists and what I had to do to get to that point. I am willing to see how I free myself from that condition.

> I see that healing must begin
> by finding Living Christ within.
> For as I see with single eye,
> each cell the light does amplify.
>
> **O Mother Mary, generate,**
> **the song that does accelerate,**
> **my mind into a peaceful state,**
> **God's perfect love I radiate.**

5. When I received my original trauma, I had a certain level of consciousness. This was a long time ago and I have gained a different perspective and greater maturity. I can now look at my original decision for how I decided to adapt to conditions on earth.

> In Mother's music I am free,
> from memories of a lesser me.

My vision in a perfect state,
that all my cells regenerate.

**O Mother Mary, generate,
the song that does accelerate,
my mind into a peaceful state,
God's perfect love I radiate.**

6. I am willing to look at my decision from a greater perspective. I am willing to see how it is limiting me, and come to the point where I can identity this as a self. I created a self that enabled me to live on earth when this condition was here, but this self also has the function of cutting off my creativity. I am willing to identify that self, look at it from the outside, realize it is not me. I am making the decision to let it die.

O Mother's Love, sweet melody,
from imperfections I AM free.
O Mother Mary, sound of sounds,
within my heart your love abounds.

**O Mother Mary, generate,
the song that does accelerate,
my mind into a peaceful state,
God's perfect love I radiate.**

7. This self thinks I cannot be at peace on earth as long as a certain condition exists. The self projects at me that I have to solve the condition before I can be at peace, but this is not the case. I – the Conscious You – see that this is just a self that is projecting this illogical decision at me, and I decide: "This is not the decision that I want to define me, define my life on earth, anymore." I decide to just let the self die without having to solve the problem that the self projects I have to solve.

Through Mother's beauty so sublime,
transcending bounds of space and time.
All cells beyond the mortal tomb,
as they are whole in Mother's womb.

> O Mother Mary, generate,
> the song that does accelerate,
> my mind into a peaceful state,
> God's perfect love I radiate.

8. As a spiritual person, I have come to feel that I need to be positive, so I tend to deny my negative feelings. It is perfectly acceptable for me to acknowledge that I have certain very intense feelings about conditions on earth. It is perfectly acceptable to bring this to my conscious awareness so I can make the calls on the energy, dissipate the energy, therefore come to see the self that is creating these feelings and just let the self die.

> In resonance with life's own song,
> in life's harmonics I belong.
> The blueprint of my perfect state
> does every cell reconsecrate.

> O Mother Mary, generate,
> the song that does accelerate,
> my mind into a peaceful state,
> God's perfect love I radiate.

9. Mother Mary, help me recognize the feelings that I have not been willing to acknowledge. Help me overcome them and be free, so that I can be at peace with being on this earth. Therefore, by being at peace, I can make a contribution to removing a certain condition.

> The tuning fork in every cell
> is now attuned to Mother's bell.
> From curse of death I AM now free,
> I claim my immortality.

> O Mother Mary, generate,
> the song that does accelerate,
> my mind into a peaceful state,
> God's perfect love I radiate.

Sealing

In the name of the Divine Mother, I call to Mother Mary for the sealing of myself and all people in my circle of influence in the creative flow of the Divine Mother, the River of Life. I call for the multiplication of my calls by all representatives of the Divine Mother, so that we form the perfect figure-eight flow of "As Above, so below." Thus, I accept that this is fully manifest, because the mouth of the Lord, the Divine Mother that I AM, has spoken it. Amen.

3 | EXPERIENCING YOURSELF ON EARTH

I AM the Ascended Master Mother Mary, and I want to follow up on my previous dictation and your discussions. I am grateful that you have been willing to share your feelings about being on earth. Whether they are positive or not so positive, it is important for you to share this and to be willing to acknowledge what feelings you have. Naturally, there are no wrong feelings. The feelings you have are the feelings you have. Surely, this is a very difficult planet, especially if you come from a background of a natural planet. If you are one of the original inhabitants of the earth and have been here for much longer, then you will not have the same feelings. You will naturally feel that this is a much more positive planet, than if you have the contrast between a natural planet and this. It is important to acknowledge feelings because, as we have said many times, you cannot truly overcome the feelings, you cannot overcome the self, until you become conscious that it exists, that it is there, that it has certain feelings.

Who is having the feeling?

Once you have brought the feelings out in the open, you can start looking at: Where do the feelings come from? You can even ask the question: "Who is feeling this way, is it me or is it a self?" Naturally, it is a self that feels this way because the feeling is related to earth. That means it is a *reactionary* feeling and only a reactionary self can have such a feeling. You, as what we have called the Conscious You, do not actually *have* feelings. There can be feelings in your emotional body and you may be experiencing the world through the coloring, through the filter, of those feelings, but you are not actually *having* the feeling. I understand that it feels like you are having the feeling, and the consequence of that is that the feeling is *having you*. The reason for this is that you are identified with a certain self, you have not yet come to see that it is a separate self: that it is not *you*. That is why you have the formula, that we have given you previously, on how to come to identify these selves, how to switch out of them and eventually let them die.

When you do this, and when you have made the calls for the consuming or the transformation of the energy that was stored in the self, then you can be free of that feeling. You can, therefore, be free to embrace your life on earth with a positive feeling. The reason we are asking you to bring out whatever feelings you have is so that you do not have to live the rest of your time on this planet being burdened by these very intense negative feelings. I can assure you that I myself had some very negative feelings about being on earth when I was in embodiment. There is absolutely no way I want to give you the image that I was any different than you, that I was so much higher than you that I did not have these feelings. I had many of the same feelings that you have expressed today.

Your feelings about people

If you look at what was said here, you can see that, generally speaking, there is a difference between what you feel about the earth and what you feel about people. It can be helpful for you, just in your own private considerations, to look at what you actually feel about people. You can then seek to differentiate. Is this feeling you have, for example that "people are stupid," related to *all* people or is it related to *some* people? If so, what kind of people? Often, you will find that the most intense feelings you have about people are related to the fallen beings. They were caused by the fallen beings. The fallen beings did something to you or you watched the fallen beings do something to others and this is what caused you to have very intense feelings about people. You can then begin to differentiate and see that, perhaps, it is not all people you feel this about. That means you

3 | Experiencing yourself on earth

can start having a different relationship with most people you encounter because, surely, most people you encounter are not fallen beings. (Even though many of you, not *all* of you but *many* of you, have had relationships with fallen beings in this lifetime and in many past lifetimes.)

I have said previously that I would like you to *not* look at me as if I was a fallen being, not relate to me through the images and expectations created by the fallen beings. I would also like you to relate to other people as if they are not fallen beings so that you differentiate and realize that your most intense feelings about people are related to the fallen beings. Therefore, you cannot evaluate or relate to other people, to *all* people, based on these feelings. That means you can then begin to soften up your view of people so that it is not *all* people. You are not generalizing based on the fallen beings and letting them color your view of people and your relationship to people.

There are many of you who felt that you came here partly to help other people in various ways, perhaps also to teach other people. You have all felt that, yes, you were treated in a very harsh way by the fallen beings, but many of you have felt that you were treated with indifference by the majority of the people on earth. They either did not even pay attention to you or they were somewhat hostile, not wanting to be disturbed. It is a very common feeling among avatars, among spiritual people in general, that people do not want to listen to you. They do not want to listen to you talk about your spiritual knowledge, your spiritual awareness. They do not want to be disturbed, they just want to live the same kind of life and they do not want to change. Many of you have felt alone. You have felt rejected. You have felt you do not belong here precisely because of this mechanism. This, then, does not have anything to do directly with the fallen beings, although the fallen beings have also tried to put you down because you were teaching people what the fallen beings do not want them to know. Nevertheless, the greater reaction you have had is from people who simply did not want to listen to anything you had to say, to the message you had to bring.

Free will and your feelings about people

This is a topic that will take some more work on your part before you come to this point where you can make peace with the fact, the observable fact, that most people on earth do not want to listen to a spiritual teaching. They do not, as was said earlier, actually want to escape their suffering even if you can tell them how to do so. In order to do this, you might have to consider what was said earlier about the fact that you need to develop this absolute respect for free will. It goes two ways. You have the respect for the free will of others and you have the respect for your own free will. Truly, there are two aspects to this that you need to ponder. Number one is that as an avatar coming from a natural planet, you are coming from an environment where nobody is forcing the free will of others. That is one of the main characteristics of a natural planet. The inhabitants of a natural planet have no need to force the free will of others.

You do actually have the respect for free will when you come here, but it is possible that, after having encountered the fallen beings and seeing how they actually manipulate people on earth, you can forget that respect for free will. You can even adopt the attitude that because people have been forced and manipulated by the fallen beings, it is okay for you to be somewhat forceful in seeking to awaken people. You are not manipulating them as the fallen beings are doing but you are forcing them to hear what you are saying.

There are some of you who will be able to look at some of the older teachings that we have given, on what it means to be the Christ on earth, where you are here to disturb status quo, you are not here to leave people in the same state you found them. You see Jesus who was challenging to people, overturning the tables of the money changers, challenging the scribes and Pharisees, challenging the people that he met, such as "Let him who is without sin among you cast the first stone" and other situations. You might look at this and say: "But if we are here to create a positive change and if people are so trapped by the fallen beings, then we might need to be forceful in order to even penetrate the resistance people have and be able to reach them with any kind of message." It is not that these things are invalid but the question is: From which state of mind are you doing it? What we are calling those of you, who are avatars, to do is to step up to where you can be on earth, you can do whatever you choose to do on earth, but you are not basing it on these reactionary selves, from the primal self and all the other selves you have created.

You see my beloved, it is possible for people with their outer minds to look at Jesus, to take the teachings on Christhood, and then decide with the outer mind: "This is what I'm going to do to awaken other people." Over the decades where we have given these teachings through various organizations, we have seen some people react this way. You will see that Master MORE in Kazakhstan gave his very, very profound dictation about a previous dispensation and how people got all fired up and all "blue-ray" about going out there and awakening other people [See the book *Fulfilling Your Highest Spiritual Potential*]. What you realize is that even though the goal was legitimate enough, the way it was done is that people did this based on these outer selves that they had. It was almost like for some people they had many lifetimes of frustration being on the earth and now they felt the ascended masters had given them free reign to go out and be forceful and blue-ray—and now they were going to do this to compensate for all those lifetimes of frustration. Now, they could finally achieve the goal that they had set.

You see, my beloved, these people were not at peace with being on earth. Jesus was not always at peace either when he challenged people. This does not mean that you cannot rise to the point where you can be on earth and you can perhaps (if this is what is in your Divine plan and what you feel), challenge people but you are doing it from a state of peace. You are, as the messenger said earlier, not trying to change other people in order to avoid having a negative feeling in yourself or about yourself because you have resolved the feeling in yourself. You have gotten rid of these separate selves and therefore you are at peace when you are interacting with other people.

Forcing people for their own good

How, then, do you come to the point where you are at peace interacting with other people no matter how they react to you? You need to go through the process that the messenger described and realize that before he came here, he thought he was coming here to change the earth but he was willing to come to the realization that this was not the highest understanding of why he came to earth. In reality, he came to earth to change himself, to have a certain experience and therefore come to that full acceptance of free will that he did not quite have, and that many of you did not have, on a natural planet.

It is an enigma! On a planet like earth, where you see that the fallen beings are constantly manipulating and forcing the free will of humanity, how do you counteract that? How do you deal with that? How far can you push other people's free will, supposedly for their own good? This messenger was willing to recognize one simple fact: Although there are fallen beings who are maliciously manipulating the free will of humanity, there are many fallen beings who actually believe that they are manipulating people's free will for people's own good. They believe that they are fighting for some legitimate cause and that the goal is so important that it justifies the means of forcing the free will of these people who just do not know better.

You can even recognize that the fallen beings, in trying to manipulate people on earth, have much the same frustration that you have had, namely that people just do not respond, that they are not interested in changing, that they want to live the same kind of life lifetime after lifetime. You can come to realize that you cannot, as an avatar, allow yourself to have the attitude that the ends can justify the means, that it is okay to push people for their own good. This you can come to realize only when you ponder this very fact: free will is absolute. The Creator has created a creation and sent self-aware beings in there and given them an absolute free will, and they have the free will to explore everything that can be done with free will.

One aspect of this is that when you have complete free will, you do not start out with the highest level of consciousness. You start out with a very point-like, very narrow, sense of self and you are exercising your free will based on that self. In fact, regardless of where you are at in consciousness, even whether you are an ascended master or not, you are always exercising your free will based on your current sense of self. *That* is all you can do.

The question is: How *separate* does that self see itself compared to other beings? You all grow up in an environment where you are not alone, there are other beings there. The central enigma about free will is: "How do I balance my own free will with the free will of the other beings around me?" This is the central enigma and you do not actually resolve that until you ascend. Therefore, I am not expecting you, at your present level of consciousness (whatever level you are at), to necessarily resolve this fully. I expect you to ponder it and move towards really accepting free will and what it means.

How far into separation do you have to go?

What you realize here is that when the Creator gave free will to the co-creators, he gave them the freedom to explore anything that can be done with free will. One of the things that can be done with free will is that you can act as a separate self. The question really is: How far into separation do you need to go before you realize that this is not what you want to do anymore?

3 | Experiencing yourself on earth

In a sense, you could say that the fallen beings are kind of explorers. They are exploring: How far can you go into separation before you cannot stand it anymore? You could say that somebody has to go into separation in order for the collective awareness to have that sense of: What are the consequences of making choices in separation? You can go into a more philosophical discussion and say: Are these people exercising *free* will? Does the fallen being have a *free* will because it sees it based on a very separate sense of self?

That is not what I want to go into here. What I want to say is that you have free will in the sense that no matter what self you have, no matter what self you have developed, you are allowed to make any choices you can see from that self. Those choices have consequences and you are going to experience those consequences. That is, sort of, the safety mechanism. The more you go into separation, the more dense you make your environment, the more of a struggle it becomes to exercise your will through that separate self. That is what can, then, eventually get you to the point where you say: "There must be a higher way to exercise my will than this. There must be a more *free* will than what I have right now."

What you can do as an avatar, is you can say: "For free will to outplay itself in this unascended sphere where I am, some beings have to go as far into separation as the fallen beings have done. There had to be some planets where these beings could outplay themselves and earth is one of those planets." This, then, leaves the question of: Why did you as an avatar choose to come to this planet? You chose to come here because you wanted to also have an experience of what it is like to be on a planet where some beings have taken their "free" will into such extremes of selfishness and separation. You wanted to have that experience. This you have most likely forgotten and you have forgotten the reason why. This messenger has so far realized that he wanted to have this experience because he wanted to have the full acceptance of free will that he did not have on a natural planet, but this is not the ultimate understanding.

Experiencing yourself on a dense planet

You actually did not come here because you wanted to change other people or change the planet. You did not come here because you wanted to rescue or save anybody or because you wanted to judge the fallen beings or change the fallen beings. You did not come here only because you wanted to have a better understanding of free will. You came here because you wanted to experience your self in this kind of environment. You wanted to experience what it was like to be you in an environment as dense as earth.

You might say: "How could I be stupid enough to want this?" But it is not a matter of being stupid. You see, my beloved, there are many different beings on natural planets. There are many different kinds of natural planets. The one described in the *My Lives* book is just one example of a natural planet. There are natural planets where you see that there are certain beings who are very eager to make progress. Even on natural planets some beings are more eager to make progress than others. There can come a point where you feel you have explored a natural planet to the fullest, you have experienced everything there is to experience on a natural planet.

Yes, you could go on to another natural planet that is different from the planet you have been on so far, and you could have a different experience. Some of you became aware that there are planets that are not natural, and you simply decided: "I have experienced everything I can imagine experiencing about how I am in an environment like a natural planet but now I want to experience how I am on an unnatural planet." It is a very valid and very valuable desire because it actually helps raise the collective consciousness of the entire sphere. You have these beings (who have gone as far as you can go on natural planets) and who say: "In order to reach a higher level of self-mastery, I want to experience a completely different environment because I want to experience how I am, how I react, how I see myself in that kind of environment."

We have given you the teachings before that in order to descend into embodiment on a planet like earth, you have to descend to the 48th level. You have to go through all the levels above the 48th, take on one illusion at a time until you have taken on all the illusions at the 48th level. Then, you come into embodiment for the first time as an avatar at that level, and you are looking at the planet through that level of consciousness, reacting to the planet through that level of consciousness.

My beloved, *nothing went wrong here*. Do you understand? Nothing went wrong in this process. You simply did what had to be done for you to take embodiment on an unnatural planet. It was not *stupid*. It was not *wrong*. It was a choice you made. What you wanted to experience was actually exactly what you have experienced on earth, namely that you came here with a certain level of consciousness that corresponded to the planet. We might say that the 48th level of consciousness is sort of the ground state, the default state, on earth. This is what you descended to in order to have the experience of what it was like to be you on planet earth. What you really wanted was to experience: "What is it like to be me on earth?" And *that* you have experienced. You may say, my beloved: "But was it really *me* who experienced this? If I experienced it through the 48th level of consciousness, if I had the birth trauma (which you say is inevitable but nevertheless was very painful) and I created the primal self and all these other selves and I have experienced the planet through this, have I really experienced what it is like to be me?"

I understand, my beloved, that you cannot instantly switch because I tell you this but you can certainly ponder this. You can gradually come to that point where you realize that even though many of the experiences you have had on earth have been colored by a certain state of consciousness, a certain outer self, you have still, behind it all, had the experience of what it is like to be you in an environment like this. This goes beyond the outer selves and the reactions of the outer selves. This will require some work for you to connect to this.

Connecting to your basic spirituality

We have told you before about connecting to the basic humanity but we can say that, beyond that, it is a matter of connecting to your basic spirituality, your basic individuality. We have called it your I AM Presence, we have said your real individuality is contained in the I AM Presence. Nevertheless my beloved, what is it? Where is it you have experienced being you in an environment like earth? It is not in the outer self. It is not in the primal self, it is not even in the Conscious You. What has experienced being you in an environment like earth, is your I AM Presence. At that level, you have had the experience of what it is like to be you on earth. You have had that since you first came here.

Obviously, I realize you do not connect to this consciously. You have had a different experience at the level of the Conscious You where you have identified with these outer selves, with the four lower bodies and you have experienced through that filter. What we are telling you is that with the teachings we have given you on overcoming the primal self, overcoming all these other selves, you can actually come to a point where you can experience while you are in embodiment, you (the Conscious You) can experience what your I AM Presence is experiencing. You can experience being you, being the I AM Presence in embodiment on earth, while you are in embodiment on earth. *That* experience is the ultimate way to make peace with being on earth.

Now, I would submit to you, that *most* of you, in fact I would say *all* of you, have in glimpses had that experience of what it is like to be you on earth. You have had this very subtle sense sometimes, of looking at life in a different way. Perhaps it has been a sense of love, a sense of being connected, a sense of looking at earth without the normal filter of judgments and just seeing the beauty, perhaps the beauty of nature, perhaps the beauty of people, perhaps the beauty of a sleeping baby. Whatever it may be, there are these moments where you see some kind of beauty.

Behind this can even be this sense that you are completely neutral about what is happening on earth. You are not analyzing or judging it. You are just experiencing it. You are experiencing it, not through all of these separate selves. You are actually experiencing it as the being you really are. There is no judgment, there is no analysis, there is no goal. There is nothing you *have* to do. You are just experiencing earth. This is an experience you can gradually come to have more and more often. You are in this, we may call it, neutral state of mind but we can also describe it in other ways. You can say you are in a state of oneness, you are in the state of connection, you are not feeling you are alone here on earth. You are not feeling you do not belong here because you have a connection to your I AM Presence, therefore you belong anywhere when you have that connection.

It is perfectly understandable that most of you have not felt at home on this planet. *I* did not feel at home when I was in embodiment. Even in my last embodiment, I did not feel at home. When I stood there in front of that cross and watched my son die, I did not feel at home on this planet at all. I just wanted to get out of here. Nevertheless, I also had moments where I felt that connection, I felt that sense of oneness and I was at peace with being here. It is possible for you – when you continue to work on these separate selves and get rid of that primal self – to come to that point where you can say: "Why did I actually choose to come to earth? Because I, the greater being that I AM, wanted to experience myself in this type of environment."

When you are not being pulled into reactionary patterns by all of these separate selves, you can have that experience. Regardless of how the planet is, of how difficult it is, how difficult people are, you feel you are being yourself on this planet. I fully understand that for most of you this will start when you are alone, when you are in a meditative, peaceful state of mind where there is nothing outside that disturbs you. Then, you can have

3 | Experiencing yourself on earth

these glimpses of this higher awareness. I also submit to you, even though *I* did not realize that in my last embodiment, Jesus did not realize it in his last embodiment, I still submit to you that it is possible for most of you in this lifetime to come to the point where you feel that way all the time. It just becomes the backdrop for your experience on earth.

You may still have certain situations that are very intense where you are not really consciously aware that this feeling is there. You are focused on the situation you have to deal with. Once the situation is taken care of, you can learn to switch back into being aware of that greater sense of connection so that you never feel that you are alone here. You never feel you do not belong here because you realize earth is not your home. Nothing in the material octave is your home. Your I AM Presence is your home. When you are connected to that I AM Presence, you are at home anywhere because the outer environment does not really matter.

What should or should not happen on earth

What is it going to take for you to move towards that state? I know I am setting a high goal. I am not expecting you to achieve it in five minutes. What is it going to take to start? You have to ponder, first of all, free will. When you understand what I said, that earth is simply a planet for beings who have chosen to explore how far you can go into separation before you cannot stand it anymore, you can see it really is meaningless to have a sense of what *should* or *should not* happen on a planet like earth.

You can have a certain memory of a natural planet. You can look at earth and see how much people are suffering because of war, conflict or this or that. You can say people should not be suffering, therefore these manifestations should not be here. This is a valid concern on a *natural* planet but it is not valid on an *unnatural* planet. It is not constructive. It only puts you in a non-constructive frame of mind that prevents you from being at peace with being on earth. The moment you judge that something should not be happening on earth, at that very moment, you have put yourself in a box in which you cannot be at peace.

You need to find a way to shift your mind so you realize that whatever is happening on earth is what somebody has chosen to manifest because they needed that experience. If you have total respect for free will – and you need to have that to be at peace on a planet like this – you can say: "I need to allow these people to suffer as they have chosen to suffer.

Obviously, I also need to respect my own free will so that I do not have to suffer the way they suffer. I do not have to feel empathy with them. I do not even have to feel compassion for them. I do not even have to put my attention on their suffering if that takes away my peace."

What I am saying here is that it is necessary for you to go through a phase where, as we have said before, you select *out* certain things in your life that are not constructive for your growth. You are saying: "Right now, it is not constructive for me to feel pity or compassion for people who are suffering. Therefore, it is acceptable for me that I do not put my attention on their suffering."

This may not be forever, but it is necessary for you in order to work through this mechanism that I am describing where you feel that things should not have happened and this takes away your peace. In order for you to find peace, it is acceptable and necessary that you go through a period where you basically ignore people's suffering and you are focusing on overcoming all of these separate selves, these reactionary selves. There may come a day where you have attained a degree of inner peace. Now, you can go back out and seek to help people, challenge people or whatever you feel, but you are doing it from a state of inner peace rather than from a state of non-peace, a state of frustration, a state where you are constantly judging that this should not be here.

You are not stupid

You see my beloved, what the messenger said earlier is indeed true. When you feel that you are stupid for having come to earth, then you automatically start judging that other people are stupid for not responding to you and not letting you help them. This also means that you are keeping yourself in a certain box where you are judging yourself that you could be stupid or wrong for coming to earth.

My beloved, first of all, it is the fallen beings who have put this standard on the earth and you have come to accept the standard of the fallen beings. You are now judging yourself as the fallen beings judge you, not as the ascended masters look at you. More than that, it is also, my beloved, that you are not respecting your own free will. As I said: Why did you choose to come to earth? Because you wanted to experience yourself in this environment. My beloved, how could that choice possibly be wrong? What could ever be wrong with wanting to experience yourself in a specific

3 | Experiencing yourself on earth

environment? That is what a co-creator is all about. Certainly, when you come to the higher levels of awareness, it is about experiencing yourself in a specific environment and by seeing how you respond to that environment, you grow. There could never be anything wrong about this choice. It is simply a very valid and valuable choice. You chose to help raise your sphere by coming to a planet like earth and experiencing yourself here.

You may say: "But what about my desire to help raise the earth, is that not what we are all about as co-creators, raising the entire sphere and obviously an unnatural planet needs to be raised?" This is correct, but the question is: How do you help raise the earth, a planet like earth? Not by *doing* something! If you do not remember it, go through Nada's book again where she talks about being here without doing and how people have created all of these problems by *doing* forcefully. How do you actually raise the earth? By being here, by *being* here.

It is not so much what you can *do* or *say* on the outer that will change the earth. It is the very fact that you have come into embodiment and, therefore, you are to some degree an anchor point and an open door for the I AM Presence. If you really want to make a contribution to changing earth, then become more and more of an open door for the I AM Presence. Just let the light shine. Do not have a judgement in the outer mind of what you *should* do or what you *should not* do, how the light should shine, what changes should happen, how other people should react. Just let the light shine, my beloved. That is the real way to change the earth. It was never meant that you should come down here at the 48th level of consciousness and be able to be a completely open door for your I AM Presence. It was a process because you are taking on the 48th level of consciousness and demonstrating how to rise above it.

My beloved, look back at your lives, look at where you are now. Why are you sitting here listening to this? Because you have already demonstrated the process of how to raise your consciousness, you have already demonstrated this in your life up to this point. I am not saying that you are wrong or lacking or you have not done enough. I am only saying you can actually take this further and come to a point where you demonstrate how to start at a certain level of consciousness and attain inner peace and be at peace with being on a planet like this. *That* is your highest potential, that is what most of you defined in your Divine plan as your highest potential. You wanted to come here and demonstrate being at peace.

Therefore, there is no blame, there is no saying you have done anything wrong. You have done exactly what you needed to do. You just need to take those steps further so that you attain that inner peace where you can actually enjoy experiencing yourself on this planet that you call earth. As difficult as it is, you can avoid been pulled into all of these difficulties but still experience your Self and experience how your I AM Presence looks at earth, experiences earth. *That* my beloved is peace.

Regardless of how this planet is, rest assured that from the moment you first took embodiment here, no matter what the Conscious You or the outer self has experienced, your I AM Presence has been in complete peace about everything that has happened on earth. Your I AM Presence knows that the real you cannot be affected by anything that could ever happen on earth. You knew this before you came and *that,* my beloved, is why it was not such a stupid choice to come here. You have just forgotten this awareness. We have given you the tools to reclaim it and therefore reclaim that peace that you had before you came.

4 | INVOKING THE MEMORY OF WHY I CAME HERE

In the name I AM THAT I AM, Jesus Christ, I call to all representatives of the Divine Mother, especially Mother Mary, to help me remember my original purpose for coming to earth, including…

[Make personal calls.]

Part 1

1. I am willing to acknowledge what feelings I have about being here on earth. There are no wrong feelings. The feelings I have are the feelings I have, and this is a very difficult planet.

> O Blessed Mary's Song of Life,
> consuming every form of strife.
> As I attune to sound so fair,
> each cell is healthy, I declare.

> **O Mother Mary, generate,**
> **the song that does accelerate,**
> **my mind into a peaceful state,**
> **God's perfect love I radiate.**

2. It is important to acknowledge my feelings because I cannot overcome the feelings, I cannot overcome the self, until I become conscious that it exists, that it is there, that it has certain feelings.

> As life's own song I ever hear,
> it does consume all sense of fear.
> In tune with Mother's symphony,
> from all diseases I AM free.

> **O Mother Mary, generate,**
> **the song that does accelerate,**
> **my mind into a peaceful state,**
> **God's perfect love I radiate.**

3. I am willing to look at where the feelings come from. I am willing to ask: "Who is feeling this way, is it me or is it a self?"

> In Mother's love I do transcend,
> and all my struggles hereby end.
> For when with Mother's eye I see,
> no imperfection touches me.

> **O Mother Mary, generate,**
> **the song that does accelerate,**
> **my mind into a peaceful state,**
> **God's perfect love I radiate.**

4. It is a self that feels this way because the feeling is related to earth. It is a *reactionary* feeling and only a reactionary self can have such a feeling.

> I see that healing must begin
> by finding Living Christ within.
> For as I see with single eye,
> each cell the light does amplify.

> **O Mother Mary, generate,**
> **the song that does accelerate,**
> **my mind into a peaceful state,**
> **God's perfect love I radiate.**

5. I, as the Conscious You, do not *have* feelings. There can be feelings in my emotional body and I may be experiencing the world through the coloring of those feelings, but I am not actually *having* the feeling.

> In Mother's music I am free,
> from memories of a lesser me.
> My vision in a perfect state,
> that all my cells regenerate.
>
> **O Mother Mary, generate,**
> **the song that does accelerate,**
> **my mind into a peaceful state,**
> **God's perfect love I radiate.**

6. It feels like I am having the feeling, and the consequence is that the feeling is *having me*. The reason is that I am identified with a certain self, I have not yet come to see that it is a separate self, that it is not me.

> O Mother's Love, sweet melody,
> from imperfections I AM free.
> O Mother Mary, sound of sounds,
> within my heart your love abounds.
>
> **O Mother Mary, generate,**
> **the song that does accelerate,**
> **my mind into a peaceful state,**
> **God's perfect love I radiate.**

7. I am willing to identify these selves, switch out of them and let them die. Mother Mary, consume the energy that was stored in the self, so I can be free of that feeling and I can embrace my life on earth with a positive feeling.

Through Mother's beauty so sublime,
transcending bounds of space and time.
All cells beyond the mortal tomb,
as they are whole in Mother's womb.

O Mother Mary, generate,
the song that does accelerate,
my mind into a peaceful state,
God's perfect love I radiate.

8. I will not live the rest of my time on this planet being burdened by these very intense negative feelings.

In resonance with life's own song,
in life's harmonics I belong.
The blueprint of my perfect state
does every cell reconsecrate.

O Mother Mary, generate,
the song that does accelerate,
my mind into a peaceful state,
God's perfect love I radiate.

9. There is a difference between what I feel about the earth and what I feel about people. I am willing to look at what I feel about people.

The tuning fork in every cell
is now attuned to Mother's bell.
From curse of death I AM now free,
I claim my immortality.

O Mother Mary, generate,
the song that does accelerate,
my mind into a peaceful state,
God's perfect love I radiate.

Part 2

1. The most intense feelings I have about people are related to the fallen beings. They were caused by the fallen beings. The fallen beings did something to me or I watched the fallen beings do something to others and this is what caused me to have very intense feelings about people.

> O Blessed Mary's Song of Life,
> consuming every form of strife.
> As I attune to sound so fair,
> each cell is healthy, I declare.
>
> **O Mother Mary, generate,**
> **the song that does accelerate,**
> **my mind into a peaceful state,**
> **God's perfect love I radiate.**

2. I differentiate and see that it is not all people I feel this about. Mother Mary, help me have a different relationship with most people I encounter because most people are not fallen beings.

> As life's own song I ever hear,
> it does consume all sense of fear.
> In tune with Mother's symphony,
> from all diseases I AM free.
>
> **O Mother Mary, generate,**
> **the song that does accelerate,**
> **my mind into a peaceful state,**
> **God's perfect love I radiate.**

3. I will soften up my view of people so that it is not *all* people. I am not generalizing based on the fallen beings and letting them color my view of people and my relationship to people.

> In Mother's love I do transcend,
> and all my struggles hereby end.

For when with Mother's eye I see,
no imperfection touches me.

**O Mother Mary, generate,
the song that does accelerate,
my mind into a peaceful state,
God's perfect love I radiate.**

4. I have felt that I was treated with indifference by the majority of the people on earth. They did not pay attention to me or they were hostile, not wanting to be disturbed.

I see that healing must begin
by finding Living Christ within.
For as I see with single eye,
each cell the light does amplify.

**O Mother Mary, generate,
the song that does accelerate,
my mind into a peaceful state,
God's perfect love I radiate.**

5. I have felt that people do not want to listen to me. They do not want to listen to my spiritual knowledge and awareness. They do not want to be disturbed, they just want to live the same kind of life and they do not want to change.

In Mother's music I am free,
from memories of a lesser me.
My vision in a perfect state,
that all my cells regenerate.

**O Mother Mary, generate,
the song that does accelerate,
my mind into a peaceful state,
God's perfect love I radiate.**

6. I have felt alone, felt rejected. I have felt I do not belong here, that people do not want to listen to anything I have to say, to the message I have to bring.

> O Mother's Love, sweet melody,
> from imperfections I AM free.
> O Mother Mary, sound of sounds,
> within my heart your love abounds.
>
> **O Mother Mary, generate,**
> **the song that does accelerate,**
> **my mind into a peaceful state,**
> **God's perfect love I radiate.**

7. Mother Mary, help me make peace with the fact that most people on earth do not want to listen to a spiritual teaching. They do not want to escape their suffering even if I can tell them how to do so.

> Through Mother's beauty so sublime,
> transcending bounds of space and time.
> All cells beyond the mortal tomb,
> as they are whole in Mother's womb.
>
> **O Mother Mary, generate,**
> **the song that does accelerate,**
> **my mind into a peaceful state,**
> **God's perfect love I radiate.**

8. Mother Mary, help me develop this absolute respect for free will, so I respect the free will of others and I respect my own free will.

> In resonance with life's own song,
> in life's harmonics I belong.
> The blueprint of my perfect state
> does every cell reconsecrate.
>
> **O Mother Mary, generate,**
> **the song that does accelerate,**

    my mind into a peaceful state,
    God's perfect love I radiate.

9. Mother Mary, help me see if, after having encountered the fallen beings and seeing how they manipulate people, I have lost my respect for free will. Help me see if I adopted the attitude that because people have been forced and manipulated by the fallen beings, it is okay for me to be forceful in seeking to awaken people.

    The tuning fork in every cell
    is now attuned to Mother's bell.
    From curse of death I AM now free,
    I claim my immortality.

    O Mother Mary, generate,
    the song that does accelerate,
    my mind into a peaceful state,
    God's perfect love I radiate.

Part 3

1. Mother Mary, help me step up to where I can be on earth, I can do whatever I choose to do on earth, but I am not basing it on these reactionary selves, from the primal self and all the other selves I have created.

    O Blessed Mary's Song of Life,
    consuming every form of strife.
    As I attune to sound so fair,
    each cell is healthy, I declare.

    O Mother Mary, generate,
    the song that does accelerate,
    my mind into a peaceful state,
    God's perfect love I radiate.

2. Mother Mary, help me see if I have had many lifetimes of frustration and after finding the teachings, I felt the ascended masters had given me free reign to go out and be forceful in order to achieve the goal I had set.

> As life's own song I ever hear,
> it does consume all sense of fear.
> In tune with Mother's symphony,
> from all diseases I AM free.
>
> **O Mother Mary, generate,**
> **the song that does accelerate,**
> **my mind into a peaceful state,**
> **God's perfect love I radiate.**

3. Mother Mary, help me rise to the point where I can be on earth and I can challenge people, but I am doing it from a state of peace. I am not trying to change other people in order to avoid having a negative feeling in myself or about myself.

> In Mother's love I do transcend,
> and all my struggles hereby end.
> For when with Mother's eye I see,
> no imperfection touches me.
>
> **O Mother Mary, generate,**
> **the song that does accelerate,**
> **my mind into a peaceful state,**
> **God's perfect love I radiate.**

4. I am willing to resolve the feeling in myself and get rid of these separate selves and therefore be at peace when I am interacting with other people.

> I see that healing must begin
> by finding Living Christ within.
> For as I see with single eye,
> each cell the light does amplify.
>
> **O Mother Mary, generate,**
> **the song that does accelerate,**

> my mind into a peaceful state,
> God's perfect love I radiate.

5. Mother Mary, help me come to the point where I am at peace interacting with other people no matter how they react to me.

> In Mother's music I am free,
> from memories of a lesser me.
> My vision in a perfect state,
> that all my cells regenerate.
>
> **O Mother Mary, generate,**
> **the song that does accelerate,**
> **my mind into a peaceful state,**
> **God's perfect love I radiate.**

6. Mother Mary, help me see if, before I came here, I thought I was coming here to change the earth. I am willing to come to the realization that this was not the highest understanding of why I came to earth. In reality, I came to earth to change myself, to have a certain experience and therefore come to that full acceptance of free will that I did not have before.

> O Mother's Love, sweet melody,
> from imperfections I AM free.
> O Mother Mary, sound of sounds,
> within my heart your love abounds.
>
> **O Mother Mary, generate,**
> **the song that does accelerate,**
> **my mind into a peaceful state,**
> **God's perfect love I radiate.**

7. I recognize that although there are fallen beings who are maliciously manipulating the free will of humanity, there are many fallen beings who actually believe that they are manipulating people's free will for people's own good. They believe that they are fighting for some legitimate cause and that the goal is so important that it justifies the means of forcing the free will of these people who just do not know better.

Through Mother's beauty so sublime,
transcending bounds of space and time.
All cells beyond the mortal tomb,
as they are whole in Mother's womb.

**O Mother Mary, generate,
the song that does accelerate,
my mind into a peaceful state,
God's perfect love I radiate.**

8. I recognize that the fallen beings, in trying to manipulate people on earth, have much the same frustration that I have had, namely that people do not respond, that they are not interested in changing, that they want to live the same kind of life lifetime after lifetime.

In resonance with life's own song,
in life's harmonics I belong.
The blueprint of my perfect state
does every cell reconsecrate.

**O Mother Mary, generate,
the song that does accelerate,
my mind into a peaceful state,
God's perfect love I radiate.**

9. I will *not* allow myself to have the attitude that the ends can justify the means, that it is okay to push people for their own good. Mother Mary, help me fully accept that free will is absolute. The Creator has created a creation and sent self-aware beings in there and given them an absolute free will, and they have the free will to explore everything that can be done with free will.

The tuning fork in every cell
is now attuned to Mother's bell.
From curse of death I AM now free,
I claim my immortality.

**O Mother Mary, generate,
the song that does accelerate,**

my mind into a peaceful state,
God's perfect love I radiate.

Part 4

1. I have complete free will, but I do not start out with the highest level of consciousness. I start out with a point-like, narrow sense of self and I am exercising my free will based on that self.

O Blessed Mary's Song of Life,
consuming every form of strife.
As I attune to sound so fair,
each cell is healthy, I declare.

**O Mother Mary, generate,
the song that does accelerate,
my mind into a peaceful state,
God's perfect love I radiate.**

2. The central enigma about free will is: "How do I balance my own free will with the free will of the other beings around me?" Mother Mary, help me ponder this enigma and move towards accepting free will and what it means.

As life's own song I ever hear,
it does consume all sense of fear.
In tune with Mother's symphony,
from all diseases I AM free.

**O Mother Mary, generate,
the song that does accelerate,
my mind into a peaceful state,
God's perfect love I radiate.**

3. When the Creator gave free will to co-creators, he gave them the freedom to explore anything that can be done with free will. One of the things that can be done with free will is that we can act as a separate self. The

question is: How far into separation do we need to go before we realize that this is not what we want to do anymore?

> In Mother's love I do transcend,
> and all my struggles hereby end.
> For when with Mother's eye I see,
> no imperfection touches me.
>
> **O Mother Mary, generate,**
> **the song that does accelerate,**
> **my mind into a peaceful state,**
> **God's perfect love I radiate.**

4. We have free will in the sense that no matter what self we have, no matter what self we have developed, we are allowed to make any choices we can see from that self. Those choices have consequences and we are going to experience those consequences.

> I see that healing must begin
> by finding Living Christ within.
> For as I see with single eye,
> each cell the light does amplify.
>
> **O Mother Mary, generate,**
> **the song that does accelerate,**
> **my mind into a peaceful state,**
> **God's perfect love I radiate.**

5. The more we go into separation, the more dense we make our environment, the more of a struggle it becomes to exercise our will through that separate self. I have had enough of this struggle and I say: "There must be a higher way to exercise my will than this. There must be a more *free* will than what I have right now."

> In Mother's music I am free,
> from memories of a lesser me.
> My vision in a perfect state,
> that all my cells regenerate.

> **O Mother Mary, generate,**
> **the song that does accelerate,**
> **my mind into a peaceful state,**
> **God's perfect love I radiate.**

6. For free will to outplay itself in this unascended sphere, some beings have to go as far into separation as the fallen beings have done. There had to be some planets where these beings could outplay themselves and earth is one of those planets.

> O Mother's Love, sweet melody,
> from imperfections I AM free.
> O Mother Mary, sound of sounds,
> within my heart your love abounds.

> **O Mother Mary, generate,**
> **the song that does accelerate,**
> **my mind into a peaceful state,**
> **God's perfect love I radiate.**

7. Mother Mary, help me see why I chose to come to this planet. Help me see that I wanted to have an experience of what it is like to be on a planet where some beings have taken their "free" will into such extremes of selfishness and separation.

> Through Mother's beauty so sublime,
> transcending bounds of space and time.
> All cells beyond the mortal tomb,
> as they are whole in Mother's womb.

> **O Mother Mary, generate,**
> **the song that does accelerate,**
> **my mind into a peaceful state,**
> **God's perfect love I radiate.**

8. Mother Mary, help me remember why I wanted to have that experience. Help me see that I did not come here because I wanted to change other people or change the planet. I did not want to rescue or save anybody, or judge the fallen beings or change the fallen beings.

In resonance with life's own song,
in life's harmonics I belong.
The blueprint of my perfect state
does every cell reconsecrate.

**O Mother Mary, generate,
the song that does accelerate,
my mind into a peaceful state,
God's perfect love I radiate.**

9. Mother Mary, help me remember that I came here because I wanted to experience my self in this kind of environment. I wanted to experience what it was like to be me in an environment as dense as earth.

The tuning fork in every cell
is now attuned to Mother's bell.
From curse of death I AM now free,
I claim my immortality.

**O Mother Mary, generate,
the song that does accelerate,
my mind into a peaceful state,
God's perfect love I radiate.**

Part 5

1. Mother Mary, help me see if I felt I had explored a natural planet to the fullest. I had experienced everything there is to experience on a natural planet, and then I decided I wanted to experience how I am on an unnatural planet. This is a valid and valuable desire because it helps raise the collective consciousness of the entire sphere.

O Blessed Mary's Song of Life,
consuming every form of strife.
As I attune to sound so fair,
each cell is healthy, I declare.

> **O Mother Mary, generate,**
> **the song that does accelerate,**
> **my mind into a peaceful state,**
> **God's perfect love I radiate.**

2. Mother Mary, help me see if I decided: "In order to reach a higher level of self-mastery, I want to experience a completely different environment, because I want to experience how I am, how I react, how I see myself in that kind of environment."

> As life's own song I ever hear,
> it does consume all sense of fear.
> In tune with Mother's symphony,
> from all diseases I AM free.

> **O Mother Mary, generate,**
> **the song that does accelerate,**
> **my mind into a peaceful state,**
> **God's perfect love I radiate.**

3. In order to descend into embodiment on a planet like earth, I had to descend to the 48th level and take on all the illusions above the 48th level. There is *nothing wrong here*. Nothing went wrong in this process.

> In Mother's love I do transcend,
> and all my struggles hereby end.
> For when with Mother's eye I see,
> no imperfection touches me.

> **O Mother Mary, generate,**
> **the song that does accelerate,**
> **my mind into a peaceful state,**
> **God's perfect love I radiate.**

4. I simply did what had to be done for me to take embodiment on an unnatural planet. It was not *stupid*. It was not *wrong*. It was a choice I made.

> I see that healing must begin
> by finding Living Christ within.

For as I see with single eye,
each cell the light does amplify.

**O Mother Mary, generate,
the song that does accelerate,
my mind into a peaceful state,
God's perfect love I radiate.**

5. What I wanted to experience was exactly what I have experienced on earth, namely that I came here with a certain level of consciousness that corresponded to the planet. I descended to the 48th level of consciousness in order to have the experience of what it was like to be me on planet earth.

In Mother's music I am free,
from memories of a lesser me.
My vision in a perfect state,
that all my cells regenerate.

**O Mother Mary, generate,
the song that does accelerate,
my mind into a peaceful state,
God's perfect love I radiate.**

6. I wanted to experience: "What is it like to be me on earth?" And *that* I have experienced.

O Mother's Love, sweet melody,
from imperfections I AM free.
O Mother Mary, sound of sounds,
within my heart your love abounds.

**O Mother Mary, generate,
the song that does accelerate,
my mind into a peaceful state,
God's perfect love I radiate.**

7. Even though many of the experiences I have had on earth have been colored by a certain state of consciousness, a certain outer self, I have still,

behind it all, had the experience of what it is like to be me in an environment like this.

> Through Mother's beauty so sublime,
> transcending bounds of space and time.
> All cells beyond the mortal tomb,
> as they are whole in Mother's womb.
>
> **O Mother Mary, generate,**
> **the song that does accelerate,**
> **my mind into a peaceful state,**
> **God's perfect love I radiate.**

8. Mother Mary, help me connect to my basic spirituality, my basic individuality in my I AM Presence.

> In resonance with life's own song,
> in life's harmonics I belong.
> The blueprint of my perfect state
> does every cell reconsecrate.
>
> **O Mother Mary, generate,**
> **the song that does accelerate,**
> **my mind into a peaceful state,**
> **God's perfect love I radiate.**

9. Mother Mary, help me see that the "you" that has experienced being me on earth is not the outer self. It is not the primal self, it is not even the Conscious You. What has experienced being me in an environment like earth, is my I AM Presence. At that level, I have had the experience of what it is like to be me on earth. I have had that since I first came here.

> The tuning fork in every cell
> is now attuned to Mother's bell.
> From curse of death I AM now free,
> I claim my immortality.
>
> **O Mother Mary, generate,**
> **the song that does accelerate,**

> my mind into a peaceful state,
> God's perfect love I radiate.

Part 6

1. I have had a different experience at the level of the Conscious You where I have identified with these outer selves, with the four lower bodies, and I have experienced through that filter.

> O Blessed Mary's Song of Life,
> consuming every form of strife.
> As I attune to sound so fair,
> each cell is healthy, I declare.
>
> **O Mother Mary, generate,**
> **the song that does accelerate,**
> **my mind into a peaceful state,**
> **God's perfect love I radiate.**

2. Mother Mary, help me come to a point where I can experience what my I AM Presence is experiencing. I can experience being me, being the I AM Presence in embodiment on earth, while I am in embodiment on earth. *That* experience is the ultimate way to make peace with being on earth.

> As life's own song I ever hear,
> it does consume all sense of fear.
> In tune with Mother's symphony,
> from all diseases I AM free.
>
> **O Mother Mary, generate,**
> **the song that does accelerate,**
> **my mind into a peaceful state,**
> **God's perfect love I radiate.**

3. Mother Mary, help me see that I have in glimpses had the experience of what it is like to be me on earth. I have had this subtle sense of looking at life in a different way of being connected to my I AM Presence.

In Mother's love I do transcend,
and all my struggles hereby end.
For when with Mother's eye I see,
no imperfection touches me.

**O Mother Mary, generate,
the song that does accelerate,
my mind into a peaceful state,
God's perfect love I radiate.**

4. Mother Mary, help me experience the sense that I am completely neutral about what is happening on earth. I am not analyzing or judging it. I am just experiencing it. I am experiencing it, not through all of these separate selves. I am experiencing it as the being I really am.

I see that healing must begin
by finding Living Christ within.
For as I see with single eye,
each cell the light does amplify.

**O Mother Mary, generate,
the song that does accelerate,
my mind into a peaceful state,
God's perfect love I radiate.**

5. Mother Mary, help me experience the state where there is no judgment, there is no analysis, there is no goal. There is nothing I *have* to do. I am just experiencing earth.

In Mother's music I am free,
from memories of a lesser me.
My vision in a perfect state,
that all my cells regenerate.

**O Mother Mary, generate,
the song that does accelerate,
my mind into a peaceful state,
God's perfect love I radiate.**

6. I am willing to be in a neutral state of mind, in a state of oneness, in the state of connection, where I am not feeling I am alone here on earth. I am not feeling I do not belong here because I have a connection to my I AM Presence. Therefore, I belong anywhere.

> O Mother's Love, sweet melody,
> from imperfections I AM free.
> O Mother Mary, sound of sounds,
> within my heart your love abounds.
>
> **O Mother Mary, generate,**
> **the song that does accelerate,**
> **my mind into a peaceful state,**
> **God's perfect love I radiate.**

7. I will continue to work on these separate selves, including the primal self, until I come to the point where I can say: "Why did I actually choose to come to earth? Because I, the greater being that I AM, wanted to experience myself in this type of environment."

> Through Mother's beauty so sublime,
> transcending bounds of space and time.
> All cells beyond the mortal tomb,
> as they are whole in Mother's womb.
>
> **O Mother Mary, generate,**
> **the song that does accelerate,**
> **my mind into a peaceful state,**
> **God's perfect love I radiate.**

8. When I am not being pulled into reactionary patterns by all of these separate selves, I will have the experience that regardless of how the planet is, of how difficult it is, how difficult people are, I feel I am being myself on this planet.

> In resonance with life's own song,
> in life's harmonics I belong.
> The blueprint of my perfect state
> does every cell reconsecrate.

> O Mother Mary, generate,
> the song that does accelerate,
> my mind into a peaceful state,
> God's perfect love I radiate.

9. I accept that it is possible for me in this lifetime to come to the point where I feel that way all the time. It becomes the backdrop for my experience on earth.

> The tuning fork in every cell
> is now attuned to Mother's bell.
> From curse of death I AM now free,
> I claim my immortality.

> O Mother Mary, generate,
> the song that does accelerate,
> my mind into a peaceful state,
> God's perfect love I radiate.

Part 7

1. I am willing to be aware of that greater sense of connection so that I never feel that I am alone here. I never feel I do not belong here because I realize earth is not my home. Nothing in the material octave is my home. My I AM Presence is my home. When I am connected to my I AM Presence, I am at home anywhere because the outer environment does not really matter.

> O Blessed Mary's Song of Life,
> consuming every form of strife.
> As I attune to sound so fair,
> each cell is healthy, I declare.

> O Mother Mary, generate,
> the song that does accelerate,
> my mind into a peaceful state,
> God's perfect love I radiate.

2. Earth is simply a planet for beings who have chosen to explore how far we can go into separation before we cannot stand it anymore. It is meaningless to have a sense of what *should* or *should not* happen on a planet like earth.

> As life's own song I ever hear,
> it does consume all sense of fear.
> In tune with Mother's symphony,
> from all diseases I AM free.
>
> **O Mother Mary, generate,**
> **the song that does accelerate,**
> **my mind into a peaceful state,**
> **God's perfect love I radiate.**

3. On an unnatural planet, it is not constructive to judge that suffering should not be here. It only puts me in a non-constructive frame of mind that prevents me from being at peace with being on earth. The moment I judge that something should not be happening on earth, at that very moment, I have put myself in a box in which I cannot be at peace.

> In Mother's love I do transcend,
> and all my struggles hereby end.
> For when with Mother's eye I see,
> no imperfection touches me.
>
> **O Mother Mary, generate,**
> **the song that does accelerate,**
> **my mind into a peaceful state,**
> **God's perfect love I radiate.**

4. Mother Mary, help me shift my mind so I realize that whatever is happening on earth is what somebody has chosen to manifest because they needed that experience. If I have total respect for free will, I can say: "I need to allow these people to suffer as they have chosen to suffer."

> I see that healing must begin
> by finding Living Christ within.

For as I see with single eye,
each cell the light does amplify.

**O Mother Mary, generate,
the song that does accelerate,
my mind into a peaceful state,
God's perfect love I radiate.**

5. I also need to respect my own free will so that I do not have to suffer the way they suffer. I do not have to feel empathy with them. I do not have to feel compassion for them. I do not even have to put my attention on their suffering if that takes away my peace.

In Mother's music I am free,
from memories of a lesser me.
My vision in a perfect state,
that all my cells regenerate.

**O Mother Mary, generate,
the song that does accelerate,
my mind into a peaceful state,
God's perfect love I radiate.**

6. I am willing to go through a phase where I select out certain things in my life that are not constructive for my growth. I am saying: "Right now, it is not constructive for me to feel pity or compassion for people who are suffering. Therefore, it is acceptable for me that I do not put my attention on their suffering."

O Mother's Love, sweet melody,
from imperfections I AM free.
O Mother Mary, sound of sounds,
within my heart your love abounds.

**O Mother Mary, generate,
the song that does accelerate,
my mind into a peaceful state,
God's perfect love I radiate.**

7. This is necessary for me in order to work through this mechanism where I feel that things should not have happened and this takes away my peace. In order for me to find peace, it is acceptable and necessary that I go through a period where I basically ignore people's suffering and I am focusing on overcoming all of these reactionary selves.

> Through Mother's beauty so sublime,
> transcending bounds of space and time.
> All cells beyond the mortal tomb,
> as they are whole in Mother's womb.
>
> **O Mother Mary, generate,**
> **the song that does accelerate,**
> **my mind into a peaceful state,**
> **God's perfect love I radiate.**

8. When I have attained a degree of inner peace, I can go back out and seek to help people, challenge people or whatever I feel. I will be doing it from a state of inner peace rather than from a state of non-peace, a state of frustration, a state where I am constantly judging that this should not be here.

> In resonance with life's own song,
> in life's harmonics I belong.
> The blueprint of my perfect state
> does every cell reconsecrate.
>
> **O Mother Mary, generate,**
> **the song that does accelerate,**
> **my mind into a peaceful state,**
> **God's perfect love I radiate.**

9. When I feel that I am stupid for having come to earth, then I automatically start judging that other people are stupid for not responding to me and not letting me help them. I am keeping myself in a certain box where I am judging myself that I could be stupid or wrong for coming to earth.

> The tuning fork in every cell
> is now attuned to Mother's bell.

From curse of death I AM now free,
I claim my immortality.

**O Mother Mary, generate,
the song that does accelerate,
my mind into a peaceful state,
God's perfect love I radiate.**

Part 8

1. It is the fallen beings who have put this standard on the earth, and I have come to accept the standard of the fallen beings. I am now judging myself as the fallen beings judge me, not as the ascended masters look at me.

O Blessed Mary's Song of Life,
consuming every form of strife.
As I attune to sound so fair,
each cell is healthy, I declare.

**O Mother Mary, generate,
the song that does accelerate,
my mind into a peaceful state,
God's perfect love I radiate.**

2. I chose to come to earth because I wanted to experience myself in this environment. How could that choice possibly be wrong? What could ever be wrong with wanting to experience myself in a specific environment? That is what a co-creator is all about.

As life's own song I ever hear,
it does consume all sense of fear.
In tune with Mother's symphony,
from all diseases I AM free.

**O Mother Mary, generate,
the song that does accelerate,**

> my mind into a peaceful state,
> God's perfect love I radiate.

3. When I come to the higher levels of awareness, it is about experiencing myself in a specific environment and by seeing how I respond to that environment, I grow. There could never be anything wrong about this choice. It is simply a very valid and valuable choice. I chose to help raise my sphere by coming to a planet like earth and experiencing myself here.

> In Mother's love I do transcend,
> and all my struggles hereby end.
> For when with Mother's eye I see,
> no imperfection touches me.

> **O Mother Mary, generate,**
> **the song that does accelerate,**
> **my mind into a peaceful state,**
> **God's perfect love I radiate.**

4. I also have a desire to help raise the earth, but I cannot help raise the earth by *doing* something! I need to be here without doing because people have created all of these problems by *doing* forcefully. I raise the earth by *being* here.

> I see that healing must begin
> by finding Living Christ within.
> For as I see with single eye,
> each cell the light does amplify.

> **O Mother Mary, generate,**
> **the song that does accelerate,**
> **my mind into a peaceful state,**
> **God's perfect love I radiate.**

5. It is not so much what I can *do* or *say* on the outer that will change the earth. It is the very fact that I have come into embodiment and therefore I am an anchor point and an open door for the I AM Presence.

In Mother's music I am free,
from memories of a lesser me.
My vision in a perfect state,
that all my cells regenerate.

**O Mother Mary, generate,
the song that does accelerate,
my mind into a peaceful state,
God's perfect love I radiate.**

6. I want to make a contribution to changing earth by becoming more of an open door for my I AM Presence. I will let the light shine, without having a judgement in the outer mind of what I *should* do or what I *should not* do, how the light should shine, what changes should happen, how other people should react. I will just let the light shine because that is the real way to change the earth.

O Mother's Love, sweet melody,
from imperfections I AM free.
O Mother Mary, sound of sounds,
within my heart your love abounds.

**O Mother Mary, generate,
the song that does accelerate,
my mind into a peaceful state,
God's perfect love I radiate.**

7. I have already demonstrated the process of how to raise my consciousness. I am willing to take this further and come to a point where I demonstrate how to start at a certain level of consciousness and attain inner peace and be at peace with being on a planet like this. *That* is my highest potential, that is what I defined in my Divine plan as my highest potential. I wanted to come here and demonstrate being at peace.

Through Mother's beauty so sublime,
transcending bounds of space and time.
All cells beyond the mortal tomb,
as they are whole in Mother's womb.

**O Mother Mary, generate,
the song that does accelerate,
my mind into a peaceful state,
God's perfect love I radiate.**

8. There is no blame, there is no saying I have done anything wrong. I have done exactly what I needed to do. I will attain that inner peace where I can enjoy experiencing myself on this planet. As difficult as it is, I can avoid being pulled into all of these difficulties but still experience my Self and experience how my I AM Presence looks at earth, experiences earth.

In resonance with life's own song,
in life's harmonics I belong.
The blueprint of my perfect state
does every cell reconsecrate.

**O Mother Mary, generate,
the song that does accelerate,
my mind into a peaceful state,
God's perfect love I radiate.**

9. From the moment I first took embodiment here, no matter what the Conscious You or the outer self has experienced, my I AM Presence has been in complete peace about everything that has happened on earth. My I AM Presence knows that the real me cannot be affected by anything that could ever happen on earth. I knew this before I came and that is why it was not a stupid choice to come here. I am reclaiming this awareness and I reclaim the peace that I had before I came here.

The tuning fork in every cell
is now attuned to Mother's bell.
From curse of death I AM now free,
I claim my immortality.

**O Mother Mary, generate,
the song that does accelerate,
my mind into a peaceful state,
God's perfect love I radiate.**

Sealing

In the name of the Divine Mother, I call to Mother Mary for the sealing of myself and all people in my circle of influence in the creative flow of the Divine Mother, the River of Life. I call for the multiplication of my calls by all representatives of the Divine Mother, so that we form the perfect figure-eight flow of "As Above, so below." Thus, I accept that this is fully manifest, because the mouth of the Lord, the Divine Mother that I AM, has spoken it. Amen.

5 | CLAIMING YOUR GOD-GIVEN RIGHT TO FORGET

I AM the Ascended Master MORE, and it is my joy to give you another installment up from the one I gave you last year on this very profound and very important topic of the birth trauma and how you overcome it. You might look at what Gautama Buddha said earlier in the question and answer session about time and about how, if you cannot go back in time to change what happened in the past, if you do not have a time machine, you cannot be free of the past [See the last chapter of this book]. As Gautama said, Mother Mary has indeed given you a time machine in her exercise of how to go back to experience that birth trauma [In the book *Healing Your Spiritual Traumas*].

I would like to give you one more time machine. You see my beloved, what the fallen beings want you to think is that the past is set in stone, it cannot be changed. Once you have made a certain mistake here on earth, you can never be free of it. Now, imagine that you are standing in front of a large stone wall. If you have been to the Great Wall of China, to the Pyramids, to the Wailing Wall in Jerusalem or to any of the fortifications you see here in this city of Tallinn or any of the other older cities in the world, you do not even have to imagine. You know exactly what it feels like to be standing in front of one of these massive stone walls. How can you break that down with your bare hands? Well, you cannot but why is that? Well, it is partly because the stones are hard and partly because they are glued together.

Imagine that, first of all, you could remove the mortar, you could remove the cement that keeps the stones stuck together. If the stones were loose, it is, of course, much more manageable to break down the wall. Yet, it still might be difficult, depending on the size of the stones. What if you could reduce the stones to a smaller substance, such as sand? What if you had some kind of machine that could send some kind of ray at this stone wall and suddenly all the stones crumbled and became sand?

Well, this is indeed what we have already given you the power to do with decrees and invocations. Not, of course, that you could crumble a stone wall, although theoretically if enough of you were standing in front of one of these stone walls, it would be possible to break it down. Nevertheless, we are not really interested in having our students go around breaking down stone walls around the world, possibly getting imprisoned for destroying historical monuments. We are far more interested in having you break down the walls in your own minds that are keeping you trapped and tied into a reactionary pattern with the fallen beings.

Naturally, you have the decrees and invocations that, as we have said many times, can be used to dissolve the energy and when the energy is less, it is easier for you to free yourself from the pattern. Still, as we have also said many times, there needs to be a conscious experience, a conscious decision, before you are truly free. It is not a mechanical process.

Becoming aware of the process of seeing

What I want to offer you here is this. You need to start, and it may begin slowly, but you need to start training your minds to envision, to imagine and eventually to actually see and experience what you already know intellectually, namely that the entire material world is built of energy. Imagine now, that you become aware that you had a very traumatic situation in your past and you are carrying that birth trauma with you. What is that situation made of? As Gautama Buddha said, time has moved on and the physical situation is no longer there, it has simply been erased by time. Or it has, we could say, been painted over by time, by the big paintbrush of time that has changed things into what they are now. As Gautama said: What is now, may indeed be affected by the past but nevertheless the past is no longer there as a physical reality. It is there as an imprint or an image

5 | Claiming your God-given right to forget

in your mind, in your three higher bodies, in a certain sense also in your physical body.

The question now is, how to free yourself from this imprint. What you need to start pondering is how your physical brain, your physical eyes (but especially the brain) and how your outer mind looks at, perceives situations—for that matter, perceives everything. Right now you are sitting here, you are looking at this wall behind the messenger, which is fairly solid, and what you are seeing is actually an image. We have said before that your eyes are not really seeing a wall, your eyes are simply receiving impulses coming to them, hitting the retina as light rays. The eye is not really seeing but is reacting to light rays. These create a reaction in the eye that is transformed into a signal similar to what you see in a computer with a digital signal. This signal is sent to what you call the visual cortex in the brain.

Now, the brain has the effect of helping you make sense of the physical world. The primary tool you use to help make sense of the physical world is that the brain imposes certain images upon the impulses that are coming from the eyes. The eyes are not seeing. In a sense, you could say that the brain is not seeing either. The brain is simply taking the impulses that come from the eyes, organizing them into an image that matches what the brain already has in its database. The brain, as it has been proven by many of these optical illusions that you have all seen, is not actually seeing what is in front of you. It is looking for a pattern that matches something it already has in its database. It is not looking at exactly what are the signals that are coming from the eyes, it is looking for a pattern that it can recognize. Once it has enough impulses that form a recognizable pattern, the brain actually stops reacting, stops looking at the impulses from the eyes and now it superimposes that stored pattern upon what you are seeing and saying: "Oh, this is what it is."

This, of course, has been going on here on earth for millions of years. When you come into this embodiment, your brain is not starting at zero and having to train itself and build up these images of what is this and what is that. Your brain is very much tied in to this collective momentum and so your brain already has a certain programming: This is a tree, this is a rock, this is the ocean, this is the sky, and so forth and so on. You have a database of patterns that not only *you* have seen before but that the collective consciousness has seen before. Therefore, you are used to seeing everything in terms of images and you are labelling everything, often labelling it with words, which adds another layer of complexity where the visual cortex basically recognizes shapes. The visual cortex of the brain might look at the shape of this wall and the color and the texture, but there is another aspect of the brain which then translates that into words, such as: "This is a wall." This adds another layer where there is also a very old momentum of people putting words on everything.

How you are trapped by your perception

It says in the Bible that God gave Adam the power to name every animal on earth. There are some that believe that if you know the name of a thing, you have power over the thing. The deeper reality is that when you name something, you are actually limiting yourself because you are reinforcing your mental box. Now, you think that this thing is the way you have labelled it and it will always be so. You cannot look beyond the programming, at least most people cannot. Therefore, you think: "This is the way it is." You have tied in to this collective momentum and you have built your own momentum over your past lifetimes.

When we tell you that there was a period or a situation in the past where you experienced a very traumatic situation and we give you an example, such as in the *My Lives* book where the protagonist experienced this very difficult situation, then you are so programmed, your brain is so programmed, to superimpose an image upon this, to put words upon it and to say: "This is how it was." The question now is: How do you truly become free of a situation from your past? As long as you have in your brain, even in your three higher bodies, the imprint of that situation, the images, the words that you associate with that situation, as long as they are stored there, you cannot be free of that situation from the past.

What I am telling you is that you can start retraining yourself. You can actually train your mind to override your brain. It may help you to take some of these many, many optical illusions that are out there. You have the classical one of the drawing that can look like a young beautiful woman or an old wrinkled lady, depending on how you focus on it. You have many others with different colors, different shapes and so forth and so on. If you have never really done this, it might help you to take some of these and realize that you cannot actually trust your senses. You cannot trust your *brain* because there is a certain programming there that makes it see things a certain way even though that is not the way they really are. You can also take another step and imagine what it is like to sit in a movie theatre. You are seeing something on the screen and because the movie theatre is dark, it is possible for you to become completely engrossed in it, to the point where you might even feel that you are right there in the situation that is being displayed on the screen. You are certainly so absorbed in it that you forget everything else. You can train yourself to realize that the images that are displayed on the screen, not only do they not represent a physical reality (because you know they are just images on a film strip in the projector), but even beyond that, you can train yourself to see that these are just patterns of colored dots that are projected onto the screen. You can actually come to a point where you train your eyes to go slightly out of focus and, now, instead of seeing these figures, these people or whatever is projected on the screen, you are just seeing the different fields of colored light rays that are projected onto the screen. When you work with this, you can gradually, over some time, come to the point where you can apply this to everyday life. You can train yourself to see that this wall behind the messenger is really not a wall. It is just certain light rays that form certain patterns.

You might even, as a child, have been told to take a newspaper photograph and look at it through a magnifying glass. Then, you can see that what seems to be certain fields, certain shapes, are actually made out of black dots that are arranged in various degrees of density. The darker the color, the closer the dots are together. The lighter the color, the further they are spaced apart. It is all made of black dots that simply cheat your brain into seeing an image. You can actually train yourself to focus on the dots rather than the image. You can then apply this to all situations in life, but it is not so important to apply it at this point to specific situations in life.

Breaking images of your past down to smaller units

What I desire you to start doing, is to look at situations from your past. Perhaps, you have a sense of your birth trauma and you do not feel it is resolved. Perhaps, you have another situation, even a situation from this lifetime where you feel something traumatic happened. You can now consider: When you think about that situation, what is the image that your brain brings up or that your three higher bodies bring up? What is that image? You would say, then, from a certain linear perspective that if you have a memory, if you have an image from your past, then you can never be free of that image because whatever happened in the past happened and you cannot change this. There is nothing you can do about it.

This is, of course, what the fallen beings want you to believe, not what is reality. You can train yourself to bring up these images for your inner vision. Then, you can train yourself to see them, not as the shapes and the images that you have but simply as patterns of light rays or patterns of atoms, electrons, subatomic particles—or however you can visualize this. You break the image down into a smaller component, however you can visualize this. As I said, if you are standing in front of a stone wall, you can break the stones down into sand particles that are much easier to move than the solid stones. That is what you can train yourself to do with these images from your past that might be haunting you, or that you may have suppressed but you then bring it up when you start touching on the birth trauma.

You can train yourself to consciously recognize: "This image is just an image that my brain and my emotional, mental and identity bodies are superimposing upon this." The reality is that it is not a physical situation anymore. It is just an image. That image is made up of these smaller electromagnetic light particles, these dots, these images made out of dots. You can even look at one of the paintings of the Impressionists, and at a certain distance you cannot see all of the dots they use to paint. When you go closer and closer to the painting, you begin to see the dots and if you get close enough to the painting, all you see is the dots because you cannot see the image. I am asking you here to train yourself, and this again has something to do with going into the pain. Now, it is not the pain you are going into, it is the visual image that you have in your mind.

You go closer and closer to that image until all you see are those dots. Then, you realize that the dots are the deeper reality. The images were just something superimposed by your brain and your emotional, mental and identity bodies. It is actually the dots that are the reality. You also realize that those dots are dynamic, they are fluid, they are constantly vibrating and they could as easily outpicture any other image as they could outpicture the present image. More than that, the dots could actually be set free from the matrix that has been superimposed upon them so that they return to their ground state, to a free state where they are just neutral, they are not displaying any image.

You might envision that the image is gradually dissolved into these smaller components, that the components start vibrating and moving, moving around, dissolving the shapes of the image and just taking on a uniform color. You might see that they become like the water of the ocean, or the sand of the desert, or the air of the blue sky but they become featureless, image-less. The image is dissolved, you are letting it go. It is as if you are making a decision, and you *are* making a decision at a certain point, to say: "I am letting this image die, I am letting it dissolve. I am simply forgetting it."

The secret to forgetting

My beloved, so many people around the world have situations from their past that are haunting them constantly or at least on a regular basis and they cannot seem to forget. Well, what is the secret of forgetting? It is to realize that your memories are stored (as we have said) partly as energy, emotional energy. For example, fear, anger, or whatever is stored and you can dissolve that energy with our decrees and invocations. More than that, your memories are stored as these images in your brain, in your three higher bodies. These images have been superimposed upon, you can call it quantum particles, you can call it the Ma-ter light, you can call it whatever you want. There are these particles that can take on, be organized into, various forms, various shapes, various densities and colors. You can undo the images that your mind has projected on these particles, set the particles free from the image. When you really do this, the image is no longer there and therefore, lo and behold, the memory is gone.

When you think about this, memory is something you have in the material realm, the four levels of the material realm. There has to be some vehicle that can carry the memory. How are most memories stored? As visual images. We have talked about the Akashic Records and there is a parallel of this in your three higher bodies, where there can be this storage medium, these particles, that take on a certain image and therefore maintain that shape indefinitely.

You can train yourself to go in, re-see the image but then see beyond the image and set those particles free to return to their ground state. When they are returned to their ground state, the image is dissolved and that is the vehicle for memory. When the vehicle for memory is dissolved, the memory is also dissolved, my beloved. This is how you can forget.

This might require some work for you, but what would be the fun if you did not have things to work on? You might end up getting bored here on this planet where many of you have said, there really is not that much you personally want to do or experience here, there is not that much for you. There is, of course, this, that you want to be free. Many of you want to move on. Well, you cannot move on until you are free of your memories as well.

There is, my beloved, a description in a book given through a previous dispensation where it is described that there are three students who come to my retreat in Darjeeling and they are shown a certain situation from their past, from the Akashic Records. Then, I take a jewel that I have and I use it to send light rays at this situation in the Akashic Records and erase it. This is an illustration given in the past when we were giving teachings for a lower level of consciousness. There is a reality to it in the sense that you can actually train your mind to be an open door for a light ray from a higher realm. It can be from your I AM Presence, it can be from an ascended master of your choice—and, naturally, I offer my service here. If you tune in to me and you visualize that I am sending a light ray into this image, and thereby causing these particles to start vibrating faster so they jump out of the set pattern of the image and return to their ground state, then this might also be a visualization that can help you.

Nothing is solid

You need to, first, train yourself to see that the image you have in your mind is actually made of these particles and therefore the image is fluid. It can easily be dissolved, it is not set in stone, it is not a solid wall. Of course, you can go on and realize that a wall is not solid but my concern here is not to have you perform these kind of tricks but actually to perform the really valuable feat of erasing your bad memories, either from past lives or from this life.

My beloved, this, of course, is something you were not told in kindergarten. Therefore, it may take some work, some contemplation, for you to retool your mind to actually come to accept that nothing in the physical, material world, nothing in the four realms of matter, is set in stone. Nothing is unchangeable because everything is made out of these light particles that have had a certain image superimposed upon them.

These light particles are not actually light particles, as science tells you that even subatomic particles are particles. You will know, if you have read about quantum physics, that scientists are baffled by the fact that an electron can appear as both a particle and a wave. They call it the wave-particle duality and they cannot explain it. The reality is that the idea that this subatomic something-or-other is a particle is an image that scientists carry in their minds because it relates to something you can see with the physical senses. They are carrying this image in their minds and wanting to superimpose this image upon this quantum level that they have discovered. The only way to understand the quantum level is to realize that it has no connection whatsoever to the macroscopic world that you can see with your senses.

The only way to really understand the quantum world and its relationship to the macroscopic world is to realize that the macroscopic world is not made up of shapes. It is made up of particles, or rather, these smaller entities that have had images superimposed upon them. A rock is not a rock; it is a collection of these light entities, light units, that have been forced into a certain pattern and are outpicturing that pattern. They could very well be set free from the pattern so they could return to a ground state or outpicture another pattern. Again, it may be a little too much for you to visualize that the entire physical world is made up of particles or smaller entities and is fluid, but certainly you can see that the images you hold in your mind, the images of the past, are not made up of a physical substance as solid as stone. They are, indeed, made up of a different kind of entities, and therefore they are fluid.

In reality, the entire material universe is made up of what we have called the Ma-ter Light. The Ma-ter Light has individual units that are very, very small. We might, if we want to use the terminology used by science, say that it is meaningless to talk about a particle because a particle has an extension in space. It is a dot of a certain size. The units that make up the Ma-ter Light are, although they are not infinitely small, they are so small that it certainly is beyond what you can detect with the physical senses or even with other instruments that are based on visible light, the wavelength of visible light.

You might know that a microscope can magnify small objects. They can make you see objects you cannot see with the naked eye. Nevertheless, there is a limit to what you can see in a microscope because an optical microscope can only operate with visible light. Visible light has a certain minimum wavelength and any object that is smaller than the wavelength of light, cannot be seen in an optical microscope. It is simply impossible. The same thing with these entities, units of the Ma-ter Light, they cannot be seen by any instrument created by science because these are material instruments and the Ma-ter Light is not material. It becomes material when it has an image superimposed upon it. You have in the quantum world even the situation where a particle can appear out of nowhere and disappear again. Scientists talk about a vacuum state, a quantum field, or other names where a particle can suddenly appear and disappear because it goes in and out of a certain state. Well, this is how you can visualize the Ma-ter Light. The Ma-ter Light, you could say, is not in the physical realm but it can be pulled into the physical spectrum. Then, these small dots of Ma-ter Light can be arranged into a certain pattern, but the Ma-ter Light will only remain in that pattern (in the physical) as long as something is projecting that image upon it. The reason the earth has certain manifestations that are man-made and that are persisting over time, is that the collective consciousness is constantly projecting certain images upon the Ma-ter Light.

You have unconscious memories

What I am telling you is that the reason you have a memory of the past (or a record or whatever you want to call it), is that your mind is superimposing that image on the Ma-ter Light. This prevents the units of the Ma-ter Light from returning to their ground state, from going back out of the physical. Now, you may say: "But how am I doing this when I do not have a conscious memory of my birth trauma?" You have an *unconscious* memory.

Memory is not just conscious, that is why we could say that what you remember consciously is a memory and what you are not consciously aware of is a record. We have sometimes used that distinction. You can also talk about *conscious* and *unconscious* memories. You all know that sometimes there is a certain fact that you know you have heard in the past but you cannot recall it consciously right now. Then, as you think about it, suddenly it clicks and now you remember. Well, that memory was obviously there even if it was not in your conscious mind and the same thing with these situations from the past. They are there because your subconscious mind is continually projecting a certain image upon the Ma-ter Light.

What you can train your mind to do, is to see that the image is not an image that is physical, that is unchanging. It is made up of these very small dots of Ma-ter Light. Then, you can make a conscious decision to say: "Poof" and dissolve the image. For this to happen, you may need to give a certain amount of decrees and invocations to dissolve the emotional energy. You may have to come to, as we have said, see this as a separate

5 | Claiming your God-given right to forget

self, see that there is a separate self that is actually maintaining that image, wanting to maintain that image. You may decide to stop feeding it your energy and your attention. There can, when you follow the other steps we have given you previously, come that point where all that is actually left is the memory. You have dissolved the energy, the emotional energy, you have dissolved the separate self, you have let it die, but there is still a memory that you for some reason think you have to hold on to.

In some cases, there is a self that thinks it has to hold on to the memory and you can come to see that self. It is even a matter of (sometimes) just making that conscious switch, a conscious decision: "I do not have to hold on to all of my memories of what has happened to me on this planet."

Why do you, my beloved, why do you not have to remember? The fallen ones, your ego will scream at you: "No, you cannot just forget! This happened! You did this; you have to remember it forever!" Why do you need to remember it forever? What have we told you? No matter what you have gone through on this planet and how you experienced it through the filter of your four lower bodies, your I AM Presence had an entirely different experience. That experience is the enduring outcome, the enduring result, that you wanted to achieve by being in embodiment on earth. That experience is stored forever in your casual body. That is what is real. That is what is enduring. That is what you wanted to get out of being on earth.

These memories that you have in your four lower bodies have no enduring value. Why should they endure? Why should you carry them with you? Why should you not look at them and say: "Poof, you are gone."

Just accept, my beloved, accept that you have a right to forget. You cannot forget as long as you have the misqualified energy and the separate self, but when you have dissolved both of them, you have a right to forget. It is a human right, we might say, and it should be on the list of these inalienable rights that all humans have been endowed with by their Creator. You have a divinely given right to forget.

My hope is that you will take this teaching and begin to exercise that right. Should you desire my help, I am MORE than willing to give it.

6 | INVOKING MY GOD-GIVEN RIGHT TO FORGET

In the name I AM THAT I AM, Jesus Christ, I call to all representatives of the Divine Mother, especially Master MORE to help me claim my Divine right to forget my past, including…

[Make personal calls.]

Part 1

1. The past is not set in stone. The past can indeed be changed. Any and all mistakes I have made on earth, I can be free of them.

> Master MORE, come to the fore,
> we will absorb your flame of MORE.
> Master MORE, our will so strong,
> our power centers cleared by song.
>
> **Master MORE, your Sacred Heart,**
> **from this we will no more depart,**

we are forever in your flow,
of Diamond Will that you bestow.

2. I am willing to break down the walls in my own mind that are keeping me trapped and tied into a reactionary pattern with the fallen beings.

Master MORE, your wisdom flows,
as our attunement ever grows.
Master MORE, we have a tie,
that helps us see through Serpent's lie.

**Master MORE, your Sacred Heart,
from this we will no more depart,
we are forever in your flow,
of Diamond Will that you bestow.**

3. I am envisioning, imagining and actually seeing and experiencing that the entire material world is built of energy.

Master MORE, your love so pink,
there is no purer love, we think.
Master MORE, you set us free,
from all conditionality.

**Master MORE, your Sacred Heart,
from this we will no more depart,
we are forever in your flow,
of Diamond Will that you bestow.**

4. I focus my attention on a traumatic situation from my past. Time has moved on and the physical situation is no longer there, it has been erased by time.

Master MORE, we will endure,
your discipline that makes us pure.
Master MORE, intentions true,
as we are always one with you.

> **Master MORE, your Sacred Heart,**
> **from this we will no more depart,**
> **we are forever in your flow,**
> **of Diamond Will that you bestow.**

5. The situation has been painted over by time, by the big paintbrush of time that has changed things into what they are now.

> Master MORE, our vision raised,
> the will of God is always praised.
> Master MORE, creative will,
> raising all life higher still.

> **Master MORE, your Sacred Heart,**
> **from this we will no more depart,**
> **we are forever in your flow,**
> **of Diamond Will that you bestow.**

6. What is now, may indeed be affected by the past but the past is no longer there as a physical reality. It is there as an imprint or an image in my mind, in my three higher bodies, even in my physical body.

> Master MORE, your peace is power,
> the demons of war it will devour.
> Master MORE, we serve all life,
> our flames consuming war and strife.

> **Master MORE, your Sacred Heart,**
> **from this we will no more depart,**
> **we are forever in your flow,**
> **of Diamond Will that you bestow.**

7. The brain has the effect of helping me make sense of the physical world. The primary tool I use is that the brain imposes certain images upon the impulses that are coming from the eyes. The eyes are not seeing. The brain is taking the impulses that come from the eyes, organizing them into an image that matches what the brain already has in its database.

Master MORE, we are so free,
eternal bond from you we see.
Master MORE, we find rebirth,
in flow of your eternal mirth.

**Master MORE, your Sacred Heart,
from this we will no more depart,
we are forever in your flow,
of Diamond Will that you bestow.**

8. The brain is not seeing what is in front of me. It is looking for a pattern that matches something it already has in its database, a pattern that it can recognize. Once it has enough impulses to form a recognizable pattern, the brain stops looking and superimposes that stored pattern upon what I am seeing.

Master MORE, you balance all,
the seven rays upon our call.
Master MORE, forever MORE,
we are the Spirit's open door.

**Master MORE, your Sacred Heart,
from this we will no more depart,
we are forever in your flow,
of Diamond Will that you bestow.**

9. My brain is tied in to the collective momentum so my brain already has a certain programming. I have a database of patterns that not only I have seen before but that the collective consciousness has seen before.

Master MORE, your Presence here,
filling up the inner sphere.
Life is now a sacred flow,
God Power we on all bestow.

**Master MORE, your Sacred Heart,
from this we will no more depart,
we are forever in your flow,
of Diamond Will that you bestow.**

Part 2

1. I am used to seeing everything in terms of images and I am labelling everything, often labelling it with words. This adds another layer of complexity because there is a very old momentum of people naming things with words.

> Master MORE, come to the fore,
> we will absorb your flame of MORE.
> Master MORE, our will so strong,
> our power centers cleared by song.
>
> **Master MORE, your Sacred Heart,**
> **from this we will no more depart,**
> **we are forever in your flow,**
> **of Diamond Will that you bestow.**

2. When I name something, I am limiting myself because I am reinforcing my mental box, and now I think that this thing is the way I have labelled it and it will always be so. I have tied in to this collective momentum and I have built my own momentum over past lifetimes.

> Master MORE, your wisdom flows,
> as our attunement ever grows.
> Master MORE, we have a tie,
> that helps us see through Serpent's lie.
>
> **Master MORE, your Sacred Heart,**
> **from this we will no more depart,**
> **we are forever in your flow,**
> **of Diamond Will that you bestow.**

3. How do I become free of a situation from my past? As long as I have in my brain, and in my three higher bodies, the imprint of that situation, the images, the words that I associate with that situation, as long as they are stored there, I cannot be free of that situation from the past.

Master MORE, your love so pink,
there is no purer love, we think.
Master MORE, you set us free,
from all conditionality.

**Master MORE, your Sacred Heart,
from this we will no more depart,
we are forever in your flow,
of Diamond Will that you bestow.**

4. I am retraining myself, training my mind to override my brain. I cannot trust my brain because there is a certain programming there that makes it see things a certain way even though that is not the way they really are.

Master MORE, we will endure,
your discipline that makes us pure.
Master MORE, intentions true,
as we are always one with you.

**Master MORE, your Sacred Heart,
from this we will no more depart,
we are forever in your flow,
of Diamond Will that you bestow.**

5. I am training myself to realize that the images that are displayed on the screen of my mind do not represent a physical reality. They are just patterns of colored dots that are projected by my eyes.

Master MORE, our vision raised,
the will of God is always praised.
Master MORE, creative will,
raising all life higher still.

**Master MORE, your Sacred Heart,
from this we will no more depart,
we are forever in your flow,
of Diamond Will that you bestow.**

6. I training my eyes to go slightly out of focus and, now, instead of seeing figures and people, I am seeing the different fields of colored light rays that are reaching my eyes.

> Master MORE, your peace is power,
> the demons of war it will devour.
> Master MORE, we serve all life,
> our flames consuming war and strife.
>
> **Master MORE, your Sacred Heart,**
> **from this we will no more depart,**
> **we are forever in your flow,**
> **of Diamond Will that you bestow.**

7. I am training myself to see that solid objects are not solid and they are not objects. They are just light rays that form certain patterns.

> Master MORE, we are so free,
> eternal bond from you we see.
> Master MORE, we find rebirth,
> in flow of your eternal mirth.
>
> **Master MORE, your Sacred Heart,**
> **from this we will no more depart,**
> **we are forever in your flow,**
> **of Diamond Will that you bestow.**

8. I am connecting to a situation from my past and the image that my brain brings up or that my three higher bodies bring up.

> Master MORE, you balance all,
> the seven rays upon our call.
> Master MORE, forever MORE,
> we are the Spirit's open door.
>
> **Master MORE, your Sacred Heart,**
> **from this we will no more depart,**
> **we are forever in your flow,**
> **of Diamond Will that you bestow.**

9. I am training myself to bring up these images for my inner vision. Then, I see them, not as the shapes and the images that I have, but simply as patterns of light rays or patterns of atoms, electrons, subatomic particles.

> Master MORE, your Presence here,
> filling up the inner sphere.
> Life is now a sacred flow,
> God Power we on all bestow.
>
> **Master MORE, your Sacred Heart,
> from this we will no more depart,
> we are forever in your flow,
> of Diamond Will that you bestow.**

Part 3

1. I am training myself to take images from my past that are haunting me, or that I have suppressed, and I break the image down into smaller components.

> Master MORE, come to the fore,
> we will absorb your flame of MORE.
> Master MORE, our will so strong,
> our power centers cleared by song.
>
> **Master MORE, your Sacred Heart,
> from this we will no more depart,
> we are forever in your flow,
> of Diamond Will that you bestow.**

2. I am training myself to consciously recognize: "This image is just an image that my brain and my emotional, mental and identity bodies are superimposing upon the light. The reality is that it is not a physical situation anymore. It is just an image."

> Master MORE, your wisdom flows,
> as our attunement ever grows.

Master MORE, we have a tie,
that helps us see through Serpent's lie.

**Master MORE, your Sacred Heart,
from this we will no more depart,
we are forever in your flow,
of Diamond Will that you bestow.**

3. That image is made up of these smaller electromagnetic light particles, these dots, these images made out of dots. I am training myself to go into the visual image that I have in my mind.

Master MORE, your love so pink,
there is no purer love, we think.
Master MORE, you set us free,
from all conditionality.

**Master MORE, your Sacred Heart,
from this we will no more depart,
we are forever in your flow,
of Diamond Will that you bestow.**

4. I go closer and closer to that image until all I see are those dots. Then, I realize that the dots are the deeper reality. The images were just something superimposed by my brain and my emotional, mental and identity bodies. It is actually the dots that are the reality.

Master MORE, we will endure,
your discipline that makes us pure.
Master MORE, intentions true,
as we are always one with you.

**Master MORE, your Sacred Heart,
from this we will no more depart,
we are forever in your flow,
of Diamond Will that you bestow.**

5. I realize that those dots are dynamic, they are fluid, they are constantly vibrating and they could as easily outpicture any other image as they could outpicture the present image.

> Master MORE, our vision raised,
> the will of God is always praised.
> Master MORE, creative will,
> raising all life higher still.
>
> **Master MORE, your Sacred Heart,**
> **from this we will no more depart,**
> **we are forever in your flow,**
> **of Diamond Will that you bestow.**

6. The dots could actually be set free from the matrix that has been superimposed upon them, so that they return to their ground state, to a free state where they are just neutral, they are not displaying any image.

> Master MORE, your peace is power,
> the demons of war it will devour.
> Master MORE, we serve all life,
> our flames consuming war and strife.
>
> **Master MORE, your Sacred Heart,**
> **from this we will no more depart,**
> **we are forever in your flow,**
> **of Diamond Will that you bestow.**

7. I am envisioning that the image is gradually dissolved into these smaller components, and the components start vibrating and moving, moving around, dissolving the shapes of the image and just taking on a uniform color.

> Master MORE, we are so free,
> eternal bond from you we see.
> Master MORE, we find rebirth,
> in flow of your eternal mirth.

> **Master MORE, your Sacred Heart,**
> **from this we will no more depart,**
> **we are forever in your flow,**
> **of Diamond Will that you bestow.**

8. I envision that they become like the water of the ocean, or the sand of the desert, or the air of the blue sky, but they become feature-less, image-less.

> Master MORE, you balance all,
> the seven rays upon our call.
> Master MORE, forever MORE,
> we are the Spirit's open door.

> **Master MORE, your Sacred Heart,**
> **from this we will no more depart,**
> **we are forever in your flow,**
> **of Diamond Will that you bestow.**

9. The image is dissolved, I am letting it go. I am making the decision to say: "I am letting this image die, I am letting it dissolve. I am simply forgetting it."

> Master MORE, your Presence here,
> filling up the inner sphere.
> Life is now a sacred flow,
> God Power we on all bestow.

> **Master MORE, your Sacred Heart,**
> **from this we will no more depart,**
> **we are forever in your flow,**
> **of Diamond Will that you bestow.**

Part 4

1. The secret of forgetting is to realize that my memories are stored partly as energy, emotional energy, that I can dissolve with decrees and invocations.

Master MORE, come to the fore,
we will absorb your flame of MORE.
Master MORE, our will so strong,
our power centers cleared by song.

**Master MORE, your Sacred Heart,
from this we will no more depart,
we are forever in your flow,
of Diamond Will that you bestow.**

2. My memories are stored as these images in my brain, in my three higher bodies. These images have been superimposed upon the quantum particles, the Ma-ter light. These particles can take on various forms, shapes, densities and colors.

Master MORE, your wisdom flows,
as our attunement ever grows.
Master MORE, we have a tie,
that helps us see through Serpent's lie.

**Master MORE, your Sacred Heart,
from this we will no more depart,
we are forever in your flow,
of Diamond Will that you bestow.**

3. I can undo the images that my mind has projected on these particles, set the particles free from the image. When I really do this, the image is no longer there and therefore the memory is gone.

Master MORE, your love so pink,
there is no purer love, we think.
Master MORE, you set us free,
from all conditionality.

**Master MORE, your Sacred Heart,
from this we will no more depart,
we are forever in your flow,
of Diamond Will that you bestow.**

6 | Invoking my God-given right to forget

4. Memory is something I have in the four levels of the material realm. There has to be some vehicle that can carry the memory. Memories are stored as visual images. In my three higher bodies is a storage medium made of particles that take on a certain image and maintain that shape indefinitely.

> Master MORE, we will endure,
> your discipline that makes us pure.
> Master MORE, intentions true,
> as we are always one with you.
>
> **Master MORE, your Sacred Heart,**
> **from this we will no more depart,**
> **we are forever in your flow,**
> **of Diamond Will that you bestow.**

5. I am training myself to go in, re-see the image but then see beyond the image and set those particles free to return to their ground state. When they are returned to their ground state, the image is dissolved and that is the vehicle for memory. When the vehicle for memory is dissolved, the memory is also dissolved.

> Master MORE, our vision raised,
> the will of God is always praised.
> Master MORE, creative will,
> raising all life higher still.
>
> **Master MORE, your Sacred Heart,**
> **from this we will no more depart,**
> **we are forever in your flow,**
> **of Diamond Will that you bestow.**

6. I am training my mind to be an open door for Master MORE sending a light ray into this image, and thereby causing these particles to start vibrating faster, so they jump out of the set pattern of the image and return to their ground state.

> Master MORE, your peace is power,
> the demons of war it will devour.

Master MORE, we serve all life,
our flames consuming war and strife.

**Master MORE, your Sacred Heart,
from this we will no more depart,
we are forever in your flow,
of Diamond Will that you bestow.**

7. I am training myself to see that the image I have in my mind is made of these particles and therefore the image is fluid. It can easily be dissolved, it is not set in stone, it is not solid.

Master MORE, we are so free,
eternal bond from you we see.
Master MORE, we find rebirth,
in flow of your eternal mirth.

**Master MORE, your Sacred Heart,
from this we will no more depart,
we are forever in your flow,
of Diamond Will that you bestow.**

8. I am training myself to erase my bad memories, either from past lives or from this life. I am retooling my mind to accept that nothing in the physical, nothing in the four realms of matter, is set in stone. Nothing is unchangeable because everything is made out of these light particles that have had a certain image superimposed upon them.

Master MORE, you balance all,
the seven rays upon our call.
Master MORE, forever MORE,
we are the Spirit's open door.

**Master MORE, your Sacred Heart,
from this we will no more depart,
we are forever in your flow,
of Diamond Will that you bestow.**

9. These light particles are not actually light particles. The macroscopic world is not made up of shapes. It is made up of these smaller entities that have had images superimposed upon them. They could be set free from the pattern so they could return to a ground state or outpicture another pattern.

> Master MORE, your Presence here,
> filling up the inner sphere.
> Life is now a sacred flow,
> God Power we on all bestow.
>
> **Master MORE, your Sacred Heart,**
> **from this we will no more depart,**
> **we are forever in your flow,**
> **of Diamond Will that you bestow.**

Part 5

1. I am training myself to see that the images I hold in my mind, the images of the past, are not made up of a physical substance as solid as stone. They are made up of a different kind of entities, and therefore they are fluid.

> Master MORE, come to the fore,
> we will absorb your flame of MORE.
> Master MORE, our will so strong,
> our power centers cleared by song.
>
> **Master MORE, your Sacred Heart,**
> **from this we will no more depart,**
> **we are forever in your flow,**
> **of Diamond Will that you bestow.**

2. The Ma-ter Light is not in the physical realm but it can be pulled into the physical spectrum. Then, these small dots of Ma-ter Light can be arranged into a certain pattern, but the Ma-ter Light will only remain in that pattern as long as something is projecting that image upon it.

Master MORE, your wisdom flows,
as our attunement ever grows.
Master MORE, we have a tie,
that helps us see through Serpent's lie.

Master MORE, your Sacred Heart,
from this we will no more depart,
we are forever in your flow,
of Diamond Will that you bestow.

3. The reason I have a memory of the past is that my mind is superimposing that image on the Ma-ter Light. This prevents the units of the Ma-ter Light from returning to their ground state, from going back out of the physical.

Master MORE, your love so pink,
there is no purer love, we think.
Master MORE, you set us free,
from all conditionality.

Master MORE, your Sacred Heart,
from this we will no more depart,
we are forever in your flow,
of Diamond Will that you bestow.

4. Memory is not just conscious, and my subconscious mind is continually projecting a certain image upon the Ma-ter Light.

Master MORE, we will endure,
your discipline that makes us pure.
Master MORE, intentions true,
as we are always one with you.

Master MORE, your Sacred Heart,
from this we will no more depart,
we are forever in your flow,
of Diamond Will that you bestow.

6 | Invoking my God-given right to forget

5. I am training myself to see that the image is not an image that is physical, that is unchanging. It is made up of these very small dots of Ma-ter Light. I can make a conscious decision to dissolve the image.

> Master MORE, our vision raised,
> the will of God is always praised.
> Master MORE, creative will,
> raising all life higher still.
>
> **Master MORE, your Sacred Heart,**
> **from this we will no more depart,**
> **we are forever in your flow,**
> **of Diamond Will that you bestow.**

6. I am training myself to see that there is a separate self that is maintaining that image, wanting to maintain that image. I decide to stop feeding it my energy and my attention.

> Master MORE, your peace is power,
> the demons of war it will devour.
> Master MORE, we serve all life,
> our flames consuming war and strife.
>
> **Master MORE, your Sacred Heart,**
> **from this we will no more depart,**
> **we are forever in your flow,**
> **of Diamond Will that you bestow.**

7. There is a self that thinks it has to hold on to the memory and I see that self. I am making a conscious switch, a conscious decision: "I do not have to hold on to all of my memories of what has happened to me on this planet."

> Master MORE, we are so free,
> eternal bond from you we see.
> Master MORE, we find rebirth,
> in flow of your eternal mirth.

**Master MORE, your Sacred Heart,
from this we will no more depart,
we are forever in your flow,
of Diamond Will that you bestow.**

8. No matter what I have gone through on this planet and how I experienced it through the filter of my four lower bodies, my I AM Presence had an entirely different experience. That experience is the enduring outcome, the enduring result that I wanted to achieve by being in embodiment on earth. That experience is stored forever in my casual body. That is what is real. That is what is enduring. That is what I wanted to get out of being on earth.

Master MORE, you balance all,
the seven rays upon our call.
Master MORE, forever MORE,
we are the Spirit's open door.

**Master MORE, your Sacred Heart,
from this we will no more depart,
we are forever in your flow,
of Diamond Will that you bestow.**

9. These memories that I have in my four lower bodies have no enduring value. Why should they endure? Why should I carry them with me? Why should I not look at them and say: "Poof, you are gone." I accept that I have a right to forget that I have been endowed with by my Creator. I accept that I have a divinely given right to forget.

Master MORE, your Presence here,
filling up the inner sphere.
Life is now a sacred flow,
God Power we on all bestow.

**Master MORE, your Sacred Heart,
from this we will no more depart,
we are forever in your flow,
of Diamond Will that you bestow.**

Sealing

In the name of the Divine Mother, I call to Mother Mary for the sealing of myself and all people in my circle of influence in the creative flow of the Divine Mother, the River of Life. I call for the multiplication of my calls by all representatives of the Divine Mother, so that we form the perfect figure-eight flow of "As Above, so below." Thus, I accept that this is fully manifest, because the mouth of the Lord, the Divine Mother that I AM, has spoken it. Amen.

7 | BEING CREATIVE IN A QUANTUM WORLD

I AM the Ascended Master Mother Mary, and as you are beginning to realize, it is my intention to capture your attention and leave other masters waiting in the wings for this conference. Nevertheless, we are not in competition up here in the ascended realm, contrary to what you so often see on earth where there is indeed so much competition. What is this competition born from? It is born from some very subtle ideas put out by the fallen beings who say that there is something right, there is something wrong, there is something absolute, something ultimate. Therefore, someone can be right, someone can be wrong, someone can win and someone can lose. This very mindset has infused, has found its way into, almost all aspects of society.

You might say that there is clear competition in a sporting event where they are competing about who can run the fastest, who can jump the highest and so on. In this case, there will be one person that is the winner and others that find lower places in this hierarchy that emerges. Based on what you see in sporting competitions, you might say that there is no competition between religions, at least not the same kind of competition. There is really a competition among religions about who has the ultimate truth, which one is the only true religion. If you look at the Catholic church, that claims to be the only religion that can guarantee your salvation, then it is a competitive mindset: "We are the number one, we are actually the *only one*, we are the winners and all the others are losers. Those people who are not members of our religion are the losers and will go to hell."

This infuses the mindset on this planet to a very large degree. As we have said before, the only thing the fallen beings really had to do to create a mess on earth was to project the idea that there is something that is *right* and *wrong*. There is a standard, and you need to compare everything you do or everything that happens to that standard and evaluate whether it is right or wrong.

Natural planets have no competition

What we are talking about at this conference is helping people make peace with being on earth. What I will say here does apply to the original inhabitants. I will use the example of avatars because it is the most clear-cut example. You see my beloved, one of the subtle differences between a natural planet and an unnatural planet is that on a natural planet there is no competition. We have said before that one of the central enigmas resulting from free will is to resolve this fact that you are here on this planet and there are other people in your immediate environment and even other people on the planet. How do you balance the exercise of *your* free will with the balance of the free will of everyone else?

The fallen beings have only one solution to this. It is that they seek to make their will the dominant one that everybody else conforms to. This has nothing to do with how things are on a natural planet. On a natural planet there is no competition. How do the beings on a natural planet, the co-creators on a natural planet, avoid conflict, avoid feeling these clashes? They are not actually avoiding it, they are just not producing competition because they are not in the state of separation. They do not see themselves as separate beings.

On a natural planet you do not see that you have a will that is separated from the will of all other people. You see that you are part of a whole and there are other beings who are part of that whole. How big that whole is depends on your growth level, the level of awareness you have reached. For some people on a natural planet, the whole that they are part of might be a small group that would be somewhat comparable to what you call a family on earth. There are, on natural planets, people who have just started out as co-creators and they live in these very small groups that are in many ways isolated from the rest of the people on their planet. People start out growing in a small group where they can easily balance the individual will with the will of other co-creators. They avoid having clashes because they all know each other and they know what the other person wants and they can cooperate.

As beings grow in awareness on a natural planet, they expand their awareness of the other beings on the planet and they now become aware of a larger group. What happens is that people then congregate together in places with people that have the same interests. You can even take the *My Lives* book and see how it is described that the protagonist became involved with theatre, later with government, later with spirituality. You would say that, for example, on a natural planet you could have certain cities that were dedicated to the performing arts. You could have some cities that were dedicated to music, some that were dedicated to visual arts, some to science and so forth.

The people who were interested in this would come together and they would form a certain unit. Perhaps there would be many units in a city and they would know each other and they would not be clashing, their wills would not be clashing. They would come together around a common goal that they would then pursue. Each person would know that they have a certain sphere where they exercise their individual creativity. Here, they have freedom to exercise their creativity but it also fits into a larger whole. There would be no clash between themselves and others, there is no competition; they are working together towards a common goal.

This was also what happened on earth before the descent into duality. Even those who are the original inhabitants of the earth can sense that they have within them this, very subtle, intuitive feeling that it should be possible to cooperate around a common goal without having all this conflict. What has to a large degree obscured this is the fallen beings, the standard of right and wrong. Somebody can be wrong, somebody can be right, there is only one right way. On a natural planet there is no right and wrong, there are many ways to be right, they are all right, they are all individual creative expressions. There is nothing right or wrong, the consideration does not even come to the people, to the beings, on a natural planet.

How co-creation works on a natural planet

What happens, then, when you come to a planet like earth that is an unnatural planet—how do you experience this as an avatar? On a natural planet you are working in a unit with other people, other beings. It is a harmonious unit because you have a common goal. Let us just take a practical example. You have a common goal of building a beautiful building. You have an overall vision of this building but the building requires many different skills: There are bricklayers, there are carpenters, there are painters, there are decorators, there are artists, there are metalworkers, there is this and that. All kinds of individual skills are needed to complete the building. There is no competition because each of these groups of people have their own area where they are creative, their own sphere of influence. They are not clashing with each other, they are working together on the common goal of building this building. You understand that on a natural planet there is a common space, a common vision, a common goal. Within that, there are individual areas for creativity. As an individual co-creator you are part of the whole, you know you are working with others but you also feel that you have plenty of room for your own creative expression.

What is the effect of this? It is, my beloved, that on a natural planet, a co-creator is working with the Ma-ter Light exactly as it is on earth. There is the Mat-er Light, you are using your mind to formulate an image and superimpose that image upon the Mat-er Light and the Mat-er Light, then, takes on that form. Here is the difference between a natural planet and earth. On a natural planet you are not using your physical body very much; most of what you bring forth on a natural planet is precipitated. There are some uses for the physical body (because the physical body is not seen as being separated from the three other bodies). You are aware, you are conscious, that you are co-creating with the mind, with the identity, mental and emotional mind that is bringing things into the physical. It is not, as it is on earth, where you think that practically everything you need to do to make something physical has to be done with the body or some machinery, some technology that is an extension of the body. On a natural planet you are much more aware that it is the mind. You are aware that you are co-creating by formulating images, matrices in the mind and projecting them, superimposing them, upon the Mat-er light.

When a group of people get together around a common goal, what happens is that their minds combine, they combine at the identity level and they then create within the Mat-er Light. Almost like we have said that the Creator creates, where at first the Creator creates a vacuum and then it projects a sphere in the vacuum and within that sphere forms can be created. Likewise, on a natural planet the people, who have decided to co-create, for example building a building, come together. First, they

7 | Being creative in a quantum world

meditate together and they visualize, they create, the void. They create a void and then they project with their minds a sphere. They fill the void with the Mat-er Light that has been activated to a certain stage where it is ready to take on form but the form has not yet been differentiated. All of the people who are part of this whole now know that they are working with this Mat-er Light, they have a connection in their minds. Yet at the same time, each being knows that it has its own sphere where it is working with the Mat-er Light. It is therefore using its mind to formulate the image projected onto the Mat-er Light.

How it is to come to earth

What happens on a natural planet is that the Mat-er Light very easily takes on the form that is projected upon it by an individual co-creator. There is no opposition there. What you are used to, when you come as an avatar from a natural planet, is that it is very easy for you to work with the Mat-er Light. You can very easily project a mental image onto the Mat-er Light and the Mat-er Light takes on that form. One of the big shocks you have when you come to earth as an avatar is that on earth this very easy co-creation simply is not possible. It is not possible for several reasons. One is that the Mat-er Light on a natural planet has a higher vibration than the Mat-er Light that makes up earth. The higher the vibration, the more fluid the light is, the more easily it takes on the forms that you project on it with the three higher bodies. Light of a higher vibration more easily conforms to mental images because it is not as dense, not as solidified.

You come to earth, and the first shock you encounter is how dense matter is, how dense the Mat-er Light is on earth. You also need to realize here that on earth it is quite rare (it is not unseen but it is quite rare) that a group of people can get together around a common goal, a common vision. You can say that there are examples where millions of people have been working together to, for example, build the pyramids or build a city or so forth. In most cases this has happened in a way that we might call top-down management where somebody has decided, like a dictator decides: "We are going to build this palace." Now, he forces all of the people to conform to that vision and build the palace. This does not mean that the people have bought into (as the saying goes) the vision, that they have accepted that this is what they *want* to do. They are forced to do it and so they do it. You could say that they are working together but they are not doing it with the same sense of oneness that is there on a natural planet. The result of this, my beloved, is that when people do not have a common vision, when they are not accepting that vision, when it is forced upon them, they cannot combine their minds to, first, create the void and then fill that void with the Mat-er Light that has been activated. You do not have access to this, we might call it "raw material" that very easily takes on form. It *could* be created on earth. If you had a group of people who could come together in a state of oneness and harmony, then they could create this. It would be more difficult than on a natural planet but it could be done. It has very rarely been done on earth because usually the fallen beings have been inserting themselves into the process and forcing the people to create what glorifies the fallen beings. Naturally, on a natural planet you do not see the creation of a palace that is meant for one king or one emperor to sit there on a throne and appear almighty and powerful.

On earth, you do not have a raw material that easily takes on form. At the same time that you do not have a common energy source, you do not have a situation where each co-creator, each person, has its own separate sphere where it can be creative. You do not have a common space and you do not have an individual space for co-creation. What you see on earth is that when people want to create something, they cannot create this separate sphere of activated Mat-er Light. They have to work with the common sphere, the common energy, what we have called the background or the basic vibration of the planet. This is their raw material. In other words, everybody on earth has the same raw material.

At the same time, you see that it is very difficult on earth to have your own sphere of creativity. Now, you may look at history and you may see that some people have managed to carve out a certain sphere of creativity. This may be writers who have been able to write something that is beyond the collective consciousness. It may be painters who have painted something completely new, not the way it was traditionally done. It is because these people have been able to carve out a certain space in their minds that was somewhat protected from the collective consciousness. What you also see is that these forms of creativity are individual creative efforts. A painter is sitting there in his studio painting a painting and there is nobody else there.

As soon as you have a situation where two or more people have to cooperate, then you have an entirely different dynamic. You have the dynamic where they do not have an individual space. They are all working in a common space and that means, in its essence, that what you do as

7 | Being creative in a quantum world

an individual is affected by the collective consciousness of all the people on the planet. You can, again, find situations where a group of people have managed to set themselves apart, for example in a monastery or in a remote community. They have therefore somewhat been able to insulate themselves from the collective but they are still working with that base energy that is more dense. They are still working in an environment where, even though they may have insulated themselves somewhat, they are not free of the collective consciousness so there is a constant interference from the collective consciousness.

How co-creation works on earth

Now, let us move on to consider how you actually co-create something on a planet like earth. Essentially, it is the same process as on a natural planet but there are some differences. On a natural planet you formulate an image in your conscious mind. You are using your identity mind, your mental mind, your emotional mind but you are formulating that image in your conscious mind. You are then sending an impulse into the energy system. You are sending an energy wave, or rather a complex energy wave, a matrix of energy waves that has a certain image upon it. You are sending that into (from the physical level, from your conscious mind) the emotional, mental and identity where it then cycles back through the identity, mental and emotional and into the physical. The thing is, on a natural planet there is nothing that interferes with this process. What you are sending out from the physical level, from the conscious level, comes back to the physical level in its pure form.

On earth this is entirely different. You are, with your conscious mind, formulating an image, projecting that into the emotional, mental and identity realms on earth, then it cycles back to the physical. Because earth is such an impure and dense environment, the energy wave that you are sending out encounters a lot of interference, both on its way up and on its way back down to the physical. This means that it is virtually impossible to formulate an image in your mind, send it out and have it manifest exactly as you envisioned it. This is for all practical purposes impossible.

Why is it important for you to know this as an avatar or as a spiritually advanced member of the original inhabitants of the earth? Because it is the only way you can make peace with being here. It is the only way you can avoid feeling that you are stupid, that you are inadequate, that you are not good enough. It is the only way that you can avoid judging your creative efforts based on the standard of the fallen beings, namely that it has to either be perfect or it is not good enough. This is essentially what the fallen beings have created. They have created a mindset on earth that says: If what you create is not perfect (according to some standard that is never really defined) then it is not good enough. Because of the density of the environment on earth, it is virtually impossible for anyone to formulate an image in the mind and have it be outpictured in physical circumstances. Therefore, you are, if you accept the mindset of the fallen beings, condemned to forever feeling that whatever you create is not good enough. You can never be satisfied with your co-creation, if you have this mindset of the fallen beings that it has to be perfect according to some standard.

Is anything ever good enough?

That is why I am giving you this teaching so that you can begin to re-evaluate your approach to anything you do—*anything* you do on earth. Look at being a parent and how there is a mindset in society that you are either the perfect parent or you are not good enough. What is the perfect parent? Some will say it is one who has perfect children, but you know very well that your children come in with psychology from many past embodiments that it is not your job as a parent to change or suppress. How could you ever have a perfect child—if there was such a thing? With the common attitude that is in society today, being a parent means you are condemning yourself to being dissatisfied for the rest of your life because your children are never going to live up to this standard of perfection.

The same thing if you want to be a writer. Many people have a desire to write something but they become so fixated on evaluating whether it is good enough or not, that they end up feeling: "Oh, it is never good enough," and they do not even dare to publish it. (Many of these people then end up becoming editors or critics who are evaluating other writers' work, without ever making themselves vulnerable to critique but that is another matter.)

It is actually a pattern you see in all aspects of life where you see many, many people who have this mindset that you are either perfect or you are not good enough. Therefore, they do not really dare to bring forth something from within themselves. Instead, they put themselves up in a position where they are evaluating the works of other people. They are

7 | Being creative in a quantum world

the ones who are always criticizing but they are never subject to criticism themselves. Who criticizes the critic? These people then shut off their own creativity and they reinforce the judgmental mindset of the fallen beings.

Now again, here you are as an avatar who has come to earth. You are used to, from a natural planet, that you can manifest whatever you envision. You come to earth, you envision something, you send the impulse into the four levels of the material universe but what comes back, what becomes manifest, is not exactly what you envisioned. It is so easy for many of us, in fact most of us, to then become susceptible to the mindset of the fallen beings and say: "Well, if what actually manifested is so far from what I envisioned, I must not be good enough. Suddenly, I am not good enough as a co-creator on earth because I cannot manifest what I envisioned."

What have I just told you, my beloved? On earth you do not have an unobstructed path where your vision is sent out and comes back without being interfered with. You have a very, very chaotic energetic environment where there are so many fear-based emotions, so many distorted ideas in the mental realm, so many wrong images in the identity realm. When you send an energy wave into those realms, there will be massive interference. You know very well that when two energy waves meet, they create an interference pattern that changes both waves.

We might say that when you are sending a creative impulse, that impulse is an energy wave. As it moves through the four levels of the material realm, it meets other energy waves from the collective consciousness. When the two waves interact, it changes both of them. That means when you are sending out a creative vision, it meets a negative energy but the interaction changes both waves. You have actually made a contribution to raising the collective consciousness by your creative effort but you do not see that. What you see is that what comes back to you is very far below what you envisioned, and so you feel: "Have I really done anything useful?" But you *have*. You have raised the energy that was interfering with your vision. Of course, the energy has also interfered with the vision so that it is not manifest in its pure form.

Why am I telling you this? Again, because you simply cannot judge your creative efforts here on earth, either the way you are used to doing from a natural planet or the way the fallen beings want you to judge them. You have to become aware of how you used to judge it on a natural planet, how the fallen beings want you to judge your creative efforts, and you throw away both of them and say they are not relevant on a planet like earth.

Judging your co-creative efforts on earth

This messenger grew up in an environment where he was familiar with guns so I have given him this image, which I will then use here. There are two types of ordinary guns used for hunting on earth. One is called a rifle, one is called a shotgun. A rifle fires one pellet, a shotgun fires a whole cluster of smaller pellets. You have all seen these targets, paper targets, where you have concentric rings and in the middle is the ring with the ten. When you are aiming with a rifle, it is possible to place a bullet right in the ten because there is one bullet and it has a fairly precise trajectory. Now, imagine that you are facing a paper target with a shotgun and you are told to place one little pellet right in the ten, just as you do with a rifle. Would this be possible?

It would be possible but there is no way for you to predict the effect of your shot because you are shooting out a cluster of smaller pellets that do not have a predefined, very precise trajectory, at least not one you can predict. There may be one of those hundred pellets that will hit the ten but there may also be a shot where none of them hits the ten. You may fire one hundred shots and there is not one pellet in the ten. There is nothing you can do about it. It is not a matter of how precisely you aim the gun. It is a matter of the physical reality of the gun.

What I am telling you here is that the fallen beings are saying: "You should hit the ten every time," but the gun you have is a shotgun. It gives no meaning that you should judge your efforts as if you had a rifle because you cannot be sure that you will hit the ten. It is a matter of complete coincidence, we might say, but it is certainly not an exact science whether you hit the ten or not. The fallen beings, my beloved, are asking you to do the impossible, yet judge yourself as if the impossible was possible. This simply is not realistic—it is not *realistic*. You cannot judge yourself for being imperfect because you cannot do what is impossible, it makes no sense. Yet, you have been programmed lifetime after lifetime to judge yourself precisely this way.

It is a very deep programming that is very, very strong in the collective consciousness on earth. You, my beloved, have the tools and you are ready to raise yourself above it. For some of you, it is a matter of just shifting the mind. For others, it will require some work because you have separate selves that you need to see, you need to see them for what they are and let them die. Again, you have the tools and what you will find is that when you let go of these selves, when you shift out of this idea that you should be able to do the impossible (and if you cannot do what is impossible you are imperfect), then you can find a whole new way to be at peace on earth, a whole new way to be a creative person and to put forth an effort. You can send forth an impulse and not be discouraged by what comes back because you know that your impulse has had a positive impact on raising the collective consciousness, even if what comes back is not exactly what you sent out.

Becoming more and more creative

My beloved, as you raise your consciousness, you should ideally become more and more creative. This does not mean you have to become an artist or a musician or whatever. You can become more and more creative in coming up with new ideas, better ways of doing things. You can even become creative in the sense that you become better at manifesting the daily life that you really want. It is not always a matter of manifesting something such as a piece of art. You can see daily life as an art form where you manifest the kind of life that you want to have. This is also a form of creativity.

My beloved, you look at so many artists, writers, what have you. You see how some of them have been very eccentric even somewhat crazy. Many of them have been very dissatisfied with their own creation. They have never felt that what they did was good enough. They never really painted that Mona Lisa with the exact smile that they wanted her to have. The reality here is that most of the big, famous artists, they might be admired by the public but they themselves were dissatisfied with their efforts and the reason is simple. You look at the Mona Lisa and you look at the actual painting. You cannot see the vision that Leonardo Da Vinci had in his mind when he painted it. You cannot see that what he got down on the canvas was not exactly what he had in his mind and therefore he was dissatisfied with it. The same with most other artists.

It was not exactly what they wanted. Again, on an unnatural planet it is unrealistic and non-constructive to expect that you can manifest in the physical exactly what you envision in your mind. It is simply *unrealistic*.

When you come to accept this, you can start making peace with the fact that even though you are not manifesting exactly what you envision, you are still helping to make the world a better place (as the saying goes) because you are sending out energy impulses that are raising the collective consciousness.

You can also take this further and simply realize that you are not here to bring forth some perfect creation. You are here to bring forth something that is higher than what most people can envision. Not so much higher that they cannot connect to it but demonstrating that there is a better way, there is a higher form of creativity. There is no perfection you need to reach, my beloved. It is, as we have said many, many times before, that if you are at the 96th level of consciousness, you have already raised yourself far above the collective consciousness. There is no point in coming down on yourself because you are not at the 144th level of consciousness.

You are wherever you are at—it is perfectly acceptable. We accept you for who you are at that level of consciousness. We do not demand that you should be at the 144th. We are just looking at how can we take you to the next step up. When you understand this, when you accept this, you can be at peace with being where you are at. You can also, therefore, be at peace with being on earth where your creative efforts never produce the exact result you envision. Instead of condemning yourself for it, you just accept this is the way it is.

The quantum approach to creativity

Go back to the analogy of the rifle and the shotgun. You may not be able to hit the ten with a shotgun, but surely you can hit the entire target and it is the same here on earth. You need to be satisfied with hitting the whole target, not necessarily the bulls eye. You can even take this a little bit further by looking at what scientists have discovered about the quantum world, the world of subatomic particles. They have discovered that an electron is a strange phenomenon. They have discovered there is what they call a "quantum measurement problem." You can measure the position of an electron but then, if you have a very precise knowledge of its position, you can have no knowledge of its speed, its momentum. On the other hand, you can use another method to measure its momentum but then you can know nothing about its position. You cannot know everything at once. This means you cannot predict exactly where an electron is going to be in the future. This contradicts, again, the old image of the universe as a clock where, if you knew the initial conditions, you could predict everything that happens in the future. Quantum physicists have proven now for almost a century that this simply is not possible in the quantum world. For that matter, it is not possible in the macroscopic world either. Scientists only thought it was possible because they thought that there are only very few conditions they need to consider. In reality, there are many more conditions than they were aware of in Newtonian science and therefore there were hidden variables that they could not take into account. They would not have been able to predict even at a macroscopic level, but quantum physicists have proven that it is not possible to make exact predictions. What you can do is, you can measure a large number of electrons and then you can create sort of an average so you can predict the *probability* that a single electron will be in a certain position at a certain time. You can predict probability, not the exact outcome. This is what you can use with your own creative efforts. You may formulate an image of what you want to manifest. You may send it out there but you cannot be absolutely sure that it will manifest exactly as it is. There is only a certain probability.

That means you cannot say that the exact image *should* manifest. You need to be realistic and say: "Surely, there will be interference with what I am sending out so what comes back will be somewhat distorted by that interference and it will not be exactly what I envisioned." You need to, then, come to the point where you realize that you had the best vision you could have at the time. You projected it out with as much power as you could, given your state of consciousness. What came back was simply the best that could be produced, given the conditions: your own state of consciousness and the state of the collective consciousness. Given the conditions in which you are working, this was the best possible outcome. You do not need to judge it as being imperfect or bad because it was not exactly what you envisioned. What you can then do is you can say: "Okay, there was a difference between what I envisioned and what came back, how can I minimize that difference? How can I reduce it?"

You can do that by raising your consciousness, by getting rid of some of these selves that might have caused you to have an imperfect or a lower vision than you could have, or they might have caused you to not have quite the same power to project it out. You can purify your four lower bodies so that there is as little interference as possible in your own four lower bodies. Naturally, what is in your own higher bodies will interfere with the vision you send out, even with your ability to formulate the vision.

This is what you can do, and it is valid to say: "There was a difference between what I envisioned and what I manifested. I need to work on myself and my consciousness." This does not mean you have to be dissatisfied with yourself. My beloved, even if you reach the 144th level of consciousness, you will not be able to manifest on earth exactly what you envision. Why is that? It is because, as I said, on earth, you do not have an individual sphere where your mind is the only mind that affects a certain portion of the Ma-ter Light, and therefore, whatever is in your mind is the exact form that the Ma-ter Light takes on. You are working in a common space here. You have to accept that you are on a planet with dense matter and with a dense collective consciousness.

Be content to raise the consciousness

You have to allow this to interfere with your vision because part of the purpose of being here and being creative is to raise the collective. You do that by sending out a vision that is as high as possible and allowing it to interfere, to interact with the collective. You might only see that it is the collective that lowers your vision but the reality is that your vision also raises the collective. This is part of what it means to be a co-creator on an unnatural planet. As a co-creator on a natural planet you have your own sphere, you can manifest exactly what is in your mind. That is not the situation on an unnatural planet. You do not have your own sphere, therefore you are not manifesting exactly what you envision. Nevertheless, by going through the process, the creative process, you are helping raise the collective consciousness.

This messenger was in his early years as a messenger somewhat dissatisfied by the fact that his books had not become best-sellers (or rather, not *his* books because he did not see them that way, but the books of the masters). He thought: "Why won't all people want to read the ascended masters' teachings?" He has also learned to realize that this was simply an unrealistic vision. It is unrealistic to expect that all people on earth are ready for the teachings of the ascended masters so why should you expect that an ascended master book will become a best-seller?

Best-sellers are ones that correspond to people's level of consciousness. Otherwise they will not be able to see that there is something in the book, they cannot even recognize it. He has learned to realize that he cannot evaluate his efforts as a messenger based on whether it is a best-seller or not. He can simply be content with the fact that the books are in the physical octave where they can be read both now and in later decades. It is not a matter of how many people, because your success as a co-creator in the physical octave does not depend on the recognition from the 80% of the general population. I trust you can see that it does not depend on the recognition of the lowest 10%, especially the fallen beings. As a co-creator with a spiritual awareness you will never, ever gain recognition from the fallen beings. It simply will not happen, my beloved. You will never get it so expecting it is just an unrealistic expectation. You have to let it go.

Recognizing you cannot please some people

You have to come to the point where you recognize there are people on this planet that you cannot please. Some of you may have close family members who belong to this category. It is not a matter of necessarily saying they are fallen beings but it is a matter of acknowledging: "I can never please that person. So why am I bothering? Why do I not move on to people that I can have a positive interaction with? Why do I have to be around people who are critical or negative or always demanding more? I have a right to move on to people that I resonate with instead of people who are disturbed by my vibration and want to put me down." When you can stop judging yourself based on the standard of the fallen beings or the opinions of other people, who may be influenced by the standard of the fallen beings, then you can start feeling that you can actually be creative on earth.

You can actually be at peace with being creative even if your creative efforts never really manifest what you can envision. You need to recognize here that when you are an avatar or an advanced spiritual student (even if you are one of the original inhabitants of the earth), you are able to envision something that is far beyond what the average person can envision, what is far beyond what is in the collective consciousness. Naturally, when you send out that impulse into the four levels of the material universe, it will meet interference from the collective consciousness because it will meet a lot of lower energy. It is not a disaster. It is not a failure on your part that it did not manifest exactly as you envisioned it. You should realize that it still has a positive effect and therefore your creative efforts are still worthwhile.

A higher motivation for being creative

Of course, when you do realize this, when you make these shifts, you come to the point where you are not any longer being creative because you want to: 1. Manifest a particular result. 2. Have the recognition and validation of other people.

This no longer motivates you. Money no longer motivates you. What motivates you is what I said in an earlier discourse where I said the real purpose of you coming to earth is to experience yourself here. You can come to a point where you are being creative and the reward for your creativity is not what is physically manifested, it is not the recognition, it is not the money. It is the experience of knowing that you have made the effort in this particular environment. You have made the effort—you have manifested something that is higher than was there before.

This is a reward where you simply gain that experience. You can come to a point where you can experience (even though you are in physical embodiment) how your I AM Presence experiences earth. When you experience how your I AM Presence experiences your creative efforts, then that is the highest form of reward for your efforts. The effort itself becomes its own reward. It becomes a self-reinforcing process where you are constantly reaching higher, not from a sense of lack but from a sense that you know you can accomplish something. Knowing what you have accomplished gives you the knowledge that you can accomplish more. You are not dissatisfied, not constantly feeling it is not good enough, you feel it is actually good enough what you have created.

Because you created that, now you can see that you can create something that is higher and you can continue to do this. Not from a sense of deficit but from a sense of abundance, a sense that you are full. You are full. You do not have a "hole" inside yourself that you are seeking to fill. Now, the joy is to feel that the glass is overflowing. It is that constant sense that the chalice of your creativity is overflowing and being sent into your environment. *That,* gives you the sense of joy, the sense of fulfilment and the sense of being full to overflowing. *That,* I desire you to have, my beloved, and I hope some of you will use these teachings to attain it. For it is what you decided in your Divine plans that you wanted to attain as your highest potential for this lifetime.

8 | INVOKING QUANTUM CREATIVITY

In the name I AM THAT I AM, Jesus Christ, I call to all representatives of the Divine Mother, especially Mother Mary, to help me overcome all conditions in my psychology that block the free flow of creativity through my four lower bodies, including…

[Make personal calls.]

Part 1

1. The competition on earth is born from the fallen beings who say that there is something *right,* there is something *wrong,* therefore, someone can be right, someone can be wrong, someone can win and someone can lose.

> O Blessed Mary's Song of Life,
> consuming every form of strife.
> As I attune to sound so fair,
> each cell is healthy, I declare.

**O Mother Mary, generate,
the song that does accelerate,
my mind into a peaceful state,
God's perfect love I radiate.**

2. The only thing the fallen beings really had to do to create a mess on earth was to project the idea that there is something that is right and wrong. There is a standard, and you need to compare everything you do or everything that happens to that standard and evaluate whether it is right or wrong.

As life's own song I ever hear,
it does consume all sense of fear.
In tune with Mother's symphony,
from all diseases I AM free.

**O Mother Mary, generate,
the song that does accelerate,
my mind into a peaceful state,
God's perfect love I radiate.**

3. One of the central enigmas resulting from free will is to resolve the fact that I am here on this planet and there are other people in my environment. How do I balance the exercise of *my* free will with the free will of everyone else?

In Mother's love I do transcend,
and all my struggles hereby end.
For when with Mother's eye I see,
no imperfection touches me.

**O Mother Mary, generate,
the song that does accelerate,
my mind into a peaceful state,
God's perfect love I radiate.**

4. The fallen beings have only one solution to this. They seek to make their will the dominant one that everybody else conforms to.

I see that healing must begin
by finding Living Christ within.
For as I see with single eye,
each cell the light does amplify.

**O Mother Mary, generate,
the song that does accelerate,
my mind into a peaceful state,
God's perfect love I radiate.**

5. I have an intuitive feeling that it should be possible to cooperate around a common goal without having all this conflict. What has obscured this is the fallen beings, the standard of right and wrong, saying somebody can be wrong, somebody can be right, there is only one right way.

In Mother's music I am free,
from memories of a lesser me.
My vision in a perfect state,
that all my cells regenerate.

**O Mother Mary, generate,
the song that does accelerate,
my mind into a peaceful state,
God's perfect love I radiate.**

6. On a natural planet there is no right and wrong, there are many ways to be right, they are all right, they are all individual creative expressions. There is nothing right or wrong, the consideration does not even come to the beings on a natural planet.

O Mother's Love, sweet melody,
from imperfections I AM free.
O Mother Mary, sound of sounds,
within my heart your love abounds.

**O Mother Mary, generate,
the song that does accelerate,
my mind into a peaceful state,
God's perfect love I radiate.**

7. On a natural planet it is very easy to work with the Mat-er Light. I can easily project a mental image onto the Mat-er Light and the light takes on that form.

> Through Mother's beauty so sublime,
> transcending bounds of space and time.
> All cells beyond the mortal tomb,
> as they are whole in Mother's womb.
>
> **O Mother Mary, generate,**
> **the song that does accelerate,**
> **my mind into a peaceful state,**
> **God's perfect love I radiate.**

8. On earth this very easy co-creation is not possible, partly because the Mat-er Light is more dense and partly because people on earth rarely come together in oneness around a common goal.

> In resonance with life's own song,
> in life's harmonics I belong.
> The blueprint of my perfect state
> does every cell reconsecrate.
>
> **O Mother Mary, generate,**
> **the song that does accelerate,**
> **my mind into a peaceful state,**
> **God's perfect love I radiate.**

9. On earth it is virtually impossible to formulate an image in my mind, send it out and have it manifest exactly as I envisioned it. This is for all practical purposes impossible.

> The tuning fork in every cell
> is now attuned to Mother's bell.
> From curse of death I AM now free,
> I claim my immortality.
>
> **O Mother Mary, generate,**
> **the song that does accelerate,**

**my mind into a peaceful state,
God's perfect love I radiate.**

Part 2

1. Knowing this is the only way I can make peace with being here. It is the only way I can avoid feeling that I am stupid, that I am inadequate, that I am not good enough. It is the only way that I can avoid judging my creative efforts based on the standard of the fallen beings, namely that it has to either be perfect or it is not good enough.

O Blessed Mary's Song of Life,
consuming every form of strife.
As I attune to sound so fair,
each cell is healthy, I declare.

**O Mother Mary, generate,
the song that does accelerate,
my mind into a peaceful state,
God's perfect love I radiate.**

2. The fallen beings have created a mindset that says: If what I create is not perfect (according to some standard that is never really defined) then it is not good enough.

As life's own song I ever hear,
it does consume all sense of fear.
In tune with Mother's symphony,
from all diseases I AM free.

**O Mother Mary, generate,
the song that does accelerate,
my mind into a peaceful state,
God's perfect love I radiate.**

3. Because of the density of the environment on earth, it is virtually impossible for anyone to formulate an image in the mind and have it be

outpictured in physical circumstances. Therefore, if I accept the mindset of the fallen beings, I am condemned to forever feeling that whatever I create is not good enough. I can never be satisfied with my co-creation, if I have this mindset of the fallen beings that it has to be perfect according to some standard.

> In Mother's love I do transcend,
> and all my struggles hereby end.
> For when with Mother's eye I see,
> no imperfection touches me.

> **O Mother Mary, generate,**
> **the song that does accelerate,**
> **my mind into a peaceful state,**
> **God's perfect love I radiate.**

4. I am re-evaluating my approach to anything I do on earth. I am letting the self die that has the mindset that I am either perfect or I am not good enough.

> I see that healing must begin
> by finding Living Christ within.
> For as I see with single eye,
> each cell the light does amplify.

> **O Mother Mary, generate,**
> **the song that does accelerate,**
> **my mind into a peaceful state,**
> **God's perfect love I radiate.**

5. I am letting the self die that is afraid to bring forth something from within myself, the self that is always criticizing but is never subject to criticism.

> In Mother's music I am free,
> from memories of a lesser me.
> My vision in a perfect state,
> that all my cells regenerate.

> O Mother Mary, generate,
> the song that does accelerate,
> my mind into a peaceful state,
> God's perfect love I radiate.

6. I will no longer shut off my own creativity and I will no longer reinforce the judgmental mindset of the fallen beings.

> O Mother's Love, sweet melody,
> from imperfections I AM free.
> O Mother Mary, sound of sounds,
> within my heart your love abounds.

> **O Mother Mary, generate,**
> **the song that does accelerate,**
> **my mind into a peaceful state,**
> **God's perfect love I radiate.**

7. I am letting the self die that is susceptible to the mindset of the fallen beings. I consciously reject the fallen mindset that I am not good enough as a co-creator on earth because I cannot manifest what I envisioned.

> Through Mother's beauty so sublime,
> transcending bounds of space and time.
> All cells beyond the mortal tomb,
> as they are whole in Mother's womb.

> **O Mother Mary, generate,**
> **the song that does accelerate,**
> **my mind into a peaceful state,**
> **God's perfect love I radiate.**

8. On earth I do not have an unobstructed path where my vision is sent out and comes back without being interfered with. I have a very chaotic energetic environment where there are so many fear-based emotions, so many distorted ideas in the mental realm, so many wrong images in the identity realm. When I send an energy wave into those realms, there will be massive interference.

In resonance with life's own song,
in life's harmonics I belong.
The blueprint of my perfect state
does every cell reconsecrate.

O Mother Mary, generate,
the song that does accelerate,
my mind into a peaceful state,
God's perfect love I radiate.

9. When I am sending out a creative vision, it meets a negative energy but the interaction changes both waves. I have actually made a contribution to raising the collective consciousness by my creative effort but I do not see that. I now accept that I have done something useful by raising the collective consciousness.

The tuning fork in every cell
is now attuned to Mother's bell.
From curse of death I AM now free,
I claim my immortality.

O Mother Mary, generate,
the song that does accelerate,
my mind into a peaceful state,
God's perfect love I radiate.

Part 3

1. I will no longer judge my creative efforts here on earth, either the way I am used to doing from a natural planet or the way the fallen beings want me to judge them. I am aware of how I used to judge it on a natural planet, how the fallen beings want me to judge my creative efforts, and I throw away both of them because they are not relevant on earth.

O Blessed Mary's Song of Life,
consuming every form of strife.

As I attune to sound so fair,
each cell is healthy, I declare.

**O Mother Mary, generate,
the song that does accelerate,
my mind into a peaceful state,
God's perfect love I radiate.**

2. The fallen beings are asking me to do the impossible, yet judge myself as if the impossible was possible. This simply is not realistic and I will not judge myself for being imperfect because I cannot do what is impossible, it makes no sense.

As life's own song I ever hear,
it does consume all sense of fear.
In tune with Mother's symphony,
from all diseases I AM free.

**O Mother Mary, generate,
the song that does accelerate,
my mind into a peaceful state,
God's perfect love I radiate.**

3. I have been programmed lifetime after lifetime to judge myself this way. It is a very deep programming that is very strong in the collective consciousness on earth. I am raising myself above it by shifting the mind and letting my separate selves die.

In Mother's love I do transcend,
and all my struggles hereby end.
For when with Mother's eye I see,
no imperfection touches me.

**O Mother Mary, generate,
the song that does accelerate,
my mind into a peaceful state,
God's perfect love I radiate.**

4. I am letting go of these selves and shifting out of this idea that I should be able to do the impossible, and if I cannot do what is impossible I am imperfect.

> I see that healing must begin
> by finding Living Christ within.
> For as I see with single eye,
> each cell the light does amplify.
>
> **O Mother Mary, generate,**
> **the song that does accelerate,**
> **my mind into a peaceful state,**
> **God's perfect love I radiate.**

5. I am finding a whole new way to be at peace on earth, a whole new way to be a creative person and to put forth an effort. I can send forth an impulse and not be discouraged by what comes back, because I know that my impulse has had a positive impact on raising the collective consciousness, even if what comes back is not exactly what I sent out.

> In Mother's music I am free,
> from memories of a lesser me.
> My vision in a perfect state,
> that all my cells regenerate.
>
> **O Mother Mary, generate,**
> **the song that does accelerate,**
> **my mind into a peaceful state,**
> **God's perfect love I radiate.**

6. As I raise my consciousness, I become more and more creative in coming up with new ideas, better ways of doing things. I am becoming creative in the sense that I become better at manifesting the daily life that I really want. I see daily life as an art form where I manifest the kind of life that I want to have.

> O Mother's Love, sweet melody,
> from imperfections I AM free.

O Mother Mary, sound of sounds,
within my heart your love abounds.

**O Mother Mary, generate,
the song that does accelerate,
my mind into a peaceful state,
God's perfect love I radiate.**

7. On an unnatural planet it is unrealistic and non-constructive to expect that I can manifest in the physical exactly what I envision in my mind. I accept this, and I make peace with the fact that even though I am not manifesting exactly what I envision, I am still helping to make the world a better place by sending out energy impulses that are raising the collective consciousness.

Through Mother's beauty so sublime,
transcending bounds of space and time.
All cells beyond the mortal tomb,
as they are whole in Mother's womb.

**O Mother Mary, generate,
the song that does accelerate,
my mind into a peaceful state,
God's perfect love I radiate.**

8. I realize that I am not here to bring forth some perfect creation. I am here to bring forth something that is higher than what most people can envision. Not so much higher that they cannot connect to it but demonstrating that there is a better way, there is a higher form of creativity.

In resonance with life's own song,
in life's harmonics I belong.
The blueprint of my perfect state
does every cell reconsecrate.

**O Mother Mary, generate,
the song that does accelerate,
my mind into a peaceful state,
God's perfect love I radiate.**

9. There is no perfection I need to reach. I have already raised myself above the collective consciousness. Wherever I am at—it is perfectly acceptable.

> The tuning fork in every cell
> is now attuned to Mother's bell.
> From curse of death I AM now free,
> I claim my immortality.

> **O Mother Mary, generate,**
> **the song that does accelerate,**
> **my mind into a peaceful state,**
> **God's perfect love I radiate.**

Part 4

1. The ascended masters accept me for who I am at this level of consciousness. They do not demand that I should be at the 144th level. They are looking at how they can help me take the next step up.

> O Blessed Mary's Song of Life,
> consuming every form of strife.
> As I attune to sound so fair,
> each cell is healthy, I declare.

> **O Mother Mary, generate,**
> **the song that does accelerate,**
> **my mind into a peaceful state,**
> **God's perfect love I radiate.**

2. I understand and accept this, and I am at peace with being where I am at. I am at peace with being on earth where my creative efforts never produce the exact result I envision. Instead of condemning myself for it, I accept that this is the way it is.

> As life's own song I ever hear,
> it does consume all sense of fear.

In tune with Mother's symphony,
from all diseases I AM free.

**O Mother Mary, generate,
the song that does accelerate,
my mind into a peaceful state,
God's perfect love I radiate.**

3. Quantum physicists have proven that it is not possible to make exact predictions. I can formulate an image of what I want to manifest. I can send it out there but I cannot be sure that it will manifest exactly as it is. There is only a certain probability.

In Mother's love I do transcend,
and all my struggles hereby end.
For when with Mother's eye I see,
no imperfection touches me.

**O Mother Mary, generate,
the song that does accelerate,
my mind into a peaceful state,
God's perfect love I radiate.**

4. I cannot say that the exact image should manifest. I need to be realistic and say: "Surely, there will be interference with what I am sending out, so what comes back will be somewhat distorted by that interference and it will not be exactly what I envisioned."

I see that healing must begin
by finding Living Christ within.
For as I see with single eye,
each cell the light does amplify.

**O Mother Mary, generate,
the song that does accelerate,
my mind into a peaceful state,
God's perfect love I radiate.**

5. I realize that I had the best vision I could have at the time. I projected it out with as much power as I could, given my state of consciousness. What came back was simply the best that could be produced, given my own state of consciousness and the state of the collective consciousness.

> In Mother's music I am free,
> from memories of a lesser me.
> My vision in a perfect state,
> that all my cells regenerate.
>
> **O Mother Mary, generate,**
> **the song that does accelerate,**
> **my mind into a peaceful state,**
> **God's perfect love I radiate.**

6. Given the conditions in which I am working, this was the best possible outcome. I do not need to judge it as being imperfect or bad because it was not exactly what I envisioned. I say: "Okay, there was a difference between what I envisioned and what came back, how can I minimize that difference? How can I reduce it?"

> O Mother's Love, sweet melody,
> from imperfections I AM free.
> O Mother Mary, sound of sounds,
> within my heart your love abounds.
>
> **O Mother Mary, generate,**
> **the song that does accelerate,**
> **my mind into a peaceful state,**
> **God's perfect love I radiate.**

7. I am raising my consciousness by getting rid of some of these selves that might have caused me to have an imperfect or a lower vision than I could have, or that might have caused me to not have quite the same power to project it out.

> Through Mother's beauty so sublime,
> transcending bounds of space and time.

All cells beyond the mortal tomb,
as they are whole in Mother's womb.

**O Mother Mary, generate,
the song that does accelerate,
my mind into a peaceful state,
God's perfect love I radiate.**

8. I am purifying my four lower bodies so that there is as little interference as possible in my own four lower bodies. I say: "There was a difference between what I envisioned and what I manifested. I need to work on myself and my consciousness."

In resonance with life's own song,
in life's harmonics I belong.
The blueprint of my perfect state
does every cell reconsecrate.

**O Mother Mary, generate,
the song that does accelerate,
my mind into a peaceful state,
God's perfect love I radiate.**

9. This does not mean I have to be dissatisfied with myself. On earth, I do not have an individual sphere where my mind is the only mind that affects the Ma-ter Light. I am working in a common space and I accept that I am on a planet with dense matter and with a dense collective consciousness.

The tuning fork in every cell
is now attuned to Mother's bell.
From curse of death I AM now free,
I claim my immortality.

**O Mother Mary, generate,
the song that does accelerate,
my mind into a peaceful state,
God's perfect love I radiate.**

Part 5

1. I allow this to interfere with my vision because part of the purpose of being here and being creative is to raise the collective. I do that by sending out a vision that is as high as possible and allowing it to interfere, to interact with the collective.

> O Blessed Mary's Song of Life,
> consuming every form of strife.
> As I attune to sound so fair,
> each cell is healthy, I declare.
>
> **O Mother Mary, generate,**
> **the song that does accelerate,**
> **my mind into a peaceful state,**
> **God's perfect love I radiate.**

2. The collective lowers my vision but my vision also raises the collective. This is part of what it means to be a co-creator on an unnatural planet. By going through the creative process, I am helping raise the collective consciousness.

> As life's own song I ever hear,
> it does consume all sense of fear.
> In tune with Mother's symphony,
> from all diseases I AM free.
>
> **O Mother Mary, generate,**
> **the song that does accelerate,**
> **my mind into a peaceful state,**
> **God's perfect love I radiate.**

3. My success as a co-creator in the physical octave does not depend on the recognition from the 80% of the general population. It does not depend on the recognition of the lowest 10%, especially the fallen beings. As a co-creator with a spiritual awareness I will never gain recognition from the fallen beings.

> In Mother's love I do transcend,
> and all my struggles hereby end.
> For when with Mother's eye I see,
> no imperfection touches me.
>
> **O Mother Mary, generate,**
> **the song that does accelerate,**
> **my mind into a peaceful state,**
> **God's perfect love I radiate.**

4. I recognize there are people on this planet that I cannot please. I acknowledge: "I can never please that person. So why am I bothering? Why do I not move on to people that I can have a positive interaction with? Why do I have to be around people who are critical or negative or always demanding more? I have a right to move on to people that I resonate with instead of people who are disturbed by my vibration and want to put me down."

> I see that healing must begin
> by finding Living Christ within.
> For as I see with single eye,
> each cell the light does amplify.
>
> **O Mother Mary, generate,**
> **the song that does accelerate,**
> **my mind into a peaceful state,**
> **God's perfect love I radiate.**

5. I stop judging myself based on the standard of the fallen beings or the opinions of other people, and I start feeling that I can actually be creative on earth.

> In Mother's music I am free,
> from memories of a lesser me.
> My vision in a perfect state,
> that all my cells regenerate.
>
> **O Mother Mary, generate,**
> **the song that does accelerate,**

my mind into a peaceful state,
God's perfect love I radiate.

6. I am at peace with being creative even if my creative efforts never really manifest what I can envision. I recognize that when I am an advanced spiritual student, I am able to envision something that is far beyond what the average person can envision and far beyond what is in the collective consciousness.

> O Mother's Love, sweet melody,
> from imperfections I AM free.
> O Mother Mary, sound of sounds,
> within my heart your love abounds.

> **O Mother Mary, generate,**
> **the song that does accelerate,**
> **my mind into a peaceful state,**
> **God's perfect love I radiate.**

7. When I send that impulse into the four levels of the material universe, it will meet interference from the collective consciousness because it will meet a lot of lower energy. It is not a disaster. It is not a failure on my part that it did not manifest exactly as I envisioned it. It still has a positive effect and therefore my creative efforts are still worthwhile.

> Through Mother's beauty so sublime,
> transcending bounds of space and time.
> All cells beyond the mortal tomb,
> as they are whole in Mother's womb.

> **O Mother Mary, generate,**
> **the song that does accelerate,**
> **my mind into a peaceful state,**
> **God's perfect love I radiate.**

8. I am no longer being creative because I want to manifest a particular result or have the recognition and validation of other people. This no longer motivates me. Money no longer motivates me.

In resonance with life's own song,
in life's harmonics I belong.
The blueprint of my perfect state
does every cell reconsecrate.

**O Mother Mary, generate,
the song that does accelerate,
my mind into a peaceful state,
God's perfect love I radiate.**

9. What motivates me is that the real purpose of me coming to earth is to experience myself here.

The tuning fork in every cell
is now attuned to Mother's bell.
From curse of death I AM now free,
I claim my immortality.

**O Mother Mary, generate,
the song that does accelerate,
my mind into a peaceful state,
God's perfect love I radiate.**

Part 6

1. I am being creative and the reward for my creativity is not what is physically manifested, it is not the recognition, it is not the money.

O Blessed Mary's Song of Life,
consuming every form of strife.
As I attune to sound so fair,
each cell is healthy, I declare.

**O Mother Mary, generate,
the song that does accelerate,
my mind into a peaceful state,
God's perfect love I radiate.**

2. My reward is the experience of knowing that I have made the effort in this particular environment. I have made the effort—I have manifested something that is higher than what was here before.

> As life's own song I ever hear,
> it does consume all sense of fear.
> In tune with Mother's symphony,
> from all diseases I AM free.
>
> **O Mother Mary, generate,**
> **the song that does accelerate,**
> **my mind into a peaceful state,**
> **God's perfect love I radiate.**

3. I want to experience how my I AM Presence experiences earth.

> In Mother's love I do transcend,
> and all my struggles hereby end.
> For when with Mother's eye I see,
> no imperfection touches me.
>
> **O Mother Mary, generate,**
> **the song that does accelerate,**
> **my mind into a peaceful state,**
> **God's perfect love I radiate.**

4. When I experience how my I AM Presence experiences my creative efforts, then that is the highest form of reward for my efforts.

> I see that healing must begin
> by finding Living Christ within.
> For as I see with single eye,
> each cell the light does amplify.
>
> **O Mother Mary, generate,**
> **the song that does accelerate,**
> **my mind into a peaceful state,**
> **God's perfect love I radiate.**

5. The effort itself becomes its own reward. It becomes a self-reinforcing process where I am constantly reaching higher, but not from a sense of lack but from a sense that I know I can accomplish something.

> In Mother's music I am free,
> from memories of a lesser me.
> My vision in a perfect state,
> that all my cells regenerate.
>
> **O Mother Mary, generate,**
> **the song that does accelerate,**
> **my mind into a peaceful state,**
> **God's perfect love I radiate.**

6. Knowing what I have accomplished gives me the knowledge that I can accomplish more. I am not dissatisfied, not constantly feeling it is not good enough, I feel it *is* actually good enough what I have created.

> O Mother's Love, sweet melody,
> from imperfections I AM free.
> O Mother Mary, sound of sounds,
> within my heart your love abounds.
>
> **O Mother Mary, generate,**
> **the song that does accelerate,**
> **my mind into a peaceful state,**
> **God's perfect love I radiate.**

7. Because I created that, now I can see that I can create something that is higher and I can continue to do this. Not from a sense of deficit but from a sense of abundance, a sense that I am full.

> Through Mother's beauty so sublime,
> transcending bounds of space and time.
> All cells beyond the mortal tomb,
> as they are whole in Mother's womb.
>
> **O Mother Mary, generate,**
> **the song that does accelerate,**

my mind into a peaceful state,
God's perfect love I radiate.

8. I am full. I do not have a "hole" inside myself that I am seeking to fill. The joy is to feel that the glass is overflowing. It is that constant sense that the chalice of my creativity is overflowing and being sent into my environment.

In resonance with life's own song,
in life's harmonics I belong.
The blueprint of my perfect state
does every cell reconsecrate.

O Mother Mary, generate,
the song that does accelerate,
my mind into a peaceful state,
God's perfect love I radiate.

9. *That,* gives me the sense of joy, the sense of fulfilment and the sense of being full to overflowing. *That,* I desire to have, and I will use these teachings to attain it. It is what I decided in my Divine plan that I wanted to attain as my highest potential for this lifetime.

The tuning fork in every cell
is now attuned to Mother's bell.
From curse of death I AM now free,
I claim my immortality.

O Mother Mary, generate,
the song that does accelerate,
my mind into a peaceful state,
God's perfect love I radiate.

Sealing

In the name of the Divine Mother, I call to Mother Mary for the sealing of myself and all people in my circle of influence in the creative flow of the Divine Mother, the River of Life. I call for the multiplication of my calls by all representatives of the Divine Mother, so that we form the perfect figure-eight flow of "As Above, so below." Thus, I accept that this is fully manifest, because the mouth of the Lord, the Divine Mother that I AM, has spoken it. Amen.

9 | TEACHING YOURSELF TO ERASE MEMORIES

I AM the Ascended Master MORE, and I would like to build on what I gave you yesterday, and what Mother Mary has given you, and direct it to the topic of how you can overcome your past. One of you mentioned to the messenger today that he still feels that he is stuck in the past, living in the past, looking back to the past, perhaps even longing for some lost paradise that you experienced some time in the past. Many, many spiritual people throughout the world have this feeling that they have lost something and, of course, you *have* lost something. You have lost the innocence you had before you came here and, in a sense, our teachings could be said to be an attempt to help you regain and reclaim that innocence.

Now, how do you get free of this sense of living in the past, of an attachment to the past? Well, we have, of course, given you many tools and teachings already. It is clear that when you dissolve the energy that pulls you, the emotional energy that pulls you towards thinking about certain situations from the past, this will help you be free. When you dissolve certain selves, when you see, for example, that if you were exposed to a trauma, you created a self in response to it, in reaction to it. When you come to identify that self and let it die, you are free from at least that situation.

Overcoming the fear of making decisions

More than that, there are certain selves that are not really created by you in reaction to a specific situation. They are created in reaction to what it feels like to be in embodiment on a planet as dense as earth. We might even say that these selves are very much there in the collective consciousness. It is difficult to not be affected by them, especially after you receive a birth trauma and you are shocked by the conditions on earth being so different than what you had envisioned before you came here. It is easy for you to take on some of these collective selves that have been created over a long period of time and which, as we have said before, were created in order to deal with the situation that people feel they cannot live with. You cannot live with the situation, you cannot escape it so you have to find a way to deal with it, and be able to at least live even if you cannot live well or live in a peaceful manner.

There are certain selves that have floated around out there in the collective consciousness for a long time and one of these selves is, of course, (building on what Mother Mary said) that you are either perfect or you are no good. It is a self that causes people to feel that if you had done something that was labeled by yourself or by other people as a mistake, then you cannot escape that. You even have religion often being used to set up a standard for how people should behave. If you do something that your religion labels as a sin, you feel like you are stained forever by that sin. You even have the concept of original sin, saying that you were born into sin because of what your parents did or what your forefathers did, going all the way back to Adam and Eve. Clearly, you can see that such ideas are in complete violation of the reality of free will, but let us not even go into that. Let us just stay focused here on the fact that there are various selves that want you to think that once you have made what you accepted as a mistake, you cannot be free of it and, as we have said before, you cannot undo that physical situation.

How can you, then, be free of your past? Well, I am the Master, the Chohan, on the First Ray of God's Will, so how can you be free of your past? Ultimately, you must make a *decision* to be free. Of course, it does not help you very much that I tell you: "You must make a decision to be free of your past." Most of you will feel: "Well, how do I, do this?" You might even be afraid to make a decision. You need to realize that *will* is a very strong driving force—the will to be who you are, the will to be creative, the will to create something that is not there now.

9 | Teaching yourself to erase memories

This is all a great threat to the fallen beings and their control of this earth. They do not want you to be creative. They do not want you to come up with something that they cannot predict. If they cannot predict it, they cannot control it. They want (to use Nada's expression) to "hammer down" your creativity so that it does not upset the status quo of their society where they are in control. One of the ways they do this is this standard that you are either perfect or no good and they make you feel that you have made a mistake and how did you make that mistake? By making a decision.

There is a self that has been in the collective consciousness for a long time, saying that it is dangerous to make decisions, that you should actually, as an individual, stop making decisions. You should follow the norms, follow the standards, follow the rules, do what everybody else is doing. In a sense, you are still making decisions but you are making decisions within a very narrowly defined framework. You are not making *creative* decisions—decisions that are new, that are an experiment. You are "doing," making the same decisions that other people have made. This self projects at you that if you do this, you are safe, you will stay within a norm, you will not make a mistake, you will not be condemned, you will not be put down. You see here that there is a very strong collective self that wants people to not make individual creative decisions. "You don't make a decision—you can't make a mistake," is what this self says.

Deciding not to be afraid to decide

Naturally, if you have come to earth as a co-creator, as an avatar, or if you are one of the original inhabitants who have grown to a certain level of consciousness, you cannot be at peace if you go into this state of mind. If you take this self into your four lower bodies, you cannot be at peace with being on earth because you know very well that you are not fulfilling your purpose for being here. You are not fulfilling your highest potential, you are not growing; you are not transcending yourself. You cannot be at peace with this. As long as you are not willing to make decisions, you cannot be at peace—it is *that* simple. What do you need to do to overcome this catch-22, this stalemate? Well my beloved, you need to make decisions—it is *that* simple.

Now, here is where even the teachings we give you can sometimes give you a slightly distorted perspective. Even going back to the 1930s when Saint Germain first released the techniques for invoking the violet flame, you saw some ascended master students who reasoned that all they needed to do was to give enough violet flame and one day they would wake up and be ready to ascend. Of course, this has never been the way it has really happened. As we have said before, it is not a mechanical path.

You could take the teachings that we have given you now and you could say: "Well, I just need to invoke enough energy through invocations and decrees that I dissolve the emotional energy that pulls me back to the past, and then I need to dissolve these selves and then one day I will be free of my past." Of course, dissolving the energy, removing the selves will help lessen the pull that the past has on you. But what is the "you" that the past has a pull on? We have called it the Conscious You, simply to signify here that there is a part of your lower being, the being that is in embodiment, that is not your four lower bodies, that is not your separate selves, that is not your sense of personality—it is beyond it. This is what gives you the self-awareness that helps you step back from your present situation, your present sense of identity, and decide that you want to change.

Every time you come to identify: "Oh, I have a separate self in my being that projects that here is a problem I have to solve," what is it that is able to realize this? It is the Conscious You. It is that part of you that has the ability to be conscious of your consciousness, be conscious of what is going on in your consciousness. You see that your outer personality, for example, is totally enveloped in your day-to-day situation. Your outer personality cannot step back and say: "It's time to do something differently." That is what the Conscious You can do when it becomes conscious of this ability. It can step back.

A separate self cannot step back, it cannot say: "Oh, I want to dissolve myself." The Conscious You *can* step back and say: "I want to dissolve that self because it is not *my* self, it is not who I am." Every time you become aware that there is a separate self, it is the Conscious You that is using its ability to be conscious of what is going on in your mind. You might say that it is the part of your mind that can be conscious of the rest of the mind. This is just one expression.

What does it take to let a separate self die? Well, the Conscious You must make that decision, and what is the decision you have to make in order to let any self die? Well, as we have said, there is a self that projects that there is a problem that you need to deal with. Say for example, to build on Mother Mary's latest discourse, that there is a separate self that projects that you need to be perfect or you are no good. The self cannot ever question this, it will keep projecting at you that you need to strive to become better and better so that you can be perfect. Or, there is another self that will project that when you are not perfect (which, of course, you never are), then you should feel bad about yourself. There is another self that projects that you should stop trying because you are obviously not good enough, there is something wrong with you, and so forth.

These selves cannot ever overcome their programing. What the Conscious You needs to do is to see the illusion behind what the self is projecting, see that the problem projected by the self has no reality to it and, for that matter, it has no solution. There *is* no solution. What is perfection? It has never been defined because it cannot be defined because it is a meaningless concept. Therefore, my beloved, it is an unsolvable problem. You can never become perfect. When the Conscious You sees this, then the Conscious You can make the decision: "I no longer want to have my attention tied up in trying to solve this impossible problem." And you let the self die.

The way out of the past

It is a little bit different, perhaps, with overcoming your past. Even though there is also a self that projects that you cannot be free of the past, what is the problem that this self is projecting? It is not quite as simple of a problem because the self is not really projecting that there is something you need to solve—because there *is not* something to solve. The past, according to this self, is set in stone and you can never be free of it. What the self is really projecting is that you should feel bad for what happened in the past and you should continue to do so. There is not really a problem to solve there, in the sense that the self is not giving you a way out.

Some of these other selves, they are giving you a way out, at least the illusion that one day you could become perfect. This self is not giving you a way out because you cannot change your past, according to what it is projecting. Of course, you can come to see that this is also an impossible situation but most people have been programmed over lifetimes to believe that there is some truth here, in the sense that you cannot change what happened in the past, you cannot undo what you did. If you made a so-called mistake, you cannot undo it.

What can you, then, do to circumvent this problem, to come to see it in a different light? You can build on what I gave you in my latest discourse where I said that everything that you do is done with the basic energy, the basic form of Ma-ter light, that makes up the four lower bodies of earth, the four realms of the material universe on earth. There is a certain energy and everything you do is done with that energy. That energy is simply, like we have said, much like the dots on a screen that can turn on and off, that can take on different colors and shapes, that can be arranged into different patterns.

As I said, you need to start training yourself that you see the energy behind the images that your mind is projecting upon the energy. Of course, this is not quite as simple of a task as we are making it out to be because, again, for a very long time, the collective consciousness has been solidified around certain images, for example, that something is a sin and something is wrong. You should feel bad about having done something wrong and you should feel that you could never be redeemed from having made certain mistakes. All of these things, many, many things, are in the collective consciousness, but you can still train yourself to realize that everything is made with energy and that the energy is just energy—it is *just* energy.

You may look at a certain situation, as I gave the example of a movie screen where you are seeing certain images on the screen but it is really patterns of light. You may look at a certain situation from your past through a specific self that says you made a mistake, and you can never be redeemed and you should feel bad. You may think that this situation *did* happen so it has some objective reality. It is not just a subjective thing. "No, the situation *did* happen. Other people saw it happen. God saw it happen." The eye in the sky that is seeing everything, saw it happen and God is forever holding the image of you making this mistake and you can never be free of it. Other people are forever holding the image of this mistake and you can never be free of it. In other words, what has been projected by these selves and by the fallen beings is that a situation that happened in the past has some objective reality. Here is where you can begin to question this and realize a very, very simple truth.

Your past has no objective reality

God, as we have said: the Creator God, does not even look at anything that happens in an unascended sphere. Until a sphere has ascended, the Creator is not looking at it whatsoever. The Creator's consciousness is so intense that it would have various effects on this and the Creator has given its co-creators free will. Basically, an unascended sphere is where the Creator creates a sphere and sends co-creators into it and says: "Now, go and do whatever you want in this sphere because I will not look at it." When a sphere ascends, then the Creator will look but until a sphere has ascended, the Creator is not looking. The real God is not judging you, is not condemning you and is not holding on to the image of what you did in the past. What kind of god is holding on? Well, the false god created by the fallen beings but is this the god you need to be concerned about? I think not, my beloved, when you know what you know.

If God is not holding an image of what happened in the past, where would then that image exist of what you did in the past? Where would an objective image exist? Well, you might say: "in the Akashic Records."

Yes, there is a record of what you did in the past in the Akashic Records, but that record is not a record of what you saw or what the fallen beings saw or what other people saw. That record is a record of the energy waves, the patterns of energy waves. The Akashic Records, they are just recording, they are not making any judgements of how you saw that situation. The images you put on it, the judgements you put upon it that this was a mistake, this is *not* recorded in the Akashic Records. The patterns of energy waves are recorded there but that is all. The Akashic Records are not looking at this consciously and making judgements about what you did, that it was wrong and how you should feel about it.

Where are these ideas (that you did something wrong), where are they located, then? Well, they might be located in the minds of other people, some of which might be fallen beings. Is what is in the minds of other people, and certainly in the minds of fallen beings, is that objective? Nay, this is a completely subjective judgment. There is one more place where the record of your past mistakes can be located and that is in your own four lower bodies, in your own mind—but is *that* objective? Nay, it is not an objective reality because it is totally dependent on the contents of your consciousness, including your separate selves that color your perception.

You see what I am saying, my beloved? There is no *objective* reality to what you did in the past. There is a certain pattern of energy waves in the Akashic Records, yes, but the whole idea that you are a sinner, that you are a bad person, that you made some mistake, *this* has no objective reality whatsoever. It is not recorded anywhere. We of the ascended masters are not like the God of the Old Testament. We are not holding an image of you either. We may see certain things that you do but we are not judging you with the human consciousness. We are not judging you at all. We are just looking at you from our perspective, which we have now given you many glimpses of is very different from the perspective of human beings. Again, what you did in your past does not exist in any objective reality whatsoever. It is only you or other people that can make it have some enduring existence. This is, of course, one of the, we might say, graces of reincarnation. If you had a lifespan of a thousand years and there were people you had known for a thousand years, they might still lift a finger and say: "Remember what you did 992 years ago?" With the short lifespan you have, at least they only have so many decades to point the finger at. You see here, there is a reality that comes in with reincarnation and it is simply this: You can take with you from lifetime to lifetime your personal subjective images of what you did in a past life, you can carry them with you in your four lower bodies. Most of the time, you are not conscious of it but you can carry them with you. Other people do not carry those images with them. They might carry some sense of their relationship with you but not the specifics.

Knowing where memories are stored

In other words, if you take a situation that happened to you 300 years ago and that involved two other people, you could put yourself into a hypnotic regression and go back to that past life and reclaim that memory. You could take the two other people, go back to that past life and reclaim and reawaken their memory of that lifetime and they would remember what *they* did and how they saw the situation. They would not remember the specifics of what *you* did and how you saw the situation. Understand here, you are carrying with you from past lives what *you* did and how you looked at it, but it is not so that other people can remember what you did 300 years ago. You need to recognize here that your memory of the past really only exists in *your* four lower bodies.

As we have said before, you do not have the power to change other people's four lower bodies, but you *do* have the power to take command over your own four lower bodies and clear them of whatever you want to clear them of. Back to my statement that the Akashic Records do not record how you looked at what you did, they only record a certain pattern of energy waves. Now, imagine that you are taking a walk in a local park where there is a playground for children and you become aware that there are some very loud noises in there and you go closer to investigate. You see an adult man who is standing there, looking down on the sandbox and yelling very loudly. You go in there and you realize that this is a father who is talking to his two-year old son who has built a little sand castle in the sandbox. He is blaming his two-year old son that he has created a bad sand castle, and it is wrong of him because it can never be erased, and he has damaged the sand, and he has made a big mistake and all of these things that the father is spouting out at the child. The child looks very scared and does not like being yelled at.

You first feel very disturbed by this situation but, then, you realize that what the father is really saying is that the child has made a mistake that can never be erased by making this sand castle. Suddenly, without thinking about it, you step in there and you say: "My good man, take a look at this," and you take your hand and whisk away the sand castle so the sand is returned to its pristine condition. It has no shape on it, it is just sand. You say: "So, are you still going to blame your child for having made a mistake that could never be erased?" The father, of course, does not know what to say so you walk on and as you are walking out of there you are thinking: "Hah, I really told him off, didn't I?"

Then, to your surprise, you notice that there is a mirror standing there and suddenly you look in the mirror and you realize: "Oh, am I doing the same to myself? Am I yelling at myself for having created a sand castle, having made a mistake that could never be erased, when in reality anything I have done on this planet is done with energy that is as pliable as sand and could as easily be returned to its undifferentiated state as the sand that I just whisked away?" You realize this is exactly what, not *you*, have been doing but what a *specific separate self* in your being has been doing, not only in this lifetime but probably in many lifetimes, perhaps for two million years. This is one of the strongest collective selves here on earth, and it makes people think that once they have made a sand castle that was labeled "wrong" or "bad" that sand castle can never be erased.

Deciding to erase the sand castle

But it is a *sand castle*. I do not care whatsoever what you might have done in a past life. Some ascended master students have had visions or glimpses or regressions to past lives where they have seen that they did something that caused the downfall of an entire civilization. I do not care what you have done, my beloved, it was still a sand castle and it can be whisked away. What will it take to whisk it away? Well, in many cases when you have done something that affected other people, you have created what we have called karma, which is really just a form of misqualified energy. You can do various things to this. You can make amends to other people and many of you have already done this in past lives. Whomever you may have hurt in the distant past, you have already compensated for this in your past life.

You can give invocations and decrees to dissolve the energy. You can dissolve the self that caused you to do what you did and, my beloved, there are many of you who have already done a lot of these things in past lives. There are many of you who can use the tools we have given you and very quickly get to a point where you have compensated, you have done what you need to do to be free of the past, except for one thing and that one thing is to make the conscious decision that you will whisk away the sand castle. The sand castle is the image you are holding in your mind that you are superimposing upon the sand, the energy, the Ma-ter Light. It is, as I said, your memory of an event. *That* is the image you are holding and when you become conscious of having done something in the past that is still burdening you, you use the tools, you do what you need to do. You must be aware, you must be sensitive to the fact, that there comes that point where the only thing, the *absolutely only* thing, that is left to do is to whisk away the image you are holding in your mind.

That requires you to make a decision, a decision to stop holding on to this image of yourself as being a bad person, having made a mistake and all of these things. Did you recognize what I just said a few minutes ago? The Creator is not looking at what you do in an un-ascended sphere. The Creator has said: "An un-ascended sphere is a cosmic sandbox." There is nothing you could do that could hurt the sand, there is nothing you could do that could ever become permanent. Just whisk away that image you are holding in your mind of yourself as a bad person, as a sinner, as a failure or as not having a right to be here, not wanting to be here, hating to be here—all of these images. There comes that point where you simply have to look at an image and whisk it away. There is nothing to solve, there is nothing to do here, just simply whisk it away and allow yourself to forget that the image ever existed.

Questioning the reality of the "real world"

You can train your mind to look beyond the images and see the pulsating, vibrating energy behind it. You can even train your mind to see that the physical world is a theatre. When you walk up on the stage and go behind the set pieces, you see that it is all make-believe. There is nothing here that is real, there is nothing here that is permanent. It only looks real from a certain perspective, namely the perspective of the audience. What is the purpose of a play in a theatre? Well, it is to give the audience a specific kind of experience. If you are watching Shakespeare's Hamlet and there are good actors who understand how to live themselves into the part, then you can live yourself into the role and you can gain a unique experience from watching that performance. It is exactly the same with anything and everything that happens in what you call the "real world."

Possibly the greatest illusion ever foisted upon humankind by the fallen beings is that what is happening on earth is the "real world." There is nothing real about it in an objective sense. The entire purpose of the earth is to give lifestreams a particular experience. Of course, my beloved, in order to have that experience, you must *believe* it is real. As an advanced spiritual student there comes that point where you are ready to question the reality of the experience that everybody else is having. Is there an objective world? Is the world there when no one is looking, as the quantum physicists are asking? The answer is that the energy is there but the images that are created in people's minds when they look at the energy, is not there. It has no objective reality.

Erasing the past

Do you understand, my beloved, what I am saying here? No, you do not and that is why you need to ponder this and ponder it. If a tree falls in the forest and there is nobody there, does it make a sound? If a tree falls, there are certain energy waves that make up what you call a tree, that are moving until they interact with the energy waves that make up the ground. This creates an interference pattern that sends out other energy waves that you perceive as sound. The energy waves are still there but it is not a *sound*. It is just energy waves.

Now, you take a situation, and we are in Eastern Europe so let us look at the Soviet occupation of Eastern Europe. If there had been no people there, would it have happened? Well, if there *had* been no people, it would not have happened, there would have been no one to make it happen. The point of it is, was there some objective event that took place? Yes, there was. There was a certain pattern, a certain interaction, a very complicated pattern of energy waves but the experience that people had was not at the level of the energy waves, it was in people's minds. They called it something, they looked at it in a certain way.

I am not blaming anybody here, my beloved. I am not blaming the people of Eastern Europe for feeling oppressed and suppressed by the Soviet Union. I am not blaming them, but I am saying that there was an objective situation, in the sense that some people perpetrated what you call the occupation of Eastern Europe, the suppression of the people in other nations. Some people were the instruments for doing this in the physical realm. The way the people experienced this was a product of an interference pattern, an interaction, between the energy waves set in motion by the Soviet occupational forces and the energy waves in the minds of the people who were occupied. There was an experience that people had on both sides but it was not an *objective* experience. It is, in fact, possible for you to step back and gain an entirely different perspective on this. Instead of seeing the events that people have collectively agreed upon took place, you can come to see the energy waves and see that the energy waves are like sand in the sandbox. Regardless of how many people were involved with this event, the energies could easily be erased, returned to their ground state.

Now, of course, this would be a complicated matter because all of the people involved would have to decide to let go of their images of the past. If, say the people in Estonia, would come together, look at their past and say: "We are going to collectively let go of any feelings we have about the past. We are going to completely let these feelings go. We are not even going to forgive the Russians for what they did to us. We are going to let go of the entire idea that there is anything to forgive. We are going to whisk away the images we are holding." If the people were to do this, the nation of Estonia could very, very quickly become completely free of its past. I am not saying this is a likely scenario to occur within the next couple of weeks.

Nevertheless, what I *am* saying is that the only way that any group of people or any individual is going to become free of the past is to come to the point where they say: "Whatever happened was just a sand castle. It was as insignificant in the longer cosmic perspective as a sand castle. It was just an interaction of energy waves. It is meaningless to hold an image of it, to call it right or wrong, to call it this or that. The real question here is, do we want to be free of it or do we not? And if we want to be free, there is nothing we have to solve here. We do not have to punish anybody. We do not have to change anything in the past that cannot be changed. We just have to realize that what is keeping us tied to the past is our image of it. We have to decide to whisk it away. Then, we are free."

Of course, they would have to do the cleanup work of all the energies to be consumed and the selves to be resolved and all of this stuff. I am not saying it is *likely*, my beloved, I am saying it is *possible* and I am saying it so that you, on an individual level, can realize that whereas it would be complicated to get other people to agree on this, there is absolutely nothing stopping you from looking at your own past. You can let go of any images you become aware of, as you use our tools to go back into the traumas of past lives to see the situation in the theatre, to see that performance, to see that being that is frozen in time and the other beings that are frozen in time because of you holding an image of it. You can see it and just let it go, let it all melt away, my beloved. This is what you have the power to do and you can use these tools.

Whisking away the memory image

As I am saying to you now, there comes a point where you have used the tools enough that the only thing that is left is that you become aware that you, in your mind, are holding on to an image and you are deciding to whisk it away. What are you actually deciding to do, when you take Mother Mary's very, very profound discourse, that what brought you to this planet was that *you* wanted, your I AM Presence wanted, to experience itself on this planet, in this environment. Well, the selves you have, the image you have of the past of having made a mistake in the past, is blocking you from experiencing yourself on this planet. You are not experiencing your real self, you are experiencing life on earth through a particular self.

We have said that the Conscious You is pure awareness, which is just words, but the Conscious You is in a sense neutral about being on earth. It has a certain curiosity about being on earth. What would it be like to experience that situation? That is why you have gone into many situations in past lives, because the Conscious You said: "What would I feel like, how would I experience myself in that situation?" When you take on and create these separate selves, then your experience is colored by the selves. What we are telling you is that you can come back to the point where the Conscious You, as pure awareness, as a neutral self, is just experiencing (neutrally) conditions. You can also reach up and experience how your I

AM Presence is experiencing that situation. This is the ultimate frame of reference that allows you to step away from being so identified with the conditions you are facing, both *inside* your four lower bodies and *outside* your four lower bodies.

We have told you that you have these selves in your four lower bodies. What are these selves? They are made up of energy waves of this Ma-ter Light, these points that had a certain pattern superimposed upon them. A self is, then, just an image and you can look at a self and you can decide to whisk that self away. We have told you before that you let the self die but if it helps you to look at the self as an image and imagine you are just erasing that image as a sand castle in the sandbox, then use that visualization instead. Whatever works for you.

You need to find some way to come to identify that the only reality here, the only thing that is left, is the image and you are erasing it. You are letting it go. This, my beloved, is not so difficult to do when you use all the tools you have. I totally admit that it cannot be done in five minutes. There are none of you that can do it instantly, but so what. If you have been in embodiment on this earth for two million years, and in a few years you can overcome all of these momentums, all of these selves you have taken in, then that is really very, very fast. It really is almost in the blink of an eye when you consider the cosmic time scale.

Overcoming impatience

Left for me is only one thing. I know I have already given you a lot, but I am Master MORE so I will give you more and it is simply this. To some degree, this applies to the original inhabitants of the earth who have reached a certain level, but it first of all applies to avatars. If you look at an avatar who has come to earth and has been here a long time (two million years is not the time span for all of you but for some of you). Anyway, you have all been here for a long time. What is the one characteristic that you see in all avatars? It is simply this, my beloved: impatience. You are all very, very impatient.

First of all, you are impatient with yourselves. Again, this is not said to blame you. My beloved, if you had known me when I was in physical embodiment, you would have seen impatience taken almost to an extreme. If you had seen Saint Germain. You can even see in the story of Jesus how he got impatient with his disciples. My beloved, we are not blaming you but we are saying you can all benefit from being aware that you have a tendency to be very impatient with yourselves. You feel that when you are told that you can accomplish something, you should be able to do it by snapping your fingers. Give yourself a little bit of time—give yourself a little bit of time.

You might even consider that the fallen beings are quite experienced in trying to derail the Christhood and the growth of spiritual beings, especially avatars. They are quite skilled at this. When you reach a certain level of awareness, they are trying to actually make you take on certain selves that will derail your continued growth. One of these selves is this idea that makes you impatient, that you should be able to achieve something very quickly. You can come to see this as a separate self and just let it go, my beloved. Give yourself some time. Meditate on Gautama Buddha who is really the master who can help you overcome impatience, who can help you realize that time, although it is there, it does not matter so much. Does it take five minutes or does it take five years? It does not matter so much and therefore you can overcome that impatience. You can give yourself a little bit of time.

I am saying this because for most of you, the problem is not that you will become indulgent and say: "Oh Master MORE says I have plenty of time, so I am just going to relax and not give any invocations and not read any books about the primal self, I am not going to worry about it. I am just going to enjoy life and have a cup of chocolate." That is not the danger for most of you. It is for *some* and you see many in the New Age field who are precisely in that state of mind: "It's all good, so let's all just relax and enjoy life." Nevertheless, *your* problem is that you are impatient and what does impatience do to you? It prevents you from being at peace with being here.

What is the topic of our conference: being at peace with being on earth. Be aware of the impatience, see that it is a self and just decide that you do not need to be so hard on yourself. You do not need to accomplish everything in five minutes because in a certain sense, time is *not*. Time is a collective illusion created by the collective consciousness. It is allowed to exist because for some people the idea that time could run out is the only thing that motivates them to stop doing what they are doing now. With this, I have completed what I want to give you (in this installment at least) and therefore I want to thank you for your attention.

I want to let you know, my beloved, that with the number of people you are, both here and on the broadcast, you have actually already had a major impact on the collective consciousness both in Eastern Europe and in all of the nations that you are connected to or live in. These invocations we have given you are quite powerful, are quite profound and they have a very dramatic affect, especially when they are given by a greater number of people so that there is that multiplication factor. I can assure you that you have already accomplished a very great work during this conference and for this, I simply want to extend our gratitude and our recognition. [The participants at the conference gave the invocations from *Healing Your Spiritual Traumas*.]

10 | INVOKING THE ERASING OF MEMORIES

In the name I AM THAT I AM, Jesus Christ, I call to all representatives of the Divine Mother, especially Master MORE, to help me learn how to erase memories, including...

[Make personal calls.]

Part 1

1. There is a self in me that feels that it is stuck in the past, living in the past, looking back to the past, even longing for some lost paradise from some time in the past.

> Master MORE, come to the fore,
> we will absorb your flame of MORE.
> Master MORE, our will so strong,
> our power centers cleared by song.
>
> **Master MORE, your Sacred Heart,
> from this we will no more depart,**

> we are forever in your flow,
> of Diamond Will that you bestow.

2. I have this feeling that I have lost something, and I *have* lost the innocence I had before I came here. The masters are seeking to help me regain and reclaim that innocence.

> Master MORE, your wisdom flows,
> as our attunement ever grows.
> Master MORE, we have a tie,
> that helps us see through Serpent's lie.
>
> **Master MORE, your Sacred Heart,
> from this we will no more depart,
> we are forever in your flow,
> of Diamond Will that you bestow.**

3. There are certain selves that are not created by me in reaction to a specific situation. They are created in reaction to what it feels like to be in embodiment on a planet as dense as earth.

> Master MORE, your love so pink,
> there is no purer love, we think.
> Master MORE, you set us free,
> from all conditionality.
>
> **Master MORE, your Sacred Heart,
> from this we will no more depart,
> we are forever in your flow,
> of Diamond Will that you bestow.**

4. These selves are in the collective consciousness and it is difficult to not be affected by them, especially after I receive a birth trauma and I am shocked by the conditions on earth being so different than what I had envisioned before I came here.

> Master MORE, we will endure,
> your discipline that makes us pure.

Master MORE, intentions true,
as we are always one with you.

**Master MORE, your Sacred Heart,
from this we will no more depart,
we are forever in your flow,
of Diamond Will that you bestow.**

5. I have taken on some of these collective selves that have been created over a long period of time, and which were created in order to deal with the situation that people feel they cannot live with.

Master MORE, our vision raised,
the will of God is always praised.
Master MORE, creative will,
raising all life higher still.

**Master MORE, your Sacred Heart,
from this we will no more depart,
we are forever in your flow,
of Diamond Will that you bestow.**

6. There are certain selves that have floated around in the collective consciousness for a long time. There are selves that want me to think that once I have made what I accepted as a mistake, I cannot be free of it because I cannot undo that physical situation.

Master MORE, your peace is power,
the demons of war it will devour.
Master MORE, we serve all life,
our flames consuming war and strife.

**Master MORE, your Sacred Heart,
from this we will no more depart,
we are forever in your flow,
of Diamond Will that you bestow.**

7. In order to be free of my past, I ultimately must make a *decision* to be free. Will is a very strong driving force—the will to be who I am, the will to be creative, the will to create something that is not there now.

> Master MORE, we are so free,
> eternal bond from you we see.
> Master MORE, we find rebirth,
> in flow of your eternal mirth.
>
> **Master MORE, your Sacred Heart,**
> **from this we will no more depart,**
> **we are forever in your flow,**
> **of Diamond Will that you bestow.**

8. Creativity is a great threat to the fallen beings and their control of this earth. They do not want me to be creative. They do not want me to come up with something that they cannot predict.

> Master MORE, you balance all,
> the seven rays upon our call.
> Master MORE, forever MORE,
> we are the Spirit's open door.
>
> **Master MORE, your Sacred Heart,**
> **from this we will no more depart,**
> **we are forever in your flow,**
> **of Diamond Will that you bestow.**

9. The fallen beings say that when I made mistakes, it was because I made decisions. There is a self in the collective consciousness that says it is dangerous to make decisions, that I, as an individual, should stop making decisions. I should follow the norms, follow the standards, follow the rules, do what everybody else is doing.

> Master MORE, your Presence here,
> filling up the inner sphere.
> Life is now a sacred flow,
> God Power we on all bestow.

**Master MORE, your Sacred Heart,
from this we will no more depart,
we are forever in your flow,
of Diamond Will that you bestow.**

Part 2

1. This self says I can still make decisions but only within a narrow framework. This is not making *creative* decisions—decisions that are new, that are an experiment. This self projects that if I stay within the norm, I am safe.

Master MORE, come to the fore,
we will absorb your flame of MORE.
Master MORE, our will so strong,
our power centers cleared by song.

**Master MORE, your Sacred Heart,
from this we will no more depart,
we are forever in your flow,
of Diamond Will that you bestow.**

2. Given my level of consciousness, I cannot be at peace if I go into this state of mind. If I take this self into my four lower bodies, I cannot be at peace with being on earth because I know that I am not fulfilling my purpose for being here. I am not fulfilling my highest potential, I am not growing; I am not transcending myself.

Master MORE, your wisdom flows,
as our attunement ever grows.
Master MORE, we have a tie,
that helps us see through Serpent's lie.

**Master MORE, your Sacred Heart,
from this we will no more depart,
we are forever in your flow,
of Diamond Will that you bestow.**

3. I cannot be at peace with this. As long as I am not willing to make decisions, I cannot be at peace. In order to overcome this catch-22, this stalemate, I have to make decisions—and I am willing to make those decisions.

> Master MORE, your love so pink,
> there is no purer love, we think.
> Master MORE, you set us free,
> from all conditionality.
>
> **Master MORE, your Sacred Heart,**
> **from this we will no more depart,**
> **we are forever in your flow,**
> **of Diamond Will that you bestow.**

4. The "you" that the past has a pull on is the Conscious You. This is a part of my lower being that is not my four lower bodies, that is not my separate selves, that is not my sense of personality—it is beyond it. This is what gives me the self-awareness that helps me step back from my present situation, my present sense of identity, and decide that I want to change.

> Master MORE, we will endure,
> your discipline that makes us pure.
> Master MORE, intentions true,
> as we are always one with you.
>
> **Master MORE, your Sacred Heart,**
> **from this we will no more depart,**
> **we are forever in your flow,**
> **of Diamond Will that you bestow.**

5. It is the Conscious You that can come to identify: "Oh, I have a separate self in my being that projects that there is a problem I have to solve." It is that part of me that has the ability to be conscious of my consciousness, be conscious of what is going on in my consciousness.

> Master MORE, our vision raised,
> the will of God is always praised.
> Master MORE, creative will,
> raising all life higher still.

> Master MORE, your Sacred Heart,
> from this we will no more depart,
> we are forever in your flow,
> of Diamond Will that you bestow.

6. My outer personality is totally enveloped in my day-to-day situation. My outer personality cannot step back and say: "It's time to do something differently." That is what the Conscious You can do when it becomes conscious of this ability. It can step back.

> Master MORE, your peace is power,
> the demons of war it will devour.
> Master MORE, we serve all life,
> our flames consuming war and strife.

> Master MORE, your Sacred Heart,
> from this we will no more depart,
> we are forever in your flow,
> of Diamond Will that you bestow.

7. A separate self cannot step back, it cannot say: "Oh, I want to dissolve myself." The Conscious You *can* step back and say: "I want to dissolve that self because it is not *my* self, it is not who I am."

> Master MORE, we are so free,
> eternal bond from you we see.
> Master MORE, we find rebirth,
> in flow of your eternal mirth.

> Master MORE, your Sacred Heart,
> from this we will no more depart,
> we are forever in your flow,
> of Diamond Will that you bestow.

8. Every time I become aware that there is a separate self, it is the Conscious You that is using its ability to be conscious of what is going on in my mind. The Conscious You is the part of my mind that can be conscious of the rest of the mind.

Master MORE, you balance all,
the seven rays upon our call.
Master MORE, forever MORE,
we are the Spirit's open door.

**Master MORE, your Sacred Heart,
from this we will no more depart,
we are forever in your flow,
of Diamond Will that you bestow.**

9. In order to let a separate self die, the Conscious You must make a decision. The Conscious You needs to see the illusion behind what the self is projecting, see that the problem projected by the self has no reality to it and no solution.

Master MORE, your Presence here,
filling up the inner sphere.
Life is now a sacred flow,
God Power we on all bestow.

**Master MORE, your Sacred Heart,
from this we will no more depart,
we are forever in your flow,
of Diamond Will that you bestow.**

Part 3

1. There *is* no solution, it is an unsolvable problem. When the Conscious You sees this, then the Conscious You can make the decision: "I no longer want to have my attention tied up in trying to solve this impossible problem." And I let the self die.

Master MORE, come to the fore,
we will absorb your flame of MORE.
Master MORE, our will so strong,
our power centers cleared by song.

> **Master MORE, your Sacred Heart,**
> **from this we will no more depart,**
> **we are forever in your flow,**
> **of Diamond Will that you bestow.**

2. There is a self that projects that I cannot be free of the past, but this self is not projecting that there is something I need to solve—because according to this self, the past is set in stone and I can never be free of it.

> Master MORE, your wisdom flows,
> as our attunement ever grows.
> Master MORE, we have a tie,
> that helps us see through Serpent's lie.

> **Master MORE, your Sacred Heart,**
> **from this we will no more depart,**
> **we are forever in your flow,**
> **of Diamond Will that you bestow.**

3. The self is really projecting that I should feel bad for what happened in the past and I should continue to do so. There is not really a problem to solve there, in the sense that the self is not giving me a way out.

> Master MORE, your love so pink,
> there is no purer love, we think.
> Master MORE, you set us free,
> from all conditionality.

> **Master MORE, your Sacred Heart,**
> **from this we will no more depart,**
> **we are forever in your flow,**
> **of Diamond Will that you bestow.**

4. Other selves are giving me a way out, at least the illusion that one day I could become perfect. This self is not giving me a way out because I cannot change my past, according to what it is projecting. I see that this is an impossible situation.

Master MORE, we will endure,
your discipline that makes us pure.
Master MORE, intentions true,
as we are always one with you.

**Master MORE, your Sacred Heart,
from this we will no more depart,
we are forever in your flow,
of Diamond Will that you bestow.**

5. In order to circumvent this problem, I see that everything I do is done with the basic energy, the basic form of Ma-ter light, that makes up the four realms of the material universe.

Master MORE, our vision raised,
the will of God is always praised.
Master MORE, creative will,
raising all life higher still.

**Master MORE, your Sacred Heart,
from this we will no more depart,
we are forever in your flow,
of Diamond Will that you bestow.**

6. There is a certain energy and everything I do is done with that energy. The energy is like the dots on a screen that can turn on and off, that can take on different colors and shapes, that can be arranged into different patterns.

Master MORE, your peace is power,
the demons of war it will devour.
Master MORE, we serve all life,
our flames consuming war and strife.

**Master MORE, your Sacred Heart,
from this we will no more depart,
we are forever in your flow,
of Diamond Will that you bestow.**

7. I am training myself to see the energy behind the images that my mind is projecting upon the energy. I realize that everything is made with energy and that the energy is just energy—it is *just* energy.

> Master MORE, we are so free,
> eternal bond from you we see.
> Master MORE, we find rebirth,
> in flow of your eternal mirth.
>
> **Master MORE, your Sacred Heart,**
> **from this we will no more depart,**
> **we are forever in your flow,**
> **of Diamond Will that you bestow.**

8. There is a self that looks at a certain situation from my past and says I made a mistake, and I can never be redeemed and I should feel bad. The self says that this situation did happen so it has some objective reality. It is not just a subjective thing.

> Master MORE, you balance all,
> the seven rays upon our call.
> Master MORE, forever MORE,
> we are the Spirit's open door.
>
> **Master MORE, your Sacred Heart,**
> **from this we will no more depart,**
> **we are forever in your flow,**
> **of Diamond Will that you bestow.**

9. What has been projected by these selves and by the fallen beings is that a situation that happened in the past has some objective reality. In reality, nothing is objective because the Creator God does not even look at anything that happens in an unascended sphere.

> Master MORE, your Presence here,
> filling up the inner sphere.
> Life is now a sacred flow,
> God Power we on all bestow.

> Master MORE, your Sacred Heart,
> from this we will no more depart,
> we are forever in your flow,
> of Diamond Will that you bestow.

Part 4

1. The Creator creates a sphere and sends co-creators into it and says: "Now, go and do whatever you want in this sphere because I will not look at it."

> Master MORE, come to the fore,
> we will absorb your flame of MORE.
> Master MORE, our will so strong,
> our power centers cleared by song.

> Master MORE, your Sacred Heart,
> from this we will no more depart,
> we are forever in your flow,
> of Diamond Will that you bestow.

2. The real God is not judging me, is not condemning me and is not holding on to the image of what I did in the past. Only the false god created by the fallen beings holds on to my past, but this is not the god I need to be concerned about.

> Master MORE, your wisdom flows,
> as our attunement ever grows.
> Master MORE, we have a tie,
> that helps us see through Serpent's lie.

> Master MORE, your Sacred Heart,
> from this we will no more depart,
> we are forever in your flow,
> of Diamond Will that you bestow.

3. If God is not holding an image of what happened in the past, where would that image exist of what I did in the past? Where would an objective image exist?

> Master MORE, your love so pink,
> there is no purer love, we think.
> Master MORE, you set us free,
> from all conditionality.
>
> **Master MORE, your Sacred Heart,**
> **from this we will no more depart,**
> **we are forever in your flow,**
> **of Diamond Will that you bestow.**

4. The Akashic Records are just recording, they are not making any judgements of how I saw that situation and the judgements I put upon it.

> Master MORE, we will endure,
> your discipline that makes us pure.
> Master MORE, intentions true,
> as we are always one with you.
>
> **Master MORE, your Sacred Heart,**
> **from this we will no more depart,**
> **we are forever in your flow,**
> **of Diamond Will that you bestow.**

5. The ideas that I did something wrong can be located in the minds of other people, some of which might be fallen beings. What is in the minds of other people is not objective. It is a completely subjective judgment.

> Master MORE, our vision raised,
> the will of God is always praised.
> Master MORE, creative will,
> raising all life higher still.
>
> **Master MORE, your Sacred Heart,**
> **from this we will no more depart,**

> we are forever in your flow,
> of Diamond Will that you bestow.

6. The record of my past mistakes can be located in my own four lower bodies, in my own mind. Yet that is not an objective reality because it is totally dependent on the contents of my consciousness, including my separate selves that color my perception.

> Master MORE, your peace is power,
> the demons of war it will devour.
> Master MORE, we serve all life,
> our flames consuming war and strife.

> **Master MORE, your Sacred Heart,
> from this we will no more depart,
> we are forever in your flow,
> of Diamond Will that you bestow.**

7. There is no objective reality to what I did in the past. There is a certain pattern of energy waves in the Akashic Records, but the idea that I am a sinner, that I am a bad person, that I made some mistake, *this* has no objective reality whatsoever. It is not recorded anywhere.

> Master MORE, we are so free,
> eternal bond from you we see.
> Master MORE, we find rebirth,
> in flow of your eternal mirth.

> **Master MORE, your Sacred Heart,
> from this we will no more depart,
> we are forever in your flow,
> of Diamond Will that you bestow.**

8. The ascended masters are not like the God of the Old Testament. They are not holding an image of me either. They are not judging me with the human consciousness. They are not judging me at all.

> Master MORE, you balance all,
> the seven rays upon our call.

Master MORE, forever MORE,
we are the Spirit's open door.

**Master MORE, your Sacred Heart,
from this we will no more depart,
we are forever in your flow,
of Diamond Will that you bestow.**

9. What I did in my past does not exist in any objective reality whatsoever. It is only me or other people that can make it have some enduring existence. I can take with me from lifetime to lifetime my personal, subjective images of what I did in a past life. I can carry them with me in my four lower bodies.

Master MORE, your Presence here,
filling up the inner sphere.
Life is now a sacred flow,
God Power we on all bestow.

**Master MORE, your Sacred Heart,
from this we will no more depart,
we are forever in your flow,
of Diamond Will that you bestow.**

Part 5

1. I am carrying with me from past lives what I did and how I looked at it, but other people cannot remember what I did. My memory of the past only exists in my four lower bodies.

Master MORE, come to the fore,
we will absorb your flame of MORE.
Master MORE, our will so strong,
our power centers cleared by song.

**Master MORE, your Sacred Heart,
from this we will no more depart,**

> we are forever in your flow,
> of Diamond Will that you bestow.

2. I do not have the power to change other people's four lower bodies but I do have the power to take command over my own four lower bodies and clear them of whatever I want to clear them of.

> Master MORE, your wisdom flows,
> as our attunement ever grows.
> Master MORE, we have a tie,
> that helps us see through Serpent's lie.
>
> **Master MORE, your Sacred Heart,
> from this we will no more depart,
> we are forever in your flow,
> of Diamond Will that you bestow.**

3. Am I yelling at myself for having created a sand castle, having made a mistake that could never be erased, when in reality anything I have done on this planet is done with energy that is as pliable as sand and could as easily be returned to its undifferentiated state as the sand in a sandbox?

> Master MORE, your love so pink,
> there is no purer love, we think.
> Master MORE, you set us free,
> from all conditionality.
>
> **Master MORE, your Sacred Heart,
> from this we will no more depart,
> we are forever in your flow,
> of Diamond Will that you bestow.**

4. I realize this is exactly what, not *I*, have been doing but what a *specific separate self* in my being has been doing, not only in this lifetime but in many lifetimes. One of the strongest collective selves on earth makes people think that once they have made a sand castle that was labeled "wrong" or "bad" that sand castle can never be erased.

Master MORE, we will endure,
your discipline that makes us pure.
Master MORE, intentions true,
as we are always one with you.

**Master MORE, your Sacred Heart,
from this we will no more depart,
we are forever in your flow,
of Diamond Will that you bestow.**

5. Whatsoever I might have done in a past life, it was only a sand castle and it can be whisked away. I will use the tools the masters have given us and get to a point where I have compensated, I have done what I need to do to be free of the past.

Master MORE, our vision raised,
the will of God is always praised.
Master MORE, creative will,
raising all life higher still.

**Master MORE, your Sacred Heart,
from this we will no more depart,
we are forever in your flow,
of Diamond Will that you bestow.**

6. Then, there is only one thing left to do, and it is to make the conscious decision that I will whisk away the sand castle. The sand castle is the image I am holding in my mind that I am superimposing upon the sand, the energy, the Ma-ter Light. It is my memory of an event.

Master MORE, your peace is power,
the demons of war it will devour.
Master MORE, we serve all life,
our flames consuming war and strife.

**Master MORE, your Sacred Heart,
from this we will no more depart,
we are forever in your flow,
of Diamond Will that you bestow.**

7. I am at the point where the only thing left to do is to whisk away the image I am holding in my mind. *That* requires me to make a decision, a decision to stop holding on to this image of myself as being a bad person, having made a mistake and so on.

> Master MORE, we are so free,
> eternal bond from you we see.
> Master MORE, we find rebirth,
> in flow of your eternal mirth.
>
> **Master MORE, your Sacred Heart,**
> **from this we will no more depart,**
> **we are forever in your flow,**
> **of Diamond Will that you bestow.**

8. The Creator is not looking at what I do in an un-ascended sphere. The Creator has said: "An un-ascended sphere is a cosmic sandbox." There is nothing I could do that could hurt the sand, there is nothing I could do that could ever become permanent.

> Master MORE, you balance all,
> the seven rays upon our call.
> Master MORE, forever MORE,
> we are the Spirit's open door.
>
> **Master MORE, your Sacred Heart,**
> **from this we will no more depart,**
> **we are forever in your flow,**
> **of Diamond Will that you bestow.**

9. I am whisking away the image I am holding in my mind of myself as a bad person, as a sinner, as a failure or as not having a right to be here, not wanting to be here, hating to be here. I am looking at an image and whisking it away. There is nothing to solve, there is nothing to do here, I am simply whisking it away and allowing myself to forget that the image ever existed.

> Master MORE, your Presence here,
> filling up the inner sphere.

Life is now a sacred flow,
God Power we on all bestow.

**Master MORE, your Sacred Heart,
from this we will no more depart,
we are forever in your flow,
of Diamond Will that you bestow.**

Part 6

1. I am training my mind to look beyond the image and see the pulsating, vibrating energy behind it.

Master MORE, come to the fore,
we will absorb your flame of MORE.
Master MORE, our will so strong,
our power centers cleared by song.

**Master MORE, your Sacred Heart,
from this we will no more depart,
we are forever in your flow,
of Diamond Will that you bestow.**

2. I am training my mind to see that the physical world is a theatre. It is all make-believe. There is nothing here that is real, there is nothing here that is permanent. It only looks real from a certain perspective, namely the perspective of the separate self.

Master MORE, your wisdom flows,
as our attunement ever grows.
Master MORE, we have a tie,
that helps us see through Serpent's lie.

**Master MORE, your Sacred Heart,
from this we will no more depart,
we are forever in your flow,
of Diamond Will that you bestow.**

3. The purpose of a play in a theatre is to give the audience a specific kind of experience. It is exactly the same with anything and everything that happens in what we call the "real world."

> Master MORE, your love so pink,
> there is no purer love, we think.
> Master MORE, you set us free,
> from all conditionality.
>
> **Master MORE, your Sacred Heart,**
> **from this we will no more depart,**
> **we are forever in your flow,**
> **of Diamond Will that you bestow.**

4. The greatest illusion ever foisted upon humankind by the fallen beings is that what is happening on earth is the "real world." There is nothing real about it in an objective sense. The entire purpose of the earth is to give lifestreams a particular experience.

> Master MORE, we will endure,
> your discipline that makes us pure.
> Master MORE, intentions true,
> as we are always one with you.
>
> **Master MORE, your Sacred Heart,**
> **from this we will no more depart,**
> **we are forever in your flow,**
> **of Diamond Will that you bestow.**

5. In order to have that experience, I must *believe* it is real. I am ready to question the reality of the experience that everybody else is having. Is there an objective world? Is the world there when no one is looking? The energy is there but the images in people's minds are not there. They have no objective reality.

> Master MORE, our vision raised,
> the will of God is always praised.
> Master MORE, creative will,
> raising all life higher still.

> Master MORE, your Sacred Heart,
> from this we will no more depart,
> we are forever in your flow,
> of Diamond Will that you bestow.

6. The only way I am going to become free of the past is to come to the point where I say: "Whatever happened was just a sand castle. It was as insignificant in the cosmic perspective as a sand castle. It was just an interaction of energy waves. It is meaningless to hold an image of it, to call it right or wrong, to call it this or that."

> Master MORE, your peace is power,
> the demons of war it will devour.
> Master MORE, we serve all life,
> our flames consuming war and strife.

> Master MORE, your Sacred Heart,
> from this we will no more depart,
> we are forever in your flow,
> of Diamond Will that you bestow.

7. The real question here is, do I want to be free of it or do I not? If I want to be free, there is nothing I have to solve here. I do not have to punish anybody. I do not have to change anything in the past that cannot be changed. I just have to realize that what is keeping me tied to the past is my image of it. I am deciding to whisk it away and then I am free.

> Master MORE, we are so free,
> eternal bond from you we see.
> Master MORE, we find rebirth,
> in flow of your eternal mirth.

> Master MORE, your Sacred Heart,
> from this we will no more depart,
> we are forever in your flow,
> of Diamond Will that you bestow.

8. There is absolutely nothing stopping me from looking at my own past. I am letting go of any image I become aware of. I see it and just let it go,

let it all melt away. I accept that I have the power and the tools to become free of my past.

> Master MORE, you balance all,
> the seven rays upon our call.
> Master MORE, forever MORE,
> we are the Spirit's open door.
>
> **Master MORE, your Sacred Heart,**
> **from this we will no more depart,**
> **we are forever in your flow,**
> **of Diamond Will that you bestow.**

9. There comes a point where I have used the tools enough that the only thing left is that I become aware that I, in my mind, am holding on to an image and I now decide to whisk it away.

> Master MORE, your Presence here,
> filling up the inner sphere.
> Life is now a sacred flow,
> God Power we on all bestow.
>
> **Master MORE, your Sacred Heart,**
> **from this we will no more depart,**
> **we are forever in your flow,**
> **of Diamond Will that you bestow.**

Part 7

1. What brought me to this planet was that I wanted, my I AM Presence wanted, to experience itself on this planet, in this environment. The selves I have, the image I have of the past is blocking me from experiencing myself on this planet. I am not experiencing my real self, I am experiencing life on earth through a particular self.

> Master MORE, come to the fore,
> we will absorb your flame of MORE.

> Master MORE, our will so strong,
> our power centers cleared by song.
>
> **Master MORE, your Sacred Heart,
> from this we will no more depart,
> we are forever in your flow,
> of Diamond Will that you bestow.**

2. The Conscious You is pure awareness, and it is neutral about being on earth. It has a certain curiosity about being on earth and said: "What would I feel like, how would I experience myself in that situation?"

> Master MORE, your wisdom flows,
> as our attunement ever grows.
> Master MORE, we have a tie,
> that helps us see through Serpent's lie.
>
> **Master MORE, your Sacred Heart,
> from this we will no more depart,
> we are forever in your flow,
> of Diamond Will that you bestow.**

3. When I take on and create these separate selves, then my experience is colored by the selves. I want to come back to the point where the Conscious You, as pure awareness, as a neutral self, is neutrally experiencing life.

> Master MORE, your love so pink,
> there is no purer love, we think.
> Master MORE, you set us free,
> from all conditionality.
>
> **Master MORE, your Sacred Heart,
> from this we will no more depart,
> we are forever in your flow,
> of Diamond Will that you bestow.**

4. I also want to reach up and experience how my I AM Presence is experiencing any situation. This is the ultimate frame of reference that allows me

to step away from being so identified with the conditions I am facing, both *inside* my four lower bodies and *outside* my four lower bodies.

> Master MORE, we will endure,
> your discipline that makes us pure.
> Master MORE, intentions true,
> as we are always one with you.
>
> **Master MORE, your Sacred Heart,**
> **from this we will no more depart,**
> **we are forever in your flow,**
> **of Diamond Will that you bestow.**

5. A separate self is made up of energy waves of the Ma-ter Light, and the light has a certain pattern superimposed upon it. A self is just an image and I can look at a self and decide to whisk that self away, erasing the image as a sand castle in the sandbox.

> Master MORE, our vision raised,
> the will of God is always praised.
> Master MORE, creative will,
> raising all life higher still.
>
> **Master MORE, your Sacred Heart,**
> **from this we will no more depart,**
> **we are forever in your flow,**
> **of Diamond Will that you bestow.**

6. The only thing that is left is the image and I am erasing it. I am letting it go. I know this cannot be done in five minutes, but it can be done very quickly compared to the time I have been on earth.

> Master MORE, your peace is power,
> the demons of war it will devour.
> Master MORE, we serve all life,
> our flames consuming war and strife.
>
> **Master MORE, your Sacred Heart,**
> **from this we will no more depart,**

10 | Invoking the erasing of memories

> we are forever in your flow,
> of Diamond Will that you bestow.

7. I will not be impatient with myself and with the process. There is a self that makes me impatient, saying I should be able to achieve something very quickly. I see this as a separate self and I just let it go.

> Master MORE, we are so free,
> eternal bond from you we see.
> Master MORE, we find rebirth,
> in flow of your eternal mirth.
>
> **Master MORE, your Sacred Heart,
> from this we will no more depart,
> we are forever in your flow,
> of Diamond Will that you bestow.**

8. Impatience prevents me from being at peace with being here. I see impatience as a self, and I decide that I do not need to be so hard on myself. I do not need to accomplish everything in five minutes because in a certain sense time is *not*.

> Master MORE, you balance all,
> the seven rays upon our call.
> Master MORE, forever MORE,
> we are the Spirit's open door.
>
> **Master MORE, your Sacred Heart,
> from this we will no more depart,
> we are forever in your flow,
> of Diamond Will that you bestow.**

9. Time is a collective illusion created by the collective consciousness. It is allowed to exist because some people need it. Yet, I will accept Gautama Buddha's statement that: "Time is not." Therefore, the self that is trapped in time is not.

> Master MORE, your Presence here,
> filling up the inner sphere.

Life is now a sacred flow,
God Power we on all bestow.

**Master MORE, your Sacred Heart,
from this we will no more depart,
we are forever in your flow,
of Diamond Will that you bestow.**

Sealing

In the name of the Divine Mother, I call to Mother Mary for the sealing of myself and all people in my circle of influence in the creative flow of the Divine Mother, the River of Life. I call for the multiplication of my calls by all representatives of the Divine Mother, so that we form the perfect figure-eight flow of "As Above, so below." Thus, I accept that this is fully manifest, because the mouth of the Lord, the Divine Mother that I AM, has spoken it. Amen.

11 | SPEAKING OUT FROM A STATE OF PEACE

I AM the Ascended Master Jesus, and I wish to make some remarks here about a topic that can be confusing. I fully understand that it is confusing to some of you. It is the topic of Christhood, how you exercise your Christhood in terms of speaking out on earth. If you are in a linear mindset, you could say that these latest teachings we have given you (over this past year or a little more), contradict earlier teachings we have given you. We have said that a part of your Christhood is to speak out, and now it seems like we are saying that you should not speak out and you should instead work on your internal spirits, your separate selves and overcome them.

Now my beloved, the key to resolving what may seem like an enigma is to realize that the spiritual path has certain stages. There are certain levels of initiation that you go through on the path to Christhood. We have given you the course in self-mastery, which is designed to take people from the 48th level of consciousness to the 96th level. At the 96th level is where you begin to exercise Christhood but, of course, there is a distance from the 96th to the 144th level. You can see that, obviously, what you attain or can attain at the 96th level is not the full measure of Christhood. As you go higher and higher towards the 144th level, you are able to manifest and express higher degrees, we might call it, of Christhood.

The experiential side of Christhood

This means that when we give a teaching that is applicable for people at the 96th level or close to it, it is, of course, not the same teaching we will give for people at higher levels. When I gave, for example, the course on Christhood [*Master Keys to Personal Christhood*] and many of the early teachings that were given in this dispensation about Christhood, it was given for the beginning level of consciousness. What we are giving you now is for the higher levels of Christhood where you need to acknowledge here that there are certain things you cannot be given theoretically on the spiritual path. There needs to be an interchange between receiving teachings and gaining understanding and then practicing, expressing, those teachings and getting experience. You do not become the Christ by sitting in a classroom and receiving teachings from a teacher even if that teacher has attained Christhood. There must be a certain experiential element where you go out and have certain experiences.

What I and other masters told people to do in the early stages of this dispensation was to go out and speak out with the understanding, with the awareness, they had at the time. Now, we knew full well, of course, that people would go out with a certain amount of separate selves and they would feel a compulsion to speak out. We knew that there were some people that were very reluctant to speak out because the separate selves that they had built in past lives told them that it was very dangerous, very unsafe, to speak out and that they should not speak out at all.

We knew that there were other people who had an ambition to speak out, either because they wanted to do something important, they wanted to get acknowledged by the ascended masters, they wanted to get acknowledged by other people or the world, or various other motivations that people have. We also knew that it was necessary to give people the teaching, let them do with it whatever they wanted, because whether they spoke out or not, they would still have certain experiences that would then help them progress to the point where they would be ready for a higher teaching.

This is what has happened. A sufficient number of people have risen to the level where they are ready for the higher teachings we are giving now. We might say that a *critical* mass of you have risen to this level, but I would prefer to say that it was an *uncritical* mass of you that have risen to this level because you have risen by overcoming this critical attitude where you feel you had to criticize, judge and evaluate everything. This is precisely what characterizes the higher levels of Christhood.

Christhood is not a linear process

At the lower levels of Christhood you are beginning to have some awareness that there are many things on earth that are not, as you see it at that level, right. They are not in accordance with the higher vision, they are not in accordance with how things should be and they should be changed. As we have now said about avatars who come to this planet feeling they have to change things on earth, in the beginning stages of Christhood you very much go out with the attitude that you have to change something. You have to make people see what they are not seeing and you have to make a difference and create a change.

This is exactly the attitude that many avatars had when they came to earth. You actually need to have this experience in this lifetime in order to tie back in to this momentum. There are other avatars who came to this earth and did not speak out, did not want to speak out and decided that they do not want to speak out on this planet. Some of these people have not gone out and spoken out but it has still given you the experience that you had the teaching and what are you doing with it.

There is absolutely nothing wrong with this. As we have said many, many times, you have a right to be at a certain level of consciousness and you have a right to express yourself based on that level of consciousness—nothing wrong with it, no blame from our part whatsoever. As Nada so carefully explained in her book, we accept you at whatever level of consciousness you are at and are only looking at how we can help you ascend to the next level up.

This, of course, does not mean that we want you to remain at the lower level of Christhood for the rest of your lifetime. We want you to have a certain experience at the lower levels that, then, combined with the teachings we give you, help you rise to higher and higher levels of Christhood. There comes a point where you have reached the level of Christhood where it is necessary to question what you have done before. I know that some people will go into a linear mindset because they want to think that if they had a true teaching given to them by an ascended master about Christhood, then that teaching is absolute and therefore all they need to do is follow that teaching for the rest of their lives.

I know there are people who want to think this way but they are simply not grasping what Christhood is about in the ongoing self-transcendence, and so I cannot cater to such people. We of the ascended masters can give certain teachings for people in this mindset. If the people do not heed the teaching, if they do not shift their attitude, then we must by the law, even the Law of Free Will, leave these people alone and not attempt to make them see what they are not willing to see.

Therefore, we then focus on those who are willing to see that there comes a point on your path of Christhood where you need to question the very things that brought you to that level of Christhood. This is not just a one-time thing. This is an ongoing thing because the higher you go towards the 144th level, the shorter are the intervals between where you need to question yourself. In fact, at the higher levels of consciousness you need to question everything at your present level in order to ascend to the next level.

The progressiveness of Christhood

What we are telling you now with these teachings on the avatar and overcoming the birth trauma, overcoming these separate selves, is that at the lower levels of Christhood it is acceptable for you (it is necessary, it is part of the path) to speak out with the level of awareness you have and with the separate selves that you have. Even if this causes you to go out and be somewhat unbalanced, perhaps too forceful, perhaps too insistent, perhaps too blue-flame, (as Master MORE calls it), it is still acceptable that you do this because you can do nothing else. It is by doing it that you get a certain feedback, you get a certain frame of reference that allows you to see that perhaps it is necessary to refine your approach.

That is what, then, opens you to say: "Okay, perhaps I have now reached a level of Christhood where the teachings that brought me here cannot bring me any further." It is essentially, like we have said before, the example of how a child starts learning to ride a bicycle and has two wheels on the side of the bicycle (training wheels) that help the child hold the balance. There should come a point where the child has learned to hold the balance on the bicycle and can throw away the training wheels. If you see an adult riding on a bicycle with training wheels, you would think that this person has missed something.

It is the same on the spiritual path. That is why we have said to you that you need to consider your modus operandi [*Healing Your Spiritual Traumas*]. You need to consider how you approach looking at earth: Is it a friendly planet, a hostile planet? Is it a friendly body, a hostile body? Is God a friendly God or a hostile God? Are the ascended masters friendly masters or hostile masters? You need to consider this. You need to look at yourself. You could even say: "Do I have a friendly view of myself or a hostile view of myself?" Where does the hostility then come from? It can only come from a separate self that is influenced by the consciousness of the fallen beings and therefore, of course, it needs to be allowed to die.

What I want to give you here in terms of Christhood and in terms of speaking out is this: Overcoming your primal self, overcoming many or most of these separate selves does not mean that you do not speak out anymore. Attaining the peace with being on earth that is our goal for this conference does not mean that you are not going to speak out. It does mean that you are going to speak out in a different way, with an entirely different attitude. You are not *driven* by a separate self to speak out. You do not have a compulsive drive to speak out. You are not speaking out with the attitude that you have to produce a certain result. You are not speaking out because you have to convince or convert other people.

You are speaking out with the attitude that you are here to give them a frame of reference that they do not have right now, and then you leave them completely free to choose what they want to do with that. You have given them what they did not have before. You have given them a foundation for making better choices, higher choices, more aware choices but you leave it up to them how or what they will choose. This is not your job within the Law of Free Will. It is to give them the option, to give them the choice, so they have a more free choice, but then to still allow them to make whatever choice they want to make. That is why it is essential that you let go of this entire relative, comparative scale of the fallen beings about perfect or imperfect, about right and wrong and all of this entire mindset. It takes some time, we realize that, but it is important that you begin to work on this so you can come to that point where, when you do speak out, you are speaking from a state of inner peace.

Speaking from inner peace

By doing this, you will accomplish two things: You will set other people free to react to what you say in any way they want. You will set yourself free to react as *you* want, regardless of what other people choose. You are not disturbed, you are not discouraged. You are not upset, you do not feel rejected if people do not take what you say. You actually feel the inner peace and the inner joy that you have said it, you have put it out there, you have made it available to people and that is the goal that you have. That is the reward: knowing that it is there in the physical and leaving people free to take it or leave it.

My beloved, it may be necessary for some of you to go through a period where you stop speaking out, if you have been speaking out, so that you simply say very little. This messenger has described how he feels, he no longer has any opinions about anything. Still, he speaks out about various topics but he does not speak out because he has an opinion that he wants validated. This is what you can come to, and the recommendations I have for you here is that you consider two things when you speak out.

One is that you can share what you think, what you feel, how you experience the topic. You can share what you do, what you have chosen to do or not do and why. You are not trying to convince anybody. You are not telling them what to do. You are simply sharing your own deliberations, your own understanding and even the process that led you to come to that understanding.

This is entirely different from going out and telling other people what they should think or believe, seeking to convince or convert. It is simply sharing your process and, as we have said many times, my beloved, regardless of what the fallen beings think, regardless of what other people think (who do not want to be disturbed by you), you do have a right to be on this planet, you do have a right to express yourself and the conclusions you have reached, the insights you have reached, the process you have gone through. You have a right to share this.

If this upsets other people, you have absolutely no need to react to it whatsoever. You can set them free to make that choice if they want, but it does not stop you, it does not discourage you. Also, it does not make you more persistent in trying to convince them. You are not speaking with the need to be validated by them or to have them agree with you. It is immaterial to you how they react to what you are saying. This is one aspect of speaking out. Share from yourself, your own insights, your own process. Share that.

Now, the other way of speaking out that I propose to you is that instead of talking about something being right or wrong, this or that, you talk about the consequences of a particular action, a particular viewpoint or a particular ideology or thought system. You can do this in various ways. Just as an example, yesterday someone asked this messenger about the problem of immigrants coming into Europe and he expressed the view that this was a consequence of the fact that the affluent nations in Europe had not done enough. They had not used their affluence to help people in Africa, in their home countries, achieve a better standard of living. Therefore, circumstances were actually forcing these affluent nations to see what they had not been willing to see and to take the responsibility that their wealth has actually given them. He expressed that the situation really forced these affluent nations to make certain choices. They could either continue to allow the immigrants to come in, with all of the consequences this has for their societies. (What do they do with so many people? Do they put them all in "concentration camps" or do they seek to integrate them, but how can you integrate people from a different culture and in those numbers?) It is clear that most nations would realize that if they continue to allow the immigrants to come in, they will overwhelm the systems they have in place.

Either this will require many more resources or their other option is to seek to stop immigration and again here are two options. You can use the navies that you have to send boats out into the Mediterranean that will sink any boat with immigrants that comes from Africa. That is one way to stop immigration but this, of course, is not in accordance with the view of themselves that most European nations have. If this is not a feasible option, what is the last option available? It is to create an entirely new approach to going into the African countries and improving the standard of living so that the people no longer want to leave. It is not so that people who are born in Africa have some universal desire, some unquenchable desire, to come to Europe. Most of them would prefer to stay in Africa because they are used to a warm climate and they really do not want to go to a country like Denmark, where it is so dark and cold in the winter. They would much prefer to stay in their countries and have a reasonable standard of living. This is what would require an entirely new approach by the European nations, even by the EU, where they truly commit resources to this instead of what they have now of foreign aid that is just a band aid and does not resolve the problem.

This is just an example of how you can talk about an issue without telling people what is right or wrong, without telling them what to believe but simply looking at the consequences. What are the consequences of what is going on? There is a situation here. You cannot remove it by snapping your fingers, so how do we deal with it? How do we look at ourselves and what does that mean for what options we could realistically choose?

The Christ has no fixed opinions

This can be transferred to many other areas of society because, my beloved, you do not necessarily have, as a Christed being, a fixed opinion of what should happen in this situation. Your overall view, as a Christed being at the higher levels of Christhood, is that you want people (all people involved, even a society or a nation or the EU or the United States or whatever) to become more aware so they can make more aware choices. This is your goal: to raise awareness, not to produce a specific outer result. The real result that you are tuned in to is the raising of awareness. At the higher levels of Christhood, you begin to gain greater attunement with the ascended masters. Therefore, you will naturally tune in to the fact that our primary goal is to raise consciousness, not to produce a specific result, as Saint Germain has said several times.

These are some very valuable pointers for those of you who are at this level. I fully realize that it is also a challenge to you because in order to go out and speak out, and be at peace and set other people free and set yourself free, it requires you to heal your birth trauma. It requires you to overcome these separate selves that give you this compulsion to influence other people. You need to, as we have said several times, overcome this mechanism of wanting to change other people in order to feel better in yourself or in order to avoid the negative feeling where you basically want to change other people in order to avoid changing yourself.

Again my beloved, why did we not give you these teachings ten years ago? Because at that time we had not yet given you the tools so that you could implement the teachings. Now, we have given you the tools and that is why we are giving you the teachings. Again, we have had to take a gradual approach. We have done this for a variety of reasons, as we have talked about, and we are very happy that this uncritical mass of you has risen to the level where you are willing to receive these teachings and ponder them, study these books, apply these techniques and really make the effort that many of you have made to heal this birth trauma.

Be not discouraged if you have not yet healed your cosmic birth trauma. Be not discouraged if you still have separate selves pop up in you. This messenger has been working more than most people on his psychology for forty years and he has overcome his birth trauma but he still has separate selves that come up. Naturally, if you have had many, many lifetimes on this earth, and in many lifetimes had very difficult experiences, then you will have created many separate selves and it will take time to work through them all. So what, my beloved?

Permission to not speak out

What I am doing with this dictation is I am giving you permission to set aside any compulsory feeling that you *should* speak out. I am giving you permission, if you want to, to step back and say: "I am going to stop speaking out for a while. I am going to zip my mouth, throw away my keyboard and not speak out. I am giving myself permission not to speak out but instead focus within on resolving the birth trauma and these separate selves that give me the compulsion to speak out, that give me the need to convince other people, this desire to be validated, to be acknowledged, this desire to produce a certain feeling in myself or avoid a negative feeling."

I am doing this because I want you to have some rest where you can heal and you can overcome this pattern, that some of you have built, of being somewhat in conflict or at least in an antagonistic relationship with many other people. It is not necessary, my beloved, to go out and provoke people in order to express your Christhood. If you look at the world, you can see there are plenty of people out there who are speaking out in an antagonistic, provocative, aggressive manner—plenty of people.

If you keep doing the same thing and expect different results, you are insane. We have plenty of people who have been speaking out this way for a long time. What we need is something different. We need a different voice. We need people who can speak out in a different way, as I have outlined, sharing yourself, talking about consequences but even beyond this, other ways of speaking out, where you, for example, talk about a higher perspective. Instead of coming across as: "Here's the only truth, here's what you *should* believe and if not, you are stupid," you can say: "But what if there is another way to look at this? What if there is a different perspective on it? How about this and this and this and this?"

This can be something that is so new, is so different, so rarely practiced, that people will be surprised and they will suddenly say: "Oh, here's something I have not heard before. Let me listen to this." It might actually do what we even said in the United States that we would like change the entire public discourse, not just in the United States but in all countries. We get rid of this public debate that is based on the journalists who, even though they claim to be objective, always have an agenda of portraying things a certain way. Or the politicians who are so trapped in their party politics of making their party the superior one that they cannot cooperate about anything.

All of this dualistic black-and-white thinking that has been driving public discourse for so long, we desire to see an alternative to this, a different voice. Quite frankly, if *you* cannot provide that different voice, who can? In order to speak with a different voice, you have to overcome those separate selves and you are the ones on the entire planet who are closest to achieving this goal. This is not said to put any pressure on you, but it is to give you a realistic assessment. Some of you will know, by just hearing or reading this: "Yes, this is part of my Divine plan. This is actually what I wanted. I never really wanted to speak out in the way that I have been doing it, that always gives me this negative reaction. I wanted to find a different voice to speak with and now I am beginning to see it. I am certainly going to work on myself until I get to the point where I find my inner voice, my true voice, and when I find it, I will speak out. I *will* speak out."

With this, my beloved, I thank you for your attention, for your presence here or on the broadcast, and I thank all of those who have embraced these new teachings from the *My Lives* book and forward and who have been willing to implement them. I know that many of you have experienced tremendous progress. Some of you have even expressed that you can hardly believe how different you feel today compared to a year ago. This is our greatest joy: to see when our students embrace a teaching and use it to come up higher where you feel better about yourself, you feel at peace. The fact that some people have attained this in a year means that all of you can attain it within a reasonable time span. There is not one person here, there is not one person who has embraced these teachings, who does not have the potential to attain that state of peace within a relatively short time span—much, much shorter than the time you have already been on the spiritual path, at least those of you who have been on the path for a few years.

Naturally, if you came in last week, it might be a different story. Nevertheless my beloved, we are very, very encouraged (if you can use that term about an ascended master who really cannot become discouraged), we are very happy about seeing the progress that all of you have made. Even though some of you might feel that you have not made enough progress, I can assure you that you *have* made progress and you are much closer to a breakthrough than you actually think. With this, you have my gratitude;

you have my Flame of Joy because it is a great joy for me to interact with you in this way and to actually experience you, my beloved: Experience *you*.

This is a great joy for me. I would say that you should, of course, not think that when I speak through a messenger, this is the only time I can experience you. I can experience you at any time but I am always respectful of free will. If you take what was said in this invocation and in my previous dictation on the modus operandi, about wanting to hide from the masters, this I, of course, respect. Some of you might actually be helped by making the decision to invite me to experience you. You might just, at certain times when you have a quiet time, close your eyes, center in your heart, and say: "Jesus, I invite you to experience me." Perhaps by doing this, you will be able to experience *me* and I think this will cause you joy.

12 | INVOKING PEACE WITH SPEAKING OUT

In the name I AM THAT I AM, Jesus Christ, I call to all representatives of the Divine Mother, especially Jesus, to help me be at peace with speaking out about how I see life, including…

[Make personal calls.]

Part 1

1. I acknowledge that there are certain things I cannot be given theoretically on the spiritual path. There needs to be an interchange between receiving teachings and then practicing, expressing, those teachings and getting experience.

> O Jesus, blessed brother mine,
> I walk the path that you outline,
> a great example to us all,
> I follow now your inner call.

**O Jesus, let the Fire of Joy,
consume the devil's subtle ploy,
transfigured is our planet earth,
the golden age is given birth.**

2. I do not become the Christ by sitting in a classroom and receiving teachings from a teacher even if that teacher has attained Christhood. There must be an experiential element where I go out and have certain experiences.

O Jesus, open inner sight,
the ego wants to prove it's right,
but this I will no longer do,
I want to be all one with you.

**O Jesus, let the Fire of Joy,
consume the devil's subtle ploy,
transfigured is our planet earth,
the golden age is given birth.**

3. I have a right to be at a certain level of consciousness and I have a right to express myself based on that level of consciousness. There is nothing wrong with it, and the masters do not blame me whatsoever. The masters accept me at whatever level of consciousness I am at and are only looking at how they can help me ascend to the next level up.

O Jesus, I now clearly see,
the Key of Knowledge given me,
my Christ self I hereby embrace,
as you fill up my inner space.

**O Jesus, let the Fire of Joy,
consume the devil's subtle ploy,
transfigured is our planet earth,
the golden age is given birth.**

4. I acknowledge that I have reached the level of Christhood where it is necessary to question what I have done before. I am willing to see that there comes a point on my path of Christhood where I need to question the very things that brought me to that level.

> O Jesus, show me serpent's lie,
> expose the beam in my own eye,
> as Christ discernment you me give,
> in oneness I forever live.
>
> **O Jesus, let the Fire of Joy,
> consume the devil's subtle ploy,
> transfigured is our planet earth,
> the golden age is given birth.**

5. This is an ongoing thing because the higher I go towards the 144th level, the shorter are the intervals between where I need to question myself. At the higher levels of consciousness, I need to question everything at my present level in order to ascend to the next level.

> O Jesus, I am truly meek,
> and thus I turn the other cheek,
> when the accuser attacks me,
> I go within and merge with thee.
>
> **O Jesus, let the Fire of Joy,
> consume the devil's subtle ploy,
> transfigured is our planet earth,
> the golden age is given birth.**

6. At the lower level of Christhood it is acceptable for me to speak out with the level of awareness I have and with the separate selves that I have. It is by doing it that I get feedback that allows me to see how to refine my approach.

> O Jesus, ego I let die,
> surrender ev'ry earthly tie,
> the dead can bury what is dead,
> I choose to walk with you instead.
>
> **O Jesus, let the Fire of Joy,
> consume the devil's subtle ploy,
> transfigured is our planet earth,
> the golden age is given birth.**

7. This eventually opens me to say: "Okay, perhaps I have now reached a level of Christhood where the teachings that brought me here cannot bring me any further."

> O Jesus, help me rise above,
> the devil's test through higher love,
> show me separate self unreal,
> my formless self you do reveal.

> **O Jesus, let the Fire of Joy,**
> **consume the devil's subtle ploy,**
> **transfigured is our planet earth,**
> **the golden age is given birth.**

8. Do I have a friendly view of myself or a hostile view of myself? Where does the hostility come from? It can only come from a separate self that is influenced by the consciousness of the fallen beings and therefore it needs to be allowed to die.

> O Jesus, what is that to me,
> I just let go and follow thee,
> with this I do pass ev'ry test,
> to find with you eternal rest.

> **O Jesus, let the Fire of Joy,**
> **consume the devil's subtle ploy,**
> **transfigured is our planet earth,**
> **the golden age is given birth.**

9. Overcoming my primal self and separate selves does not mean that I do not speak out anymore. Attaining peace with being on earth does not mean that I am not going to speak out. It does mean that I am going to speak out in a different way, with an entirely different attitude. I am not *driven* by a separate self to speak out. I do not have a compulsive drive to speak out.

> O Jesus, fiery master mine,
> my heart now melting into thine,

I love with heart and mind and soul,
the God who is my highest goal.

O Jesus, let the Fire of Joy,
consume the devil's subtle ploy,
transfigured is our planet earth,
the golden age is given birth.

Part 2

1. I am not speaking out with the attitude that I have to produce a certain result. I am not speaking out because I have to convince or convert other people. I am speaking out with the attitude that I am here to give them a frame of reference that they do not have right now, and then I leave them completely free to choose what they want to do with that.

O Jesus, blessed brother mine,
I walk the path that you outline,
a great example to us all,
I follow now your inner call.

O Jesus, let the Fire of Joy,
consume the devil's subtle ploy,
transfigured is our planet earth,
the golden age is given birth.

2. I have given them what they did not have before. I have given them a foundation for making better choices, higher choices, more aware choices, but I leave it up to them how or what they will choose.

O Jesus, open inner sight,
the ego wants to prove it's right,
but this I will no longer do,
I want to be all one with you.

O Jesus, let the Fire of Joy,
consume the devil's subtle ploy,

> transfigured is our planet earth,
> the golden age is given birth.

3. Choosing for others is not my job within the Law of Free Will. It is to give them the option, to give them the choice, so they have a more free choice, but then to still allow them to make whatever choice they want to make.

> O Jesus, I now clearly see,
> the Key of Knowledge given me,
> my Christ self I hereby embrace,
> as you fill up my inner space.
>
> **O Jesus, let the Fire of Joy,**
> **consume the devil's subtle ploy,**
> **transfigured is our planet earth,**
> **the golden age is given birth.**

4. I am letting go of this entire relative, comparative scale of the fallen beings about perfect or imperfect, about right and wrong and this entire mindset. I am speaking from a state of inner peace.

> O Jesus, show me serpent's lie,
> expose the beam in my own eye,
> as Christ discernment you me give,
> in oneness I forever live.
>
> **O Jesus, let the Fire of Joy,**
> **consume the devil's subtle ploy,**
> **transfigured is our planet earth,**
> **the golden age is given birth.**

5. I set other people free to react to what I say in any way they want. I set myself free to react as I want to, regardless of what other people choose. I am not disturbed, I am not discouraged. I am not upset, I do not feel rejected if people do not accept what I say.

> O Jesus, I am truly meek,
> and thus I turn the other cheek,

when the accuser attacks me,
I go within and merge with thee.

O Jesus, let the Fire of Joy,
consume the devil's subtle ploy,
transfigured is our planet earth,
the golden age is given birth.

6. I feel the inner peace and the inner joy that I have said it, I have put it out there, I have made it available to people and that is the goal that I have. That is the reward: knowing that it is there in the physical and leaving people free to take it or leave it.

O Jesus, ego I let die,
surrender ev'ry earthly tie,
the dead can bury what is dead,
I choose to walk with you instead.

O Jesus, let the Fire of Joy,
consume the devil's subtle ploy,
transfigured is our planet earth,
the golden age is given birth.

7. I am willing to go through a period where I am not speaking out and even feel I no longer have any opinions about anything. I do not speak out because I have an opinion that I want validated.

O Jesus, help me rise above,
the devil's test through higher love,
show me separate self unreal,
my formless self you do reveal.

O Jesus, let the Fire of Joy,
consume the devil's subtle ploy,
transfigured is our planet earth,
the golden age is given birth.

8. When I speak out, I will share what I think, what I feel, how I experience the topic. I share what I do, what I have chosen to do or not do and why.

I am not trying to convince anybody. I am not telling them what to do. I am simply sharing my own deliberations, my own understanding and even the process that led me to that understanding.

> O Jesus, what is that to me,
> I just let go and follow thee,
> with this I do pass ev'ry test,
> to find with you eternal rest.
>
> **O Jesus, let the Fire of Joy,**
> **consume the devil's subtle ploy,**
> **transfigured is our planet earth,**
> **the golden age is given birth.**

9. Regardless of what the fallen beings think, regardless of what other people think, I do have a right to be on this planet, I do have a right to express myself and the conclusions I have reached, the insights I have reached, the process I have gone through. I have a right to share this.

> O Jesus, fiery master mine,
> my heart now melting into thine,
> I love with heart and mind and soul,
> the God who is my highest goal.
>
> **O Jesus, let the Fire of Joy,**
> **consume the devil's subtle ploy,**
> **transfigured is our planet earth,**
> **the golden age is given birth.**

Part 3

1. If this upsets other people, I have absolutely no need to react to it whatsoever. I set them free to make that choice if they want, but it does not stop me, it does not discourage me.

> O Jesus, blessed brother mine,
> I walk the path that you outline,

a great example to us all,
I follow now your inner call.

**O Jesus, let the Fire of Joy,
consume the devil's subtle ploy,
transfigured is our planet earth,
the golden age is given birth.**

2. When people reject what I say, it does not make me more persistent in trying to convince them. I am not speaking with the need to be validated by them or to have them agree with me. It is immaterial to me how they react to what I am saying.

O Jesus, open inner sight,
the ego wants to prove it's right,
but this I will no longer do,
I want to be all one with you.

**O Jesus, let the Fire of Joy,
consume the devil's subtle ploy,
transfigured is our planet earth,
the golden age is given birth.**

3. Instead of talking about something being right or wrong, I talk about the consequences of a particular action, viewpoint, ideology or thought system. I talk about an issue without telling people what is right or wrong, without telling them what to believe but simply looking at the consequences.

O Jesus, I now clearly see,
the Key of Knowledge given me,
my Christ self I hereby embrace,
as you fill up my inner space.

**O Jesus, let the Fire of Joy,
consume the devil's subtle ploy,
transfigured is our planet earth,
the golden age is given birth.**

4. As a Christed being, I do not have a fixed opinion of what should happen in any situation. My overall view is that I want people to become more aware so they can make more aware choices.

> O Jesus, show me serpent's lie,
> expose the beam in my own eye,
> as Christ discernment you me give,
> in oneness I forever live.
>
> **O Jesus, let the Fire of Joy,**
> **consume the devil's subtle ploy,**
> **transfigured is our planet earth,**
> **the golden age is given birth.**

5. My goal is to raise awareness, not to produce a specific outer result. The real result that I am tuned in to is the raising of awareness. At the higher levels of Christhood, I begin to gain greater attunement with the ascended masters, and their primary goal is to raise consciousness, not to produce a specific result.

> O Jesus, I am truly meek,
> and thus I turn the other cheek,
> when the accuser attacks me,
> I go within and merge with thee.
>
> **O Jesus, let the Fire of Joy,**
> **consume the devil's subtle ploy,**
> **transfigured is our planet earth,**
> **the golden age is given birth.**

6. In order to speak out and be at peace and set other people free and set myself free, it requires me to heal my birth trauma. It requires me to overcome these separate selves that give me this compulsion to influence other people.

> O Jesus, ego I let die,
> surrender ev'ry earthly tie,
> the dead can bury what is dead,
> I choose to walk with you instead.

> O Jesus, let the Fire of Joy,
> consume the devil's subtle ploy,
> transfigured is our planet earth,
> the golden age is given birth.

7. I am willing to overcome this mechanism of wanting to change other people in order to feel better in myself or in order to avoid the negative feeling where I basically want to change other people in order to avoid changing myself.

> O Jesus, help me rise above,
> the devil's test through higher love,
> show me separate self unreal,
> my formless self you do reveal.

> O Jesus, let the Fire of Joy,
> consume the devil's subtle ploy,
> transfigured is our planet earth,
> the golden age is given birth.

8. I will not be discouraged if I have not yet healed my cosmic birth trauma. I will not be discouraged if I still have separate selves in me. I have had many lifetimes on earth, and I have created many separate selves and it will take time to work through them all.

> O Jesus, what is that to me,
> I just let go and follow thee,
> with this I do pass ev'ry test,
> to find with you eternal rest.

> O Jesus, let the Fire of Joy,
> consume the devil's subtle ploy,
> transfigured is our planet earth,
> the golden age is given birth.

9. I accept that you, Jesus, have given me permission to set aside any compulsory feeling that I *should* speak out. I accept that I can step back and say: "I am going to stop speaking out for a while. I am going to zip my mouth, throw away my keyboard and not speak out. I am giving myself permission

not to speak out but instead focus within on resolving the birth trauma and these separate selves that give me the compulsion to speak out, that give me the need to convince other people, this desire to be validated, to be acknowledged, this desire to produce a certain feeling in myself or avoid a negative feeling."

> O Jesus, fiery master mine,
> my heart now melting into thine,
> I love with heart and mind and soul,
> the God who is my highest goal.
>
> **O Jesus, let the Fire of Joy,**
> **consume the devil's subtle ploy,**
> **transfigured is our planet earth,**
> **the golden age is given birth.**

Part 4

1. I want to have some rest where I can heal and I can overcome this pattern of being in conflict or in an antagonistic relationship with other people.

> O Jesus, blessed brother mine,
> I walk the path that you outline,
> a great example to us all,
> I follow now your inner call.
>
> **O Jesus, let the Fire of Joy,**
> **consume the devil's subtle ploy,**
> **transfigured is our planet earth,**
> **the golden age is given birth.**

2. It is not necessary to provoke people in order to express my Christhood. There are plenty of people out there who are speaking out in an antagonistic, provocative, aggressive manner. What is needed is something different, a different voice.

O Jesus, open inner sight,
the ego wants to prove it's right,
but this I will no longer do,
I want to be all one with you.

O Jesus, let the Fire of Joy,
consume the devil's subtle ploy,
transfigured is our planet earth,
the golden age is given birth.

3. Jesus, teach me to speak out in a different way, sharing myself, talking about consequences, but even talking about a higher perspective, showing people there is a different perspective on the issue.

O Jesus, I now clearly see,
the Key of Knowledge given me,
my Christ self I hereby embrace,
as you fill up my inner space.

O Jesus, let the Fire of Joy,
consume the devil's subtle ploy,
transfigured is our planet earth,
the golden age is given birth.

4. Jesus, teach me how I can help change the entire public discourse, where we get rid of this public debate that is based on the journalists who, even though they claim to be objective, always have an agenda of portraying things a certain way. Or the politicians who are so trapped in their party politics of making their party the superior one that they cannot cooperate about anything.

O Jesus, show me serpent's lie,
expose the beam in my own eye,
as Christ discernment you me give,
in oneness I forever live.

O Jesus, let the Fire of Joy,
consume the devil's subtle ploy,

> transfigured is our planet earth,
> the golden age is given birth.

5. Jesus, help me see how I can provide an alternative to the dualistic black-and-white thinking that has been driving public discourse for so long. In order to speak with a different voice, I have to overcome those separate selves and I have the tools for achieving this.

> O Jesus, I am truly meek,
> and thus I turn the other cheek,
> when the accuser attacks me,
> I go within and merge with thee.

> **O Jesus, let the Fire of Joy,**
> **consume the devil's subtle ploy,**
> **transfigured is our planet earth,**
> **the golden age is given birth.**

6. Jesus, help me see if this is part of my Divine plan. This is actually what I wanted. I never really wanted to speak out in the way that I have been doing it, that always gives me this negative reaction.

> O Jesus, ego I let die,
> surrender ev'ry earthly tie,
> the dead can bury what is dead,
> I choose to walk with you instead.

> **O Jesus, let the Fire of Joy,**
> **consume the devil's subtle ploy,**
> **transfigured is our planet earth,**
> **the golden age is given birth.**

7. Jesus, help me find a different voice to speak with so I can begin to see it. I am willing to work on myself until I get to the point where I find my inner voice, my true voice, and when I find it, I *will* speak out.

> O Jesus, help me rise above,
> the devil's test through higher love,

show me separate self unreal,
my formless self you do reveal.

**O Jesus, let the Fire of Joy,
consume the devil's subtle ploy,
transfigured is our planet earth,
the golden age is given birth.**

8. Jesus, I know it is your joy to experience me and that you can experience me at any time. I therefore give up any attitude of wanting to hide from you.

O Jesus, what is that to me,
I just let go and follow thee,
with this I do pass ev'ry test,
to find with you eternal rest.

**O Jesus, let the Fire of Joy,
consume the devil's subtle ploy,
transfigured is our planet earth,
the golden age is given birth.**

9. I am making the decision to invite you to experience me, and I am indeed willing to experience you and the joy that you are. Jesus, I invite you to experience me.

O Jesus, fiery master mine,
my heart now melting into thine,
I love with heart and mind and soul,
the God who is my highest goal.

**O Jesus, let the Fire of Joy,
consume the devil's subtle ploy,
transfigured is our planet earth,
the golden age is given birth.**

Sealing

In the name of the Divine Mother, I call to Mother Mary for the sealing of myself and all people in my circle of influence in the creative flow of the Divine Mother, the River of Life. I call for the multiplication of my calls by all representatives of the Divine Mother, so that we form the perfect figure-eight flow of "As Above, so below." Thus, I accept that this is fully manifest, because the mouth of the Lord, the Divine Mother that I AM, has spoken it. Amen.

13 | GRASPING THE RADICAL NATURE OF MERCY

I AM the Ascended Master Kuan Yin, and as you know, I am the master who holds the Flame of Mercy for the earth. What, my beloved, is mercy? Well, there is a worldly view of mercy and then there is an ascended view of mercy. I, of course, aim to give you an appreciation, an experience, of the ascended view. Let us first look at the worldly view. So many times you see a situation, for example, where some aggressor has conquered a village and is about to kill a person and the person says: "Have mercy upon me." Then, the mercy is looked at as that you do not kill the person. That is supposedly being merciful. Now, how do I, as an ascended master, view mercy?

The greatest form of non-mercy

Well, what is the greatest non-mercy, the greatest lack of mercy on an unnatural planet like earth? This is something that most people have never even considered. *You* can understand this because we have given you all of the background, we have given you, but an average person would not have the vocabulary to even comprehend this. What have we told you in the teachings we have given you since the book *My Lives* and the book on the birth trauma? We have told you that you are a formless being. You have descended into a world of form. You have made decisions and those decisions have led to a physical consequence. In the ideal state, my beloved, *listen carefully,* in the ideal state as a co-creator, even on an unnatural planet, you should be able to co-create something but your co-creation does not *define* you.

You are creating something that has some endurance in time and space. You create something that lasts. It does not just appear for a second and then disappear. It lasts over time but still, even though you have created that, it should not define you. You should still be a formless being. What, of course, happens on earth? It is not said to blame anyone, just simply a statement that this is the way it works on an unnatural planet. What happens on earth is that when you create something that has a certain endurance, you begin to identify yourself based on what you have created. What also happens is that other people begin to identify you based on what you have created.

This, of course, all started with the fallen beings who very well knew that when an avatar descends to earth, you descend at the 48th level of consciousness. Therefore, you do not have full Christhood. Therefore, you will make some decisions and you will create certain things that are not the highest possible. They then created this standard that there is right and wrong, there is either perfect or no-good. Therefore, they could easily blame you that whatever you co-created was not good enough, was not perfect, was wrong according to some standard. Then, they used this very aggressively to put upon you this idea that there is something wrong with you. If your creation is wrong, that means *you* are wrong. Therefore, you gradually started reacting to these very aggressive attacks by creating these separate selves. These separate selves are *reactionary* selves, they are created to respond to a certain condition that has endurance in time and space. You have created something, you have been put down or criticized for it. You are reacting to this by creating a self and the self also has endurance. When you received the birth trauma, as we have said before, all of a sudden everything became personal, or at least life on earth became personal to you. The attacks of the fallen beings you saw as a personal attack against you.

What *is* non-mercy? What is the opposite of mercy? It is when anyone, whether yourself or someone else, holds a fixed image in their minds of you as a formless being. They are taking an image that has form, projecting it upon you, the formless being, and saying: "This is how you are." You are fixing an image of the River of Life. You are taking a snapshot of the River of Life and saying: "This is how the river is. You can know everything about the river by looking at this still image." That is what they do to you. That is what you do to yourself. This is non-mercy. Therefore, what is mercy? It is to become aware of a fixed image of a formless being, whether yourself or someone else, and just releasing it. As Master MORE described, when you see an image of something that happened in the past, you can let it go, you can whisk it away, you can give it up, surrender it. *This* is mercy.

Ascended master students who get stuck

With this, let us take a slightly different direction and talk about ascended master students. There are people who have come into an ascended master teaching and when they found the teaching, they were, of course, (as you should all realize as inevitable) at a certain level of consciousness. They had a certain psychology, they had a certain amount of separate selves and they were approaching the ascended master teaching through their present level of consciousness. Nobody has ever done anything else. Nothing wrong with it, no blame here, it is simply inevitable. You find the teachings at a certain point, you look at the teachings a certain way, through the consciousness you have at the time, through the separate selves you have at the time.

Now, what happens to some ascended master students (not all, not even the majority but what happens to *some*) is that they formulate a very strong opinion and belief about ascended masters, about our teachings and about themselves as students. They do this because they have a separate self that has a certain need. It might be a need to feel that they are good enough, that they are okay or it might be a need to feel superior. There is especially a group of students who have this need to feel that they are either superior to others or blameless, that they know and understand something that other people do not understand. When they find the teachings, they build this image of themselves as advanced students but it is a separate self that builds and holds this image.

Now, the question is: Can these students, after having been in the teachings for some time and applied the teachings, can they overcome this separate self? Some can and then they move on and they grow. Others, my beloved, *cannot* or *will not* and therefore (even though they are studying the teachings, practicing the teachings and they are making progress in other ways), there is still that original separate self that caused them to formulate the view of themselves and the teachings. That self has not been touched. Even if they have been in the teachings and been practicing them for 30-40 years, there are students whose original separate self has not even been touched. They have not started to see that this was a separate self. They are firmly convinced that the way they look at the masters, the spiritual path and themselves is the ultimate view. They do not need to change it.

What can we of the ascended masters do about such students? Well, in a sense, we do not do anything about them because they are unreachable to us. What we do is we say: "Now, it is time to bring forth a higher level of teaching, because there is a critical mass of students that are ready for it." What, then, often happens is that these people who see themselves as advanced students, their original view of the ascended masters, their original view of the spiritual path and their original view of themselves is being challenged by the new teaching. Some of them are now able to see this, to see that their original view was just coming from a separate self and they can let it go. Others are not willing to do this because they are not willing to question the image that they are superior students and they have the path firmly in their grasp, they know what it is about, what it means to be a student. These people will in many cases reject the new teaching. We have in the past seen many times where we had sponsored one organization for a time. We withdrew our sponsorship and stopped progressive revelation in that movement. We started a new one, some of the students from the old movement moved on to the new, but those who were the most (in their own mind) sophisticated and advanced students, would not move on to the new because the new one was a little bit different and therefore challenged their view of what the path was about.

This, of course, can happen even within an organization as it has recently happened for some people with the *My Lives* book and the new teachings we are giving on the primal self and the separate selves. Why am I bringing this up? Well, because these students are actually an example of non-mercy. They have not locked in to the Flame of Mercy. If you truly grasp mercy, you recognize that the spiritual path, the Path to Christhood, is a *process* that goes through several stages. You realize (when you have mercy with yourself and others) that what applies to one stage is only given in order to take you to a certain level of the path. When you come to that level, your challenge is to step up to a new level and you cannot, as other masters have said, rise to the new level by continuing to do what you did at the old level.

Having mercy upon yourself

You are at a certain point of the path. What you have been doing to get to that point was perfectly valid, but what took you to that point cannot take you beyond that point. If you do not have mercy, you tend to hold on to a fixed view of the path, of the masters, of yourself. You will see many, many students throughout the ages, who have looked at a new dispensation and found something they could point their finger at: "Oh, the masters would never say that. The masters would never express themselves that way, the masters would never talk about these topics." All of these things. This is actually an expression of non-mercy.

Now, am I saying this because I want people in embodiment to have mercy upon the ascended masters? Of course not! I do not need your mercy. *You* need your mercy because what are these students doing? They are holding themselves in a fixed image of themselves. Therefore, they are not having mercy upon themselves. Also, they are often not having mercy upon other students. They become very judgmental of those who (for example) move on. They try to, perhaps, persuade them or scare them into not moving on by all kinds of scare tactics that this is wrong, this is false, this is not the masters and so forth and so on.

There is this very rigid mindset that comes in, and it is the rigidity of the mindset that is lacking in mercy. You can look at fundamentalist Christians who have this very rigid mindset that the Bible is the word of God and that there is nothing else needed for salvation. It is a rather extreme expression of non-mercy. I know most people have never seen it that way but this is the reality. It is a complete lack of mercy with themselves and with the people they judge.

You, as ascended master students, can, of course, step up. You who are open to our teachings on the primal self, the birth trauma and all these separate selves, you can use this to say: "What is it that I need to go through here?" I have given you these other students just as an example. You do not need to dwell on it, you do not need to try to persuade them at all but you just need to look at yourself and say: "Do I have some element of non-mercy with myself or even with the way I look at other people? Am I tending to hold a fixed image of myself, of the path, of the masters?" Jesus talked about your modus operandi of how you relate to the masters. More importantly: "How do I look at myself?"

What I am bringing you to is this recognition that the spiritual path, the path to Christhood, has distinct stages, distinct phases. This means that you cannot allow yourself, as an ascended master student, to hold the image in your mind that: "I have a basic grasp of the path. It says I have to do this and then I just need to keep doing that for the rest of my life and I will make maximum progress." This simply is not the case. There comes a point where what you have been doing so far will not take you into the next phase. Therefore, you need to be flexible enough that you are willing to let go of that image of the path and of how you are as a student and say: "What do I actually need in order to grow to the next phase"?

You see my beloved, there are students who will look at anything new we bring out and judge it based on what has been brought out before. There are students (for example) who will look at a new dispensation, compare it to what was said in the previous dispensation and say: "Oh, the new cannot be right because it contradicts or goes beyond what was said in the old." Well, hello my beloved! What is the point of starting a new dispensation if it is not to say something that goes beyond what was said in the old? Be aware here that there is this tendency.

The traps set for spiritual students

This, then, allows me to bring you to the topic I really want to talk about, which is that when you start dealing with these very deep issues of the birth trauma, the primal self (and these separate selves you created right in the beginning of the time you were on earth), it is necessary to see that the fallen beings have been very clever at creating these traps for spiritual students, especially for avatars. They said: "How can we trap an avatar into holding a certain image of itself that prevents it from manifesting Christhood?" They have created these, what we might call, almost machines that are aimed at trapping people, not only avatars but certainly primarily avatars because they are the biggest threat to the fallen beings. There comes this stage where you now have to sometimes take a certain measure in order to overcome a particular separate self. It may seem that what you have to do to overcome that separate self is very different from the way you have looked at the path previously. It may seem almost *radical* in comparison to what you have done previously. This brings me to the topic of how you can be free of the mistakes you think you have made in the past. If you came here as an avatar, whether you were exposed to the same kind of trauma as described in the *My Lives* book does not matter. Some of you had different scenarios but you all, as avatars, came to a point where you felt it was a mistake for you to come to this planet. This was based on you experiencing that whatever you did and whatever you brought forth was (to use Nada's expression) "hammered down by the fallen beings" and labeled as a mistake. There is something wrong with everything you do, there is something wrong with *you*. If there is something wrong with everything you *do*, there must be something wrong with *you*. That is the mantra of the fallen beings.

My beloved, what do you have to do to overcome this separate self? Here is where you need to be flexible. Naturally, we have in our teachings said that you need to take responsibility for yourself, for your own path, for your own growth and so forth. What I will say next will, from a certain linear perspective seem to be in contradiction to this.

Stop taking responsibility for anything

Now, I am actually going to tell you that you need to stop taking responsibility for anything you have ever done on earth. Why am I telling you this? Because, my beloved, the fallen beings have manipulated you into creating a separate self that makes you feel that *you* did something wrong, but what have we told you?

Who are you? You are the Conscious You. You are a formless being. You have a right to descend to earth. You take on the form of your four lower bodies, you descend to the 48th level of consciousness. You act based on that level, you get a certain response and then, in an ideal scenario, you grow to the 49th level. You grow to the 50th level and you keep growing until you again become aware: "I am a formless being, I am not defined by form." This is what we have called the *immersion* and the *awakening*. What the fallen beings have managed to do for many of you, is to force you to create the separate self that is now holding a fixed image of yourself. Not that you are a formless being but that you are a being with a particular form and that this form is wrong according to some standard. This self has for many of you been there since your first embodiment or one of your first embodiments after you came to earth. You have been dragging this self along with you for a very, very long time, and this self is one of the primary factors that prevents you from rising to a certain level of Christhood. You cannot rise beyond a certain level on the path as long as you are dragging this self with you.

What do you have to do to overcome this self? Well, here is what I propose that you consider: Why have you done anything on earth? When you descended to the 48th level, we have told you that you take on all of these illusions that are like veils that you put on. You are seeing life through these veils, they are distorting and coloring your vision. Why did you do what you did? Did *you*, the Conscious You seeing itself as a formless being, do what you did? Nay! You the Conscious You did what you did, not by seeing yourself as a formless being but seeing yourself as a being who had form based on these illusions you had taken on. Was it actually *you* as you really are, the formless being, or was it a separate self that you had created in order to descend into physical embodiment?

Do you see what I am saying here? We have said that you received the birth trauma and you created the primal self after that, but even in order to descend to the 48th level and take embodiment, you had to create these separate selves, the soul vehicle, your four lower bodies, your three higher bodies specifically. What I am helping you see here is that there comes a point on the spiritual path where you need to deal with this.

Of course, you cannot do this at lower levels. You cannot have a new ascended master student who is ready for this teaching unless they have been prepared in past lives. Most people will not be ready for some time for this teaching but there comes a point where you have to start pondering this and realizing that: "If I really am the Conscious You, if I really am a formless being, then I am not any of my separate selves. I have only identified myself as these separate selves because I have gone inside of them and I was looking through that filter. Now, that I am beginning to get a feel that I am a formless being, it is time for me to step back and say: 'So I did something when I first came to earth. It was done in complete innocence with the best of intentions of helping other people. I was hammered down by the fallen beings and I reacted to this by creating this separate self that feels that I am wrong, or I was wrong for coming to this planet or however I express myself on this planet, it is wrong! I formulated this self and then, after I had created this self, I started making decisions through that self.'"

This is what Mother Mary partly called avoidance decisions. You have been given the impression that when you express your true being, you are wrong. You decide: "I cannot express my true being" so you start to make

13 | Grasping the radical nature of mercy

all of these decisions to avoid being proven wrong again. It is like your overall goal (or at least the overall goal for this self) is to not be wrong again so you make decisions based on this. You can say to yourself: "Yes I did something that was a mistake." It could be in this life or if you have become aware of something from a past life, you say: "Yes, I did this. From a traditional viewpoint, *I* did this, but from a higher viewpoint did *I* actually do this? Was it me, the formless being, who did this or was it actually a separate self that made the decision to do this? Who did it? Me or the separate self?"

When you start pondering this, even asking this question, you are starting to separate yourself from that separate self. Separating your *Self* from the separate self. When you have done this, you can come to the realization: "I am not that separate self, I am more, I am a formless being." You can experience glimpses of this pure awareness, the sense of being conscious without being conscious of yourself as a particular being or being conscious of a particular situation. Then, you realize: "I am not the separate self. Well, if I am not the separate self, it follows that I did not do what the separate self did." If *you* did not do what the separate self did, why should *you* feel responsible for it? *Why* should you feel responsible for it?

Can you undo what you did?

You see, what the fallen beings want you to feel is that you made this terrible mistake in the past and that proves that you are bad. You will be bad forever and ever because you can never overcome it. You can never undo what you did in the past. That proves that you are bad and you will be bad forever and ever because you can never overcome it. You can never undo what you did in the past.

True, from a certain perspective, you cannot change the fact that this *did* happen. You can, of course, use the tools we have given you to overcome the memory and so forth. I am giving you another tool here, which is to say (you say this to the devil): "Okay devil, you are saying this happened, it cannot be undone. Why are you telling *me* this? *I* did not do it. It was that separate self but that separate self is not *me*. Yes, you are right, devil, I created that separate self. I fully take responsibility for creating that separate self. You know what's the wonderful thing about that, devil? What I have created, I can un-create. *You* have no power over that separate self. Or rather, you may have power to manipulate the separate self but you did not create it and you cannot un-create it—but *I* can. I can let it die and guess what? I am letting it die and, now, that self is no more. So why are you bothering me? Go somewhere else. Find someone else to bother who still has a separate self. Get thee behind me, Satan."

You see here, there is a phase on the spiritual path where you need to take responsibility for your self. You need to give decrees and invocations to transmute the energy. You need to work on your psychology and this and that. Then, there comes that point where you need to step back, look at this from a different perspective and say: "Now, I actually need to stop taking responsibility." You are still being responsible because you are taking responsibility for having created the separate self and you have also taken responsibility for letting it die. But when, my beloved, you have let a separate self die, you are no longer responsible for the actions taken by or through that separate self. This is where you need to tune in to the true Flame of Mercy and realize: "I need to have mercy upon myself. I need to forgive myself totally and unconditionally for what I did in the past, even to the point where whatever I did in the past simply does not matter anymore." When you realize that it just does not matter, you can do what Master MORE said: You can erase the image of having done it so even the memory of it is gone.

It can be difficult to erase the image until you have forgiven yourself and tuned in to the Flame of Mercy, used the Flame of Mercy to erase the sense of guilt, shame, embarrassment, whatever it is. The Flame of Mercy that I hold is the eraser for these kinds of feelings. You can invoke it in many ways: invocations, even the mantra *Om Mani Padme Hum* and many other ways by tuning in to my Being. It is necessary to have this total forgiveness of yourself where you say: "*I* did not do this. I am a formless being and I did not do this!" Then, you are free.

Freeing yourself by forgiving all who have harmed you

This, of course, is only one side of the coin of being free. You now need to take what you have internalized about yourself and apply this to other people. Someone hurt you. You can even go to the extreme of the fallen beings that gave you the birth trauma. They did something absolutely horrible, absolutely aggressive and destructive. Now, why was it that *you* did what you did? Oh yes, you were acting through a separate self, you were blinded by a separate self. Why did the fallen beings do what they did?

13 | Grasping the radical nature of mercy

Oh yes, they *also* were acting through a separate self. What is the devil? Is it a divine being? Nay, it is a conglomerate of separate selves. There is, somewhere in there (in Satan or Lucifer or whomever), a Conscious You that is no longer conscious of it is own existence because it has been completely overwhelmed by and identified with all of these very aggressive, very negative separate selves. They are still separate selves. They have no enduring reality. They cannot ever ascend and become permanent. They are impermanent and they will be erased at some point, if not before, then certainly when the sphere ascends. You do not need to forgive a separate self because it is not ultimately real, but what you need to do is forgive all people who have harmed you.

You need to have mercy upon them, and this can most easily be practiced among the people you know in this embodiment, for example, family members, spouses or ex-spouses. You need to simply come to a point where you realize that whatever they did to you, it was not the Conscious You in that person who did this, it was a separate self. Therefore, you can forgive, you can have mercy upon that person by *not* holding the image of them that they *are* the separate self, that they are the way that the separate self treated you. You can avoid this reaction of: "This is how that person is, you *are* that kind of person." You can avoid that. You can erase that. You can come to a point where you forgive the people who have harmed you. When you do this, it is not so much to set *them* free because if you forgive somebody, they are still colored by the separate self so they are not set free. Who is set free when you forgive another person? Well, *you* are. You are set free because as long as you are holding a certain image of another person, well, how can you be free?

How can you hold an image that has form of another person? Only if you have a self that has form that is holding that image. As the Conscious You, you cannot hold a specific image of another person. If you are truly in the Conscious You and you have no separate selves (as you achieve at the 144th level of consciousness, or at least as you grow closer to that and you have fewer and fewer separate selves), you are not looking at other people in a certain way. You do not have a preconceived image or impression of how that person is. It is as if you wake up in the morning, you look over at your spouse on the other side of the bed and for a brief moment: "Who is that person? I do not know that person." You do not have any preconceived images that you are carrying along with you. You are living in the now, as they say, in the sense that every now is new. You are not demanding that the person should live up to a certain image. You are not blaming the person for what happened in the past. You are meeting that person anew every time because you are allowing yourself to be a new person every day. Even if you do not have a spouse, when you get to the higher levels of consciousness, you wake up and you look in the mirror and you say: "Who is this person?" You are free to say: "Who do I want to be today?" Most people are not free to say that because they wake up with a pattern carried over from the day before that says: "This is how you have to be today! You *have* to be this way." As you go to the higher levels, you gain more and more freedom, and naturally the omega aspect of that is that you set other people free. It may be that you know people who act the same way every day and they do not change, but *you* are not concerned about this anymore. You are just setting them free and thereby setting yourself free. You are saying: "You may act the same as you did yesterday but I am not going to react the same way I reacted yesterday. I am not going to act as you expect me to act. I am going be free to choose: 'Who do I want to be today?'"

Nobody ever did anything to you

When you have done this, reached that level of forgiving yourself, having mercy on yourself, having mercy on others, you can take another very radical step. You can come to the realization that this messenger came to some time ago where it suddenly hit him one day: "Nobody ever did anything to me." Ponder that statement. Imagine yourself saying this, looking at your history in this life and what you might have sensed in past lives. Then say: "Nobody ever did anything to me," and then monitor your reaction and see if there is some kind of voice in you that is objecting to this statement. Then, you know there is a separate self that you can look at so that you can set yourself free from it.

I have said to you that you need to stop taking responsibility for your actions. You need to also, very much, stop taking responsibility for other people's reactions to you. Naturally, when you first came to this earth, the fallen beings attacked you and they attempted to make this very, very personal: There is something wrong with *you*, you should not have done this. When you realize that the fallen beings were doing this to you because they had separate selves, then you can actually come to the point where you say: "Oh, but that means they weren't actually doing this to *me* because they were just acting based on their separate selves. If somebody else had been in my position, they would have done the same to that person, so that means it is not actually *personal* against me. It is just that I created a separate self that took this personally."

One of the absolutely most important steps you can take on the path to Christhood is to come to the point where you identify that in your being is a separate self that reacts. Whenever a certain thing happens to you (it may be that you make a mistake, that you do something you think is stupid, that you do something you think is embarrassing, that other people do not like, that upsets other people, it can be all kinds of different things for you individually). There is something you do and when you do it, you take it very, very personally that you have done this very terrible thing and made this mistake and therefore you should feel a certain way. This is just a separate self, like all of the other separate selves.

Now, mind you, my beloved, this self can be very difficult to overcome because it is the self that takes things personally. It will try to make you take it personally that you have this self that makes you take everything personally. You might have to really, almost do a trick on yourself that instead of just seeing it as a separate self, you have to step back twice and see that this is a separate self that made you feel bad about having all the other separate selves and about anything you have done. Still, when you step back enough, you see it is just a separate self.

You can actually realize that the self that takes everything personally was created in reaction to other people blaming you. You can realize that they were not blaming *you*. They were acting out their own unresolved psychology. Whatever anybody has ever done to you, they were acting out their own unresolved psychology. *Ponder that statement.* Whatever anybody ever did to you that was negative, they were acting out their own unresolved psychology. If they were acting out their own unresolved psychology and blaming you, why do you have to accept that blame and take it personally and say: "Oh, I must have been the one who upset them."

You did not create those people's separate selves. You are not responsible for them, therefore you do not need to take it personally. You do not need to feel responsible for it. You can simply recognize that it was not personal against you. They had a separate self that made them feel bad and they had another separate self that caused them to think that it was not their fault they were feeling bad. It was something you did and therefore that separate self was directing blame at you. If it had not been you, and somebody else had been there, they would have directed the blame at that other person. It is not personal towards you. It is personal *for them,* what they are directing out. It does not mean that you have to take it in and make it personal *for you*.

When you recognize this, you can take the next step, which is perhaps the most radical and say: "Well this means that nobody ever did anything to *me*." The one side of it is, nobody ever really was angry with me or blaming me. It was simply their own unresolved psychology that they directed at me. Then, you can say: "Yes. Okay, it was not personal against me when they blamed me but I still felt bad about it." Then, you can say: "But did *they* make me feel bad about it? No. I felt bad about it because I have a separate self that I created in the past that is causing me to feel bad in this particular type of situation. So nobody ever did anything to me because the only thing that ever affected me was not what other people did, it was my reaction to it. It was my inner experience of what they did that affected me, not the outer action that they took." You see my beloved, in your mind you come to the realization that there is a fundamental difference between what people did *outside* of your four lower bodies and what happens *inside* of your four lower bodies.

Your inner responsibility

Now again, there is absolutely no blame here. When you descend to the 48th level and are exposed to the aggression from the fallen beings, you can only react to that based on the 48th level of consciousness. Therefore, it is inevitable that you take it personally, that you create these separate selves to deal with it. We have all done this who have been in embodiment on an unnatural planet. There is no reason to blame yourself for having done it but you need to recognize that you have done it. Then, you need to make the switch where you, in fact, take another kind of responsibility. You are not responsible for the actions you took through a separate self but you *are* responsible for creating the separate self.

You did this based on the level of consciousness you had at the time but you have now risen to a higher level of consciousness. Therefore, you can look at that separate self again and say: "I no longer need you because today I would not react that way. Today I know more, I am more mature but I still have this self that I have carried with me for these many lifetimes but now it is time to see it, now it is time to dismiss it and thereby lock in to that Flame of Mercy, apply that Flame of Mercy and set myself free from that self that has form. I set myself free to be the formless being that I am.

13 | Grasping the radical nature of mercy

I realize that whatever people do to me, I do not have to react to it in a certain way anymore. I do not anymore have to react to it the way I used to react to it. In fact, whatever people do to me, I do not have to react to it."

There is a separate self that is very strong in the collective consciousness on earth. All people have taken it into their auras and allowed it to reside there. This separate self says that when a certain person approaches you, you *have* to react, you *have* to respond. You cannot just ignore them. What is the worst thing you could ever do to other people? It is to ignore them, to not react at all. Look at how many people are angry people and they approach you, blaming you for something. They are expecting you to argue back or to feel bad but they are expecting you to respond. My beloved, one of the funniest things you can possibly experience on earth, is to have one of these people who come at you, blaming you and then not react at all and just watch what happens when they do not get the reaction they expect.

My beloved, you have free will. Have we not told you so many times, you have free will? The fact that you are in embodiment in a family unit or in another group of people (or even meet strangers on the street), does not mean you *have* to react, you *have* to respond to them. If they come and throw something at you that you feel is not something you want to respond to, you are free *not* to respond. You are free to just walk away and not engage that person and their negativity. This is a right you have. It is a right that very, very few people have claimed. The people who have claimed it have often been labelled as eccentrics, egomaniacs, crazy people who do not respond the way people are used to.

I am not saying that you should now start going around and ignoring all people. I am saying, that you can perhaps, some of you, identify certain people in your sphere of influence that are always trying to engage you in a negative pattern, pull you into some repetitive pattern that really only has the purpose of engaging your attention so they can take your energy. You have the right to simply decide: "I am not going to respond to this anymore."

This messenger has, in the time he has been a messenger, been exposed to quite a number of people who came for various reasons, sometimes very aggressively trying to engage him in some way. In the beginning years it was a burden to him because he felt he had to be nice to everybody and he had to try to help everybody. He has learned, partly the hard way, that there are some people you cannot help. There are some people you cannot ever satisfy because they are not really interested in changing, they are just interested in engaging you. He has learned he has a right to say: "There are people I cannot help and I am choosing not to engage with them. I am not even responding to them."

My beloved, this is a right you have. When you actually think about it, if somebody approaches you, wanting to engage you in a negative pattern and you do not respond to it, what are you doing? You are being merciful towards that person. How are you being merciful? Well, what is mercy? It is when you do not hold a fixed image of yourself or other people. Here is a person who approaches you in a negative state of mind, wanting to engage you in an argument. They are expecting a certain response from you. You are saying: "I am not going to respond to this at all because if I respond the way the person expects, it will only validate that separate self and the person will not be able to see it. He will just be pulled into endlessly repeating the pattern, but if I do not respond the way he expects, then, perhaps, he will look at his reaction, he will be surprised by this and he will have an opportunity to look at his reaction and wonder why this happened. *That* could potentially set the person free. If I respond the way he expects, it is guaranteed not to set him free, but if I respond the way he does not expect, there is at least a small possibility that it might help him—and *this* is mercy." Even though the person obviously will not see it this way and might, in fact (if they use that terminology) blame you for being very merci-*less*.

Self-transcendence is an ongoing process

It is mercy when you do not hold any fixed images in your mind of other people. The consequence is that you do not hold any fixed images of how you should respond to those people, even if you have known them for your entire lifetime. You can choose to do something you have never done before. You can choose a new response that is different from your previous response and that is merciful. My beloved, it is not merciful towards yourself to think that if you found the ascended master teachings some time ago, you were in a state of consciousness at the time that helped you understand the full depth of the teachings at that point. This is not merciful. It is a misunderstanding of the spiritual path, which is an on-going process of self-transcendence.

There are people who have found ascended master teachings or other spiritual teachings and they have a separate self that blocks their vision

13 | Grasping the radical nature of mercy

of the need for on-going self-transcendence. This self actually thinks that the entire purpose of finding the ascended master teachings is to validate the person's or the self's image of superiority. There are people who have come into ascended master teachings, followed them for decades and their only purpose has been to use the teachings to validate their sense of superiority compared to other people, whether it is people who are not in the teachings or other people in the teachings. You have seen previous organizations where they created a very distinct hierarchy of those students who had been in the teachings the longest, those who where closest to the messenger, those who had some kind of position. They created this, which we can only call a *false hierarchy*, my beloved, because it was not coming from the ascended masters this sense that they were higher than everybody else.

There were certain cliques that formed of people who thought they were at a superior level compared to all others. These people sometimes have been in ascended master teachings for 30-40 years and they have never even started to see this self, which means that they, in some cases, have made very little progress in 30 or 40 years of supposedly following and applying an ascended master teaching.

Can *we* do anything about this? No, we cannot in a direct way but we can at least put out there that this can happen to people. There is always the potential that someone will be willing to see this, even though it often will be very difficult for these people because over time they have been so judgmental of others. My beloved, what is the greatest trap of this judgmentalness, which is, of course, an expression of anti-mercy? What is the greatest trap when a person is judgmental of others? Well, it is always based on a sense of superiority. "I know better, I am at a higher level, I am a more advanced student than you, therefore I can judge you and it is absolutely okay that I am judging you. It is, in fact, good for you that I am judging you." That is how these people feel so they feel superior. Now, if they come to the realization that the judgmental attitude needs to go and was not the highest, how are they going to look at this? Well, they are going to look at this through the same state of consciousness that caused them to judge others. Which means that now, they are going to start judging *themselves* as harshly as they have judged other people.

For some people it will be impossible to make that step in this lifetime. There are people (and it is not just ascended master students, you find them everywhere, in the field of science, in the field of religion) who have locked themselves in this sense of superiority. In order to overcome it, they would then have to judge themselves as harshly as they have judged others. They cannot stand the pain of that and therefore they go into denial about this for the rest of their lifetime, which means they do not make any progress. There are some of them who, then, in between lifetimes can snap out of it. There are some of them who, in between lifetimes when they choose their next embodiment, they choose to come into very humble circumstances where they have no position or where they are put down so that they can overcome the sense of superiority.

Why am I saying this? I am saying it because I hold the Flame of Mercy for earth. There is no human attribute that the Flame of Mercy cannot consume and help you overcome. If there is someone who realizes: "I have been too judgmental of others," do not hesitate to approach me. I will not judge you as you are judging yourself. I will help you overcome the sense of superiority, the sense of judging yourself because it is a separate self. There is a separate self that gives you the need to feel superior, there is a separate self that gives you the need to judge, and those two work together and the combination can be difficult to overcome. It is impossible to overcome if you do not have the antidote, which is the Flame of Mercy.

The Flame of Mercy as your frame of reference

Now, the same thing you can say for all of you. You all have a self that judges yourself and you all have another self that, in reaction to the fallen beings putting you down, is trying to build you up to say: "Well, I may have made certain mistakes but I am definitely not worthless, I have some good qualities." You will see how many people, when they first find the spiritual path, they have a need for this kind of validation. That is why, for example, they look at their numerology or astrology or anything else that makes them stand out from the crowd. They feel: "Because I have these special numbers in my name or this combination in my birth chart, then I am okay."

This is okay. It is a legitimate need at a certain stage of the path, but how are you going to overcome this unless you, as I said, start having mercy upon yourself? When you lock in to the Flame of Mercy, you realize precisely that all of these outer things are unreal. Because they are unreal, they do not actually matter.

There is, as we have said before, a need to come to the point where you can look at something that has happened on earth, something you have done on earth, and say: "So what! It does not matter, it just does not matter." It can be difficult to do this unless you have a frame of reference and, my beloved, the Flame of Mercy can give you that frame of reference. You realize that compared to the Flame of Mercy, which when you experience it is very, very real, all of this human nonsense on earth is unreal and utterly insignificant.

Do you understand what I am saying here? I am not saying I do not care about you in your present situation. I always see that you are more than whatever outer situation you are in. Therefore, I see that you can be free of it. I know also (and this is, of course, as we have said before, the secret of these teachings we have given you) that you are not going to be free of your present circumstances by doing something or by solving a problem.

As we have said now several times, the separate self projects that there is a problem that has to be solved or some condition that has to be changed. Even if you solved the problem, you would not be free of the separate self, it would just come up with another problem. The *only* solution is to step outside of the separate self and let it go.

I am offering you my Flame of Mercy to help you with this process. Whenever you are dealing with a separate self, just ask me. Just ask me: "Kuan Yin, help me see this. Kuan Yin help me experience the Flame of Mercy, help me gain a perspective, help me see this as you see it. Help me have that frame of reference of experiencing the reality of the Flame of Mercy and the unreality of the human condition.

My beloved, it has been my great joy to commune with you in this way, but it will be an even greater joy if you individually would put a little attention on me once in a while and allow me to commune with you directly in your own hearts, which I am perfectly capable of doing. You are all capable of doing it, if you will just put a little bit of attention on it and perhaps strive to go into that neutral frame of mind where you are just allowing it to unfold rather than have any preconceived opinions. If you have not been able to tune in to me before, try to meet me with a new view. Try to set *me* free, try to set *yourself* free and meet me anew and there will come a point where you *will* experience my Presence with you.

14 | INVOKING RADICAL FORGIVENESS

In the name I AM THAT I AM, Jesus Christ, I call to all representatives of the Divine Mother, especially Kuan Yin, to help me overcome all elements of non-mercy and non-forgiveness in my psychology, including…

[Make personal calls.]

Part 1

1. I am a formless being. I have descended into a world of form. I have made decisions and those decisions have led to physical consequences. As a co-creator I should be able to co-create something but my co-creation does not *define* me.

> O Kuan Yin, what sacred name,
> fill me now with Mercy's Flame.
> In giving mercy I am free,
> forgiving all is magic key.

> **In Kuan Yin's sweet melody,**
> **I am set free my Self to be.**
> **In Kuan Yin's vitality,**
> **I claim my immortality.**

2. I am creating something that has some endurance in time and space. Even though I have created that, it should not define me. I should still be a formless being.

> O Kuan Yin, I now let go,
> of all attachments here below.
> All pent-up feelings I release,
> free from emotional disease.

> **In Kuan Yin's sweet melody,**
> **I am set free my Self to be.**
> **In Kuan Yin's vitality,**
> **I claim my immortality.**

3. What happens on earth is that when I create something that has a certain endurance, I begin to identify myself based on what I have created. Other people begin to identify me based on what I have created.

> O Kuan Yin, why must I feel,
> that life falls short of my ideal?
> All expectations I give up,
> my mind is now an empty cup.

> **In Kuan Yin's sweet melody,**
> **I am set free my Self to be.**
> **In Kuan Yin's vitality,**
> **I claim my immortality.**

4. This started with the fallen beings who knew that when an avatar descends to earth, I descend at the 48th level of consciousness. I do not have full Christhood and I will make some decisions and I will create certain things that are not the highest possible.

O Kuan Yin, transcend the past,
as all resentment gone at last.
From future nothing I expect,
eternal now I won't reject.

**In Kuan Yin's sweet melody,
I am set free my Self to be.
In Kuan Yin's vitality,
I claim my immortality.**

5. The fallen beings then created this standard that there is right and wrong, there is either perfect or no-good. They could easily blame me that whatever I co-created was not good enough, was not perfect, was wrong according to their standard.

O Kuan Yin, uplifting me,
beyond Samsara's raging sea.
All safe inside your Prajna boat,
the farther shore no more remote.

**In Kuan Yin's sweet melody,
I am set free my Self to be.
In Kuan Yin's vitality,
I claim my immortality.**

6. Then, they used this very aggressively to put upon me this idea that there is something wrong with me. They say that if my creation is wrong, *I am* wrong.

O Kuan Yin, your alchemy,
with miracles you set me free.
As I forgive, I am forgiven,
by guilt I am no longer driven.

**In Kuan Yin's sweet melody,
I am set free my Self to be.
In Kuan Yin's vitality,
I claim my immortality.**

7. I started reacting to these very aggressive attacks by creating separate selves. These separate selves are *reactionary* selves, they are created to respond to a certain condition that has endurance in time and space.

> O Kuan Yin, all worries gone,
> with nothing done, no thing undone.
> Through separate self I will not do,
> and thus I rest, all one with you.

> **In Kuan Yin's sweet melody,**
> **I am set free my Self to be.**
> **In Kuan Yin's vitality,**
> **I claim my immortality.**

8. I have created something, I have been put down or criticized for it. I am reacting to this by creating a self and the self also has endurance. When I received the birth trauma, life on earth became personal to me. The attacks of the fallen beings I saw as a personal attack against me.

> O Kuan Yin, your sanity,
> now sets me free from vanity.
> For truly, what is that to me;
> I just let go and follow thee.

> **In Kuan Yin's sweet melody,**
> **I am set free my Self to be.**
> **In Kuan Yin's vitality,**
> **I claim my immortality.**

9. The opposite of mercy is when anyone, whether myself or someone else, holds a fixed image in their minds of me as a formless being. They are taking an image that has form, projecting it upon me, the formless being and saying: "This is how you are."

> O Kuan Yin, so sweet the sound,
> that emanates from holy ground.
> As I let go of ego's chore,
> I find myself on farther shore.

**In Kuan Yin's sweet melody,
I am set free my Self to be.
In Kuan Yin's vitality,
I claim my immortality.**

Part 2

1. Non-mercy is fixing an image of the River of Life. It is taking a snapshot of the River of Life and saying: "This is how the river is. You can know everything about the river by looking at this still image." That is what they do to me. That is what I do to myself.

> O Kuan Yin, what sacred name,
> fill me now with Mercy's Flame.
> In giving mercy I am free,
> forgiving all is magic key.

**In Kuan Yin's sweet melody,
I am set free my Self to be.
In Kuan Yin's vitality,
I claim my immortality.**

2. Mercy is to become aware of a fixed image of a formless being, whether myself or someone else, and releasing it. When I see an image of something that happened in the past, I can let it go, I can whisk it away, I can give it up, surrender it. *This* is mercy.

> O Kuan Yin, I now let go,
> of all attachments here below.
> All pent-up feelings I release,
> free from emotional disease.

**In Kuan Yin's sweet melody,
I am set free my Self to be.
In Kuan Yin's vitality,
I claim my immortality.**

3. I realize that when I found an ascended master teaching, I was at a certain level of consciousness. I had a certain psychology, I had a certain amount of separate selves and I was approaching the teaching through that level of consciousness. I could not do anything else.

> O Kuan Yin, why must I feel,
> that life falls short of my ideal?
> All expectations I give up,
> my mind is now an empty cup.
>
> **In Kuan Yin's sweet melody,**
> **I am set free my Self to be.**
> **In Kuan Yin's vitality,**
> **I claim my immortality.**

4. Kuan Yin, help me see if I formulated a very strong opinion and belief about ascended masters, about your teachings and about myself as a student.

> O Kuan Yin, transcend the past,
> as all resentment gone at last.
> From future nothing I expect,
> eternal now I won't reject.
>
> **In Kuan Yin's sweet melody,**
> **I am set free my Self to be.**
> **In Kuan Yin's vitality,**
> **I claim my immortality.**

5. Kuan Yin, help me see if I have a separate self that has a need to feel that I am good enough or to feel superior. Help me see if a separate self built this image of myself as an advanced student.

> O Kuan Yin, uplifting me,
> beyond Samsara's raging sea.
> All safe inside your Prajna boat,
> the farther shore no more remote.

> In Kuan Yin's sweet melody,
> I am set free my Self to be.
> In Kuan Yin's vitality,
> I claim my immortality.

6. Kuan Yin, help me see if I have such a self and then help me see it as a self. I am willing to let this self die so I can be open to a higher level of teachings.

> O Kuan Yin, your alchemy,
> with miracles you set me free.
> As I forgive, I am forgiven,
> by guilt I am no longer driven.

> In Kuan Yin's sweet melody,
> I am set free my Self to be.
> In Kuan Yin's vitality,
> I claim my immortality.

7. I recognize that if my original view of the ascended masters, of the spiritual path and of myself is being challenged by a new teaching, this is coming from a separate self and I am willing to let it go.

> O Kuan Yin, all worries gone,
> with nothing done, no thing undone.
> Through separate self I will not do,
> and thus I rest, all one with you.

> In Kuan Yin's sweet melody,
> I am set free my Self to be.
> In Kuan Yin's vitality,
> I claim my immortality.

8. I am willing to question the image that I am a superior student and that I have the path firmly in my grasp. I am willing to reach for a new understanding of the teaching that challenges this separate self.

> O Kuan Yin, your sanity,
> now sets me free from vanity.

For truly, what is that to me;
I just let go and follow thee.

**In Kuan Yin's sweet melody,
I am set free my Self to be.
In Kuan Yin's vitality,
I claim my immortality.**

9. I realize that if I hold on to an old image of myself and the path, this is a form of non-mercy. Instead, I want to lock in to the Flame of Mercy and truly grasp mercy, thereby recognizing that the spiritual path, the path to Christhood, is a *process* that goes through several stages.

O Kuan Yin, so sweet the sound,
that emanates from holy ground.
As I let go of ego's chore,
I find myself on farther shore.

**In Kuan Yin's sweet melody,
I am set free my Self to be.
In Kuan Yin's vitality,
I claim my immortality.**

Part 3

1. When I have mercy with myself and others, I realize that what applies to one stage is only given in order to take me to a certain level of the path. When I come to that level, my challenge is to step up to a new level, and I cannot rise to the new level by continuing to do what I did at the old level.

O Kuan Yin, what sacred name,
fill me now with Mercy's Flame.
In giving mercy I am free,
forgiving all is magic key.

**In Kuan Yin's sweet melody,
I am set free my Self to be.**

**In Kuan Yin's vitality,
I claim my immortality.**

2. I am at a certain point of the path. What I have been doing to get to this point was perfectly valid, but what took me to this point cannot take me beyond this point. If I do not have mercy, I tend to hold on to a fixed view of the path, of the masters, of myself.

> O Kuan Yin, I now let go,
> of all attachments here below.
> All pent-up feelings I release,
> free from emotional disease.

**In Kuan Yin's sweet melody,
I am set free my Self to be.
In Kuan Yin's vitality,
I claim my immortality.**

3. I need mercy because it is the only way to avoid holding myself in a fixed image of myself. I am willing to let go of the mindset and the selves that are rigid and therefore lacking in mercy.

> O Kuan Yin, why must I feel,
> that life falls short of my ideal?
> All expectations I give up,
> my mind is now an empty cup.

**In Kuan Yin's sweet melody,
I am set free my Self to be.
In Kuan Yin's vitality,
I claim my immortality.**

4. As an ascended master student, I am willing to step up. I am willing to look at myself and say: "Do I have some element of non-mercy with myself or even with the way I look at other people? Am I tending to hold a fixed image of myself, of the path, of the masters? How do I look at myself?"

O Kuan Yin, transcend the past,
as all resentment gone at last.
From future nothing I expect,
eternal now I won't reject.

**In Kuan Yin's sweet melody,
I am set free my Self to be.
In Kuan Yin's vitality,
I claim my immortality.**

5. The spiritual path, the path to Christhood, has distinct stages. I cannot allow myself to hold the image in my mind that: "I have a basic grasp of the path. I have to do this and then I just need to keep doing that for the rest of my life and I will make maximum progress."

O Kuan Yin, uplifting me,
beyond Samsara's raging sea.
All safe inside your Prajna boat,
the farther shore no more remote.

**In Kuan Yin's sweet melody,
I am set free my Self to be.
In Kuan Yin's vitality,
I claim my immortality.**

6. This simply is not the case. There comes a point where what I have been doing so far will not take me into the next phase. I will be flexible enough and let go of that image of the path and say: "What do I actually need in order to grow to the next phase?"

O Kuan Yin, your alchemy,
with miracles you set me free.
As I forgive, I am forgiven,
by guilt I am no longer driven.

**In Kuan Yin's sweet melody,
I am set free my Self to be.
In Kuan Yin's vitality,
I claim my immortality.**

7. The fallen beings have been very clever at creating these traps for spiritual students. They have created a kind of machines that are aimed at trapping people.

> O Kuan Yin, all worries gone,
> with nothing done, no thing undone.
> Through separate self I will not do,
> and thus I rest, all one with you.
>
> **In Kuan Yin's sweet melody,**
> **I am set free my Self to be.**
> **In Kuan Yin's vitality,**
> **I claim my immortality.**

8. There comes a stage where I have to take certain measures in order to overcome a particular separate self. It may seem that what I have to do to overcome that self is very different from the way I have looked at the path previously. It may seem almost *radical* in comparison to what I have done before.

> O Kuan Yin, your sanity,
> now sets me free from vanity.
> For truly, what is that to me;
> I just let go and follow thee.
>
> **In Kuan Yin's sweet melody,**
> **I am set free my Self to be.**
> **In Kuan Yin's vitality,**
> **I claim my immortality.**

9. There came a point where I felt it was a mistake for me to come to this planet. This was based on experiencing that whatever I did was hammered down by the fallen beings and labeled as a mistake.

> O Kuan Yin, so sweet the sound,
> that emanates from holy ground.
> As I let go of ego's chore,
> I find myself on farther shore.

**In Kuan Yin's sweet melody,
I am set free my Self to be.
In Kuan Yin's vitality,
I claim my immortality.**

Part 4

1. In order to overcome this separate self I need to be flexible. I need to stop taking responsibility for anything I have ever done on earth.

> O Kuan Yin, what sacred name,
> fill me now with Mercy's Flame.
> In giving mercy I am free,
> forgiving all is magic key.

**In Kuan Yin's sweet melody,
I am set free my Self to be.
In Kuan Yin's vitality,
I claim my immortality.**

2. The fallen beings have manipulated me into creating a separate self that makes me feel that *I* did something wrong. Yet, I am the Conscious You. I am a formless being. I have a right to descend to earth.

> O Kuan Yin, I now let go,
> of all attachments here below.
> All pent-up feelings I release,
> free from emotional disease.

**In Kuan Yin's sweet melody,
I am set free my Self to be.
In Kuan Yin's vitality,
I claim my immortality.**

3. I take on the form of my four lower bodies, I descend to the 48th level of consciousness. I act based on that level, I get a certain response and

then, in an ideal scenario, I grow until I again become aware: "I am a formless being, I am not defined by form."

> O Kuan Yin, why must I feel,
> that life falls short of my ideal?
> All expectations I give up,
> my mind is now an empty cup.

> **In Kuan Yin's sweet melody,**
> **I am set free my Self to be.**
> **In Kuan Yin's vitality,**
> **I claim my immortality.**

4. The fallen beings have managed to force me to create the separate self that is now holding a fixed image of myself. Not that I am a formless being but that I am a being with a particular form and that this form is wrong according to some standard.

> O Kuan Yin, transcend the past,
> as all resentment gone at last.
> From future nothing I expect,
> eternal now I won't reject.

> **In Kuan Yin's sweet melody,**
> **I am set free my Self to be.**
> **In Kuan Yin's vitality,**
> **I claim my immortality.**

5. This self may have been there since my first embodiment. I have been dragging this self along with me for a very long time, and this self is one of the primary factors that prevents me from rising to a higher level of Christhood. I cannot rise beyond a certain level on the path as long as I am dragging this self with me.

> O Kuan Yin, uplifting me,
> beyond Samsara's raging sea.
> All safe inside your Prajna boat,
> the farther shore no more remote.

> In Kuan Yin's sweet melody,
> I am set free my Self to be.
> In Kuan Yin's vitality,
> I claim my immortality.

6. Why have I done anything on earth? When I descended to the 48th level, I took on these illusions that are like veils that I put on. I saw life through these veils, they were distorting and coloring my vision.

> O Kuan Yin, your alchemy,
> with miracles you set me free.
> As I forgive, I am forgiven,
> by guilt I am no longer driven.

> In Kuan Yin's sweet melody,
> I am set free my Self to be.
> In Kuan Yin's vitality,
> I claim my immortality.

7. Why did I do what I did? Did *I,* the Conscious You seeing itself as a formless being, do what I did? Nay! I, the Conscious You, did what I did, not by seeing myself as a formless being but seeing myself as a being who had form based on these illusions I had taken on. Was it actually *me,* as I really am, the formless being, or was it a separate self that I had created in order to descend into physical embodiment?

> O Kuan Yin, all worries gone,
> with nothing done, no thing undone.
> Through separate self I will not do,
> and thus I rest, all one with you.

> In Kuan Yin's sweet melody,
> I am set free my Self to be.
> In Kuan Yin's vitality,
> I claim my immortality.

8. In order to descend to the 48th level and take embodiment, I had to create these separate selves, the soul vehicle, my three higher bodies. There comes a point on the spiritual path where I need to deal with this.

O Kuan Yin, your sanity,
now sets me free from vanity.
For truly, what is that to me;
I just let go and follow thee.

**In Kuan Yin's sweet melody,
I am set free my Self to be.
In Kuan Yin's vitality,
I claim my immortality.**

9. If I really am the Conscious You, if I really am a formless being, then I am not any of my separate selves. I have only identified myself as these separate selves because I have gone inside of them and I was looking through that filter.

O Kuan Yin, so sweet the sound,
that emanates from holy ground.
As I let go of ego's chore,
I find myself on farther shore.

**In Kuan Yin's sweet melody,
I am set free my Self to be.
In Kuan Yin's vitality,
I claim my immortality.**

Part 5

1. Now, that I am beginning to get a feel that I am a formless being, it is time for me to step back and say: "So I did something when I first came to earth. It was done in complete innocence with the best of intentions of helping other people. I was hammered down by the fallen beings and I reacted to this by creating this separate self that feels that I was wrong for coming to this planet. I formulated this self and then, after I had created this self, I started making decisions through that self."

O Kuan Yin, what sacred name,
fill me now with Mercy's Flame.

In giving mercy I am free,
forgiving all is magic key.

**In Kuan Yin's sweet melody,
I am set free my Self to be.
In Kuan Yin's vitality,
I claim my immortality.**

2. I was given the impression that when I expressed my true being, I was wrong. I decided: "I cannot express my true being" so I started to make all of these decisions to avoid being proven wrong again. The overall goal for this self is to not be wrong again so I made decisions based on this.

O Kuan Yin, I now let go,
of all attachments here below.
All pent-up feelings I release,
free from emotional disease.

**In Kuan Yin's sweet melody,
I am set free my Self to be.
In Kuan Yin's vitality,
I claim my immortality.**

3. I can now say: "Yes I did something that was a mistake. From a traditional viewpoint, *I* did this, but from a higher viewpoint did *I* actually do this? Was it me, the formless being, who did this or was it actually a separate self that made the decision to do this? Who did it? Me or the separate self?"

O Kuan Yin, why must I feel,
that life falls short of my ideal?
All expectations I give up,
my mind is now an empty cup.

**In Kuan Yin's sweet melody,
I am set free my Self to be.
In Kuan Yin's vitality,
I claim my immortality.**

4. By pondering this question, I am starting to separate myself from that separate self. Separating my *Self* from the separate self. When I have done this, I realize: "I am not that separate self, I am more, I am a formless being."

> O Kuan Yin, transcend the past,
> as all resentment gone at last.
> From future nothing I expect,
> eternal now I won't reject.
>
> **In Kuan Yin's sweet melody,**
> **I am set free my Self to be.**
> **In Kuan Yin's vitality,**
> **I claim my immortality.**

5. I am willing to experience glimpses of this pure awareness, the sense of being conscious without being conscious of myself as a particular being or being conscious of a particular situation.

> O Kuan Yin, uplifting me,
> beyond Samsara's raging sea.
> All safe inside your Prajna boat,
> the farther shore no more remote.
>
> **In Kuan Yin's sweet melody,**
> **I am set free my Self to be.**
> **In Kuan Yin's vitality,**
> **I claim my immortality.**

6. I am not the separate self. If I am not the separate self, it follows that I did not do what the separate self did. If *I* did not do what the separate self did, why should *I* feel responsible for it?

> O Kuan Yin, your alchemy,
> with miracles you set me free.
> As I forgive, I am forgiven,
> by guilt I am no longer driven.

**In Kuan Yin's sweet melody,
I am set free my Self to be.
In Kuan Yin's vitality,
I claim my immortality.**

7. The fallen beings want me to feel that I made this terrible mistake in the past and that proves that I am bad, and I will be bad forever because I can never overcome it. From a certain perspective, I cannot change the fact that this *did* happen.

O Kuan Yin, all worries gone,
with nothing done, no thing undone.
Through separate self I will not do,
and thus I rest, all one with you.

**In Kuan Yin's sweet melody,
I am set free my Self to be.
In Kuan Yin's vitality,
I claim my immortality.**

8. Yet, I now say to the devil: "Okay devil, you are saying this happened, it cannot be undone. Why are you telling *me* this? *I* did not do it. It was that separate self but that separate self is not *me*."

O Kuan Yin, your sanity,
now sets me free from vanity.
For truly, what is that to me;
I just let go and follow thee.

**In Kuan Yin's sweet melody,
I am set free my Self to be.
In Kuan Yin's vitality,
I claim my immortality.**

9. "Yes, you are right, devil, I created that separate self. I fully take responsibility for creating that separate self. You know what's the wonderful thing about that, devil? What I have created, I can un-create. *You* have no power over that separate self. Or rather, you may have power to manipulate the separate self but you did not create it and you cannot un-create it—but *I*

can. I can let it die and guess what? I am letting it die and now, that self is no more. So why are you bothering me? Go somewhere else. Find someone else to bother who still has a separate self. Get thee behind me, Satan."

O Kuan Yin, so sweet the sound,
that emanates from holy ground.
As I let go of ego's chore,
I find myself on farther shore.

In Kuan Yin's sweet melody,
I am set free my Self to be.
In Kuan Yin's vitality,
I claim my immortality.

Sealing

In the name of the Divine Mother, I call to Mother Mary for the sealing of myself and all people in my circle of influence in the creative flow of the Divine Mother, the River of Life. I call for the multiplication of my calls by all representatives of the Divine Mother, so that we form the perfect figure-eight flow of "As Above, so below." Thus, I accept that this is fully manifest, because the mouth of the Lord, the Divine Mother that I AM, has spoken it. Amen.

15 | INVOKING FREEDOM FROM TAKING LIFE PERSONALLY

In the name I AM THAT I AM, Jesus Christ, I call to all representatives of the Divine Mother, especially Kuan Yin, to help me overcome the selves that make me take so many things personally, including…

[Make personal calls.]

Part 1

1. There is a phase on the spiritual path where I need to take responsibility for my self. Then, there comes that point where I need to step back, look at this from a different perspective and say: "Now, I actually need to stop taking responsibility."

> O Kuan Yin, what sacred name,
> fill me now with Mercy's Flame.

> In giving mercy I am free,
> forgiving all is magic key.
>
> **In Kuan Yin's sweet melody,**
> **I am set free my Self to be.**
> **In Kuan Yin's vitality,**
> **I claim my immortality.**

2. I am still being responsible because I am taking responsibility for having created the separate self, and I have also taken responsibility for letting it die. But when I have let a separate self die, I am no longer responsible for the actions taken by or through that separate self.

> O Kuan Yin, I now let go,
> of all attachments here below.
> All pent-up feelings I release,
> free from emotional disease.
>
> **In Kuan Yin's sweet melody,**
> **I am set free my Self to be.**
> **In Kuan Yin's vitality,**
> **I claim my immortality.**

3. I now tune in to the true Flame of Mercy and realize: "I need to have Mercy upon myself. I need to forgive myself totally and unconditionally for what I did in the past, even to the point where whatever I did in the past simply does not matter anymore."

> O Kuan Yin, why must I feel,
> that life falls short of my ideal?
> All expectations I give up,
> my mind is now an empty cup.
>
> **In Kuan Yin's sweet melody,**
> **I am set free my Self to be.**
> **In Kuan Yin's vitality,**
> **I claim my immortality.**

4. When I realize that it just does not matter, I can erase the image of having done it so even the memory of it is gone.

> O Kuan Yin, transcend the past,
> as all resentment gone at last.
> From future nothing I expect,
> eternal now I won't reject.
>
> **In Kuan Yin's sweet melody,**
> **I am set free my Self to be.**
> **In Kuan Yin's vitality,**
> **I claim my immortality.**

5. It can be difficult to erase the image until I have forgiven myself and tuned in to the Flame of Mercy, used the Flame of Mercy to erase the sense of guilt, shame and embarrassment.

> O Kuan Yin, uplifting me,
> beyond Samsara's raging sea.
> All safe inside your Prajna boat,
> the farther shore no more remote.
>
> **In Kuan Yin's sweet melody,**
> **I am set free my Self to be.**
> **In Kuan Yin's vitality,**
> **I claim my immortality.**

6. Kuan Yin, I invoke your Flame of Mercy to erase these kind of feelings. Kuan Yin, I tune in to your Being, and I ask you to help me experience this total forgiveness of myself where I say: "*I did not do this. I am a formless being and I did not do this!*"

> O Kuan Yin, your alchemy,
> with miracles you set me free.
> As I forgive, I am forgiven,
> by guilt I am no longer driven.
>
> **In Kuan Yin's sweet melody,**
> **I am set free my Self to be.**

> In Kuan Yin's vitality,
> I claim my immortality.

7. I now take what I have internalized about myself and apply this to other people. Other people did what they did because *they* were acting through a separate self.

> O Kuan Yin, all worries gone,
> with nothing done, no thing undone.
> Through separate self I will not do,
> and thus I rest, all one with you.
>
> **In Kuan Yin's sweet melody,
> I am set free my Self to be.
> In Kuan Yin's vitality,
> I claim my immortality.**

8. I do not need to forgive a separate self because it is not ultimately real, but I need to forgive all people who have harmed me. I need to have mercy upon them.

> O Kuan Yin, your sanity,
> now sets me free from vanity.
> For truly, what is that to me;
> I just let go and follow thee.
>
> **In Kuan Yin's sweet melody,
> I am set free my Self to be.
> In Kuan Yin's vitality,
> I claim my immortality.**

9. I realize that whatever they did to me, it was not the Conscious You in that person who did this, it was a separate self. Therefore, I can forgive, I can have mercy upon that person by not holding the image of them that they *are* the separate self, that they are the way that the separate self treated me. I erase this reaction of: "This is how that person is, you *are* that kind of person."

15 | Invoking freedom from taking life personally

O Kuan Yin, so sweet the sound,
that emanates from holy ground.
As I let go of ego's chore,
I find myself on farther shore.

**In Kuan Yin's sweet melody,
I am set free my Self to be.
In Kuan Yin's vitality,
I claim my immortality.**

Part 2

1. Kuan Yin, help me come to the point where I forgive the people who have harmed me. When I forgive another person, I am set free because as long as I am holding a certain image of another person, how can I be free?

O Kuan Yin, what sacred name,
fill me now with Mercy's Flame.
In giving mercy I am free,
forgiving all is magic key.

**In Kuan Yin's sweet melody,
I am set free my Self to be.
In Kuan Yin's vitality,
I claim my immortality.**

2. I can hold an image that has form of another person only if I have a self that has form that is holding that image. As the Conscious You, I cannot hold a specific image of another person. If I am truly in the Conscious You and have no separate selves, I do not have a preconceived image or impression of how that person is.

O Kuan Yin, I now let go,
of all attachments here below.
All pent-up feelings I release,
free from emotional disease.

**In Kuan Yin's sweet melody,
I am set free my Self to be.
In Kuan Yin's vitality,
I claim my immortality.**

3. Kuan Yin, I want to grow towards the stage where I do not have any preconceived images that I am carrying along with me. I am living in the now, in the sense that every now is new.

O Kuan Yin, why must I feel,
that life falls short of my ideal?
All expectations I give up,
my mind is now an empty cup.

**In Kuan Yin's sweet melody,
I am set free my Self to be.
In Kuan Yin's vitality,
I claim my immortality.**

4. I am not demanding that the person should live up to a certain image. I am not blaming the person for what happened in the past. I am meeting that person anew every time because I am allowing myself to be a new person every day.

O Kuan Yin, transcend the past,
as all resentment gone at last.
From future nothing I expect,
eternal now I won't reject.

**In Kuan Yin's sweet melody,
I am set free my Self to be.
In Kuan Yin's vitality,
I claim my immortality.**

5. When I get to the higher levels of consciousness, I wake up and look in the mirror and say: "Who is this person?" I am free to say: "Who do I want to be today?"

15 | Invoking freedom from taking life personally

O Kuan Yin, uplifting me,
beyond Samsara's raging sea.
All safe inside your Prajna boat,
the farther shore no more remote.

**In Kuan Yin's sweet melody,
I am set free my Self to be.
In Kuan Yin's vitality,
I claim my immortality.**

6. Kuan Yin, help me come to the point where I do not wake up with a pattern carried over from the day before that says: "This is how I have to be today! I *have* to be this way."

O Kuan Yin, your alchemy,
with miracles you set me free.
As I forgive, I am forgiven,
by guilt I am no longer driven.

**In Kuan Yin's sweet melody,
I am set free my Self to be.
In Kuan Yin's vitality,
I claim my immortality.**

7. Kuan Yin, help me gain more and more freedom, and also set other people free. Help me say: "You may act the same as you did yesterday but I am not going to react the same way I reacted yesterday. I am not going to act as you expect me to act. I am going be free to choose: 'Who do I want to be today?'"

O Kuan Yin, all worries gone,
with nothing done, no thing undone.
Through separate self I will not do,
and thus I rest, all one with you.

**In Kuan Yin's sweet melody,
I am set free my Self to be.
In Kuan Yin's vitality,
I claim my immortality.**

8. When I have forgiven myself and others, I realize: "Nobody ever did anything to me." I will monitor myself, and if I sense an objection to this statement, I will know there is a separate self that I need to overcome.

> O Kuan Yin, your sanity,
> now sets me free from vanity.
> For truly, what is that to me;
> I just let go and follow thee.
>
> **In Kuan Yin's sweet melody,**
> **I am set free my Self to be.**
> **In Kuan Yin's vitality,**
> **I claim my immortality.**

9. I need to stop taking responsibility for my actions, but I also need to stop taking responsibility for other people's reactions to me. The fallen beings did what they did to me because they had separate selves, and therefore I say: "Oh, but that means they weren't actually doing this to *me* because they were just acting based on their separate selves. If somebody else had been in my position, they would have done the same to that person, so that means it is not actually *personal* against me. It is just that I created a separate self that took this personally."

> O Kuan Yin, so sweet the sound,
> that emanates from holy ground.
> As I let go of ego's chore,
> I find myself on farther shore.
>
> **In Kuan Yin's sweet melody,**
> **I am set free my Self to be.**
> **In Kuan Yin's vitality,**
> **I claim my immortality.**

15 | Invoking freedom from taking life personally

Part 3

1. Kuan Yin, help me identify that in my being is a separate self that reacts. Whenever a certain thing happens to me, I take it very personally that I have made this mistake and therefore I should feel a certain way.

> O Kuan Yin, what sacred name,
> fill me now with Mercy's Flame.
> In giving mercy I am free,
> forgiving all is magic key.
>
> **In Kuan Yin's sweet melody,**
> **I am set free my Self to be.**
> **In Kuan Yin's vitality,**
> **I claim my immortality.**

2. This is just a separate self, like all of the other separate selves. Because it is the self that takes things personally, it will try to make me take it personally that I have this self that makes me take everything personally.

> O Kuan Yin, I now let go,
> of all attachments here below.
> All pent-up feelings I release,
> free from emotional disease.
>
> **In Kuan Yin's sweet melody,**
> **I am set free my Self to be.**
> **In Kuan Yin's vitality,**
> **I claim my immortality.**

3. Kuan Yin, help me step back twice and see that this is a separate self that made me feel bad about having all the other separate selves and about anything I have done. Yet, it is just a separate self.

> O Kuan Yin, why must I feel,
> that life falls short of my ideal?
> All expectations I give up,
> my mind is now an empty cup.

> In Kuan Yin's sweet melody,
> I am set free my Self to be.
> In Kuan Yin's vitality,
> I claim my immortality.

4. The self that takes everything personally was created in reaction to other people blaming me. I realize that they were not blaming *me*. They were acting out their own unresolved psychology. Whatever anybody has ever done to me, they were acting out their own unresolved psychology.

> O Kuan Yin, transcend the past,
> as all resentment gone at last.
> From future nothing I expect,
> eternal now I won't reject.

> In Kuan Yin's sweet melody,
> I am set free my Self to be.
> In Kuan Yin's vitality,
> I claim my immortality.

5. Whatever anybody ever did to me that was negative, they were acting out their own unresolved psychology. If they were acting out their unresolved psychology and blaming me, why do I have to accept that blame and take it personally and say: "Oh, I must have been the one who upset them."

> O Kuan Yin, uplifting me,
> beyond Samsara's raging sea.
> All safe inside your Prajna boat,
> the farther shore no more remote.

> In Kuan Yin's sweet melody,
> I am set free my Self to be.
> In Kuan Yin's vitality,
> I claim my immortality.

6. I did not create those people's separate selves. I am not responsible for them, therefore I do not need to take it personally. I do not need to feel responsible for it.

> O Kuan Yin, your alchemy,
> with miracles you set me free.
> As I forgive, I am forgiven,
> by guilt I am no longer driven.
>
> **In Kuan Yin's sweet melody,
> I am set free my Self to be.
> In Kuan Yin's vitality,
> I claim my immortality.**

7. I recognize that it was not personal against me. They had a separate self that made them feel bad and they had another separate self that caused them to think that it was not their fault they were feeling bad. It was something I did and therefore that separate self was directing blame at me.

> O Kuan Yin, all worries gone,
> with nothing done, no thing undone.
> Through separate self I will not do,
> and thus I rest, all one with you.
>
> **In Kuan Yin's sweet melody,
> I am set free my Self to be.
> In Kuan Yin's vitality,
> I claim my immortality.**

8. If it had not been me, and somebody else had been there, they would have directed the blame at that other person. It is not personal towards me. It is personal *for them,* what they are directing out. It does not mean that I have to take it in and make it personal *for me.*

> O Kuan Yin, your sanity,
> now sets me free from vanity.
> For truly, what is that to me;
> I just let go and follow thee.
>
> **In Kuan Yin's sweet melody,
> I am set free my Self to be.
> In Kuan Yin's vitality,
> I claim my immortality.**

9. I now say: "Well, this means that nobody ever did anything to *me*." Nobody ever really was angry with me or blaming me. It was simply their own unresolved psychology that they directed at me.

> O Kuan Yin, so sweet the sound,
> that emanates from holy ground.
> As I let go of ego's chore,
> I find myself on farther shore.
>
> **In Kuan Yin's sweet melody,**
> **I am set free my Self to be.**
> **In Kuan Yin's vitality,**
> **I claim my immortality.**

Part 4

1. It was not personal against me when they blamed me but I still felt bad about it. But did *they* make me feel bad about it? No. I felt bad about it because I have a separate self that I created in the past that is causing me to feel bad in this particular type of situation.

> O Kuan Yin, what sacred name,
> fill me now with Mercy's Flame.
> In giving mercy I am free,
> forgiving all is magic key.
>
> **In Kuan Yin's sweet melody,**
> **I am set free my Self to be.**
> **In Kuan Yin's vitality,**
> **I claim my immortality.**

2. Nobody ever did anything to me because the only thing that ever affected me was not what other people did, it was my reaction to it. It was my inner experience of what they did that affected me, not the outer action that they took.

> O Kuan Yin, I now let go,
> of all attachments here below.
> All pent-up feelings I release,
> free from emotional disease.
>
> **In Kuan Yin's sweet melody,
> I am set free my Self to be.
> In Kuan Yin's vitality,
> I claim my immortality.**

3. I realize there is a fundamental difference between what people did outside of my four lower bodies and what happens inside of my four lower bodies.

> O Kuan Yin, why must I feel,
> that life falls short of my ideal?
> All expectations I give up,
> my mind is now an empty cup.
>
> **In Kuan Yin's sweet melody,
> I am set free my Self to be.
> In Kuan Yin's vitality,
> I claim my immortality.**

4. There is no blame here. When I descended to the 48th level and was exposed to the aggression from the fallen beings, I could only react to that based on the 48th level of consciousness. Therefore, it was inevitable that I took it personally, that I created these separate selves to deal with it.

> O Kuan Yin, transcend the past,
> as all resentment gone at last.
> From future nothing I expect,
> eternal now I won't reject.
>
> **In Kuan Yin's sweet melody,
> I am set free my Self to be.
> In Kuan Yin's vitality,
> I claim my immortality.**

5. There is no reason to blame myself for having done it but when I recognize that I have done it, I take another kind of responsibility. I am not responsible for the actions I took through a separate self but I am responsible for creating the separate self.

> O Kuan Yin, uplifting me,
> beyond Samsara's raging sea.
> All safe inside your Prajna boat,
> the farther shore no more remote.
>
> **In Kuan Yin's sweet melody,**
> **I am set free my Self to be.**
> **In Kuan Yin's vitality,**
> **I claim my immortality.**

6. I did this based on the level of consciousness I had at the time but I have now risen to a higher level of consciousness. Therefore, I can look at that separate self and say: "I no longer need you because today I would not react that way. Today, I know more, I am more mature."

> O Kuan Yin, your alchemy,
> with miracles you set me free.
> As I forgive, I am forgiven,
> by guilt I am no longer driven.
>
> **In Kuan Yin's sweet melody,**
> **I am set free my Self to be.**
> **In Kuan Yin's vitality,**
> **I claim my immortality.**

7. I still have this self that I have carried with me for these many lifetimes but now it is time to see it, now it is time to dismiss it and thereby lock in to that Flame of Mercy, apply that Flame of Mercy and set myself free from the self that has form.

> O Kuan Yin, all worries gone,
> with nothing done, no thing undone.
> Through separate self I will not do,
> and thus I rest, all one with you.

> **In Kuan Yin's sweet melody,**
> **I am set free my Self to be.**
> **In Kuan Yin's vitality,**
> **I claim my immortality.**

8. I set myself free to be the formless being that I am. I realize that whatever people do to me, I do not have to react to it in a certain way anymore. I do not anymore have to react to it the way I used to react to it. In fact, whatever people do to me, I do not have to react to it.

> O Kuan Yin, your sanity,
> now sets me free from vanity.
> For truly, what is that to me;
> I just let go and follow thee.

> **In Kuan Yin's sweet melody,**
> **I am set free my Self to be.**
> **In Kuan Yin's vitality,**
> **I claim my immortality.**

9. There is a separate self that is very strong in the collective consciousness on earth. It says that when a certain person approaches me, I *have* to react, I *have* to respond. I cannot just ignore them.

> O Kuan Yin, so sweet the sound,
> that emanates from holy ground.
> As I let go of ego's chore,
> I find myself on farther shore.

> **In Kuan Yin's sweet melody,**
> **I am set free my Self to be.**
> **In Kuan Yin's vitality,**
> **I claim my immortality.**

Part 5

1. I have free will. The fact that I am in embodiment and meet certain people does not mean I *have* to react. If they throw something at me that I feel is not something I want to respond to, I am free *not* to respond.

> O Kuan Yin, what sacred name,
> fill me now with Mercy's Flame.
> In giving mercy I am free,
> forgiving all is magic key.
>
> **In Kuan Yin's sweet melody,**
> **I am set free my Self to be.**
> **In Kuan Yin's vitality,**
> **I claim my immortality.**

2. I am free to just walk away and not engage that person and their negativity. This is a right I have, and I am claiming that right, even if people label me as selfish.

> O Kuan Yin, I now let go,
> of all attachments here below.
> All pent-up feelings I release,
> free from emotional disease.
>
> **In Kuan Yin's sweet melody,**
> **I am set free my Self to be.**
> **In Kuan Yin's vitality,**
> **I claim my immortality.**

3. Kuan Yin, help me identify certain people in my sphere of influence that are always trying to engage me in a negative pattern. It has the purpose of engaging my attention so they can take my energy. I now decide: "I am not going to respond to this anymore."

> O Kuan Yin, why must I feel,
> that life falls short of my ideal?

15 | Invoking freedom from taking life personally

> All expectations I give up,
> my mind is now an empty cup.
>
> **In Kuan Yin's sweet melody,**
> **I am set free my Self to be.**
> **In Kuan Yin's vitality,**
> **I claim my immortality.**

4. There are some people I cannot ever satisfy because they are not interested in changing, they are just interested in engaging me. I have a right to say: "There are people I cannot help and I am choosing not to engage with them. I am not even responding to them."

> O Kuan Yin, transcend the past,
> as all resentment gone at last.
> From future nothing I expect,
> eternal now I won't reject.
>
> **In Kuan Yin's sweet melody,**
> **I am set free my Self to be.**
> **In Kuan Yin's vitality,**
> **I claim my immortality.**

5. If somebody approaches me, wanting to engage me in a negative pattern and I do not respond to it, I am being merciful towards that person. Mercy is when I do not hold a fixed image of myself or other people.

> O Kuan Yin, uplifting me,
> beyond Samsara's raging sea.
> All safe inside your Prajna boat,
> the farther shore no more remote.
>
> **In Kuan Yin's sweet melody,**
> **I am set free my Self to be.**
> **In Kuan Yin's vitality,**
> **I claim my immortality.**

6. When a person approaches me in a negative state of mind, I can say: "I am not going to respond to this because if I respond the way the person

expects, it will only validate that separate self and the person will not be able to see it. He will just be pulled into endlessly repeating the pattern."

> O Kuan Yin, your alchemy,
> with miracles you set me free.
> As I forgive, I am forgiven,
> by guilt I am no longer driven.
>
> **In Kuan Yin's sweet melody,**
> **I am set free my Self to be.**
> **In Kuan Yin's vitality,**
> **I claim my immortality.**

7. If I do not respond the way he expects, then, perhaps, he will look at his reaction and he will be surprised by this. He will have an opportunity to look at his reaction and wonder why this happened. *That* could potentially set the person free.

> O Kuan Yin, all worries gone,
> with nothing done, no thing undone.
> Through separate self I will not do,
> and thus I rest, all one with you.
>
> **In Kuan Yin's sweet melody,**
> **I am set free my Self to be.**
> **In Kuan Yin's vitality,**
> **I claim my immortality.**

8. If I respond the way he expects, it is guaranteed not to set him free, but if I respond the way he does not expect, there is at least a small possibility that it might help him—and this is mercy.

> O Kuan Yin, your sanity,
> now sets me free from vanity.
> For truly, what is that to me;
> I just let go and follow thee.
>
> **In Kuan Yin's sweet melody,**
> **I am set free my Self to be.**

**In Kuan Yin's vitality,
I claim my immortality.**

9. I choose to not hold any fixed images of how I should respond to those people, even if I have known them for my entire lifetime. I can choose to do something I have never done before. I can choose a new response that is different from my previous response and *that* is merciful.

> O Kuan Yin, so sweet the sound,
> that emanates from holy ground.
> As I let go of ego's chore,
> I find myself on farther shore.

**In Kuan Yin's sweet melody,
I am set free my Self to be.
In Kuan Yin's vitality,
I claim my immortality.**

Part 6

1. Kuan Yin, help me see if I have a separate self that blocks my vision of the need for on-going self-transcendence. This self thinks that the entire purpose of finding the teachings is to validate the self's image of superiority. I am willing to see this self, even if it has caused me to be judgmental of others.

> O Kuan Yin, what sacred name,
> fill me now with Mercy's Flame.
> In giving mercy I am free,
> forgiving all is magic key.

**In Kuan Yin's sweet melody,
I am set free my Self to be.
In Kuan Yin's vitality,
I claim my immortality.**

2. The trap of judgmentalness is that it is based on a sense of superiority. If I come to see that I have been judgmental, I might look at this through the same state of consciousness, which means that I am going to start judging *myself* as harshly as I have judged other people.

> O Kuan Yin, I now let go,
> of all attachments here below.
> All pent-up feelings I release,
> free from emotional disease.
>
> **In Kuan Yin's sweet melody,**
> **I am set free my Self to be.**
> **In Kuan Yin's vitality,**
> **I claim my immortality.**

3. Kuan Yin, I know you hold the Flame of Mercy for earth. There is no human attribute that the Flame of Mercy cannot consume and help me overcome. Even if I have been too judgmental of others, I will not hesitate to approach you.

> O Kuan Yin, why must I feel,
> that life falls short of my ideal?
> All expectations I give up,
> my mind is now an empty cup.
>
> **In Kuan Yin's sweet melody,**
> **I am set free my Self to be.**
> **In Kuan Yin's vitality,**
> **I claim my immortality.**

4. Kuan Yin, I know you will not judge me as I am judging myself. Help me overcome the sense of superiority, the sense of judging myself, and see that it is a separate self.

> O Kuan Yin, transcend the past,
> as all resentment gone at last.
> From future nothing I expect,
> eternal now I won't reject.

> **In Kuan Yin's sweet melody,**
> **I am set free my Self to be.**
> **In Kuan Yin's vitality,**
> **I claim my immortality.**

5. There is a separate self that gives me the need to feel superior, there is a separate self that gives me the need to judge, and those two work together. Yet I can overcome the combination when I have the antidote, which is the Flame of Mercy.

> O Kuan Yin, uplifting me,
> beyond Samsara's raging sea.
> All safe inside your Prajna boat,
> the farther shore no more remote.

> **In Kuan Yin's sweet melody,**
> **I am set free my Self to be.**
> **In Kuan Yin's vitality,**
> **I claim my immortality.**

6. I see that when I first found the path, I had a self that had a strong need for outer validation. I am not going to overcome this unless I start having mercy upon myself. I lock in to the Flame of Mercy, and I realize that all of these outer things are unreal. Because they are unreal, they do not actually matter.

> O Kuan Yin, your alchemy,
> with miracles you set me free.
> As I forgive, I am forgiven,
> by guilt I am no longer driven.

> **In Kuan Yin's sweet melody,**
> **I am set free my Self to be.**
> **In Kuan Yin's vitality,**
> **I claim my immortality.**

7. Kuan Yin, help me look at something that has happened on earth, something I have done and say: "So what! It does not matter, it just does

not matter." Help me realize that compared to the Flame of Mercy, which is very real, all of this human nonsense on earth is unreal and utterly insignificant.

> O Kuan Yin, all worries gone,
> with nothing done, no thing undone.
> Through separate self I will not do,
> and thus I rest, all one with you.
>
> **In Kuan Yin's sweet melody,**
> **I am set free my Self to be.**
> **In Kuan Yin's vitality,**
> **I claim my immortality.**

8. Kuan Yin, I am accepting your Flame of Mercy to help me stop taking life personally. I am asking you: "Kuan Yin, help me see this. Kuan Yin, help me experience the Flame of Mercy, help me gain a perspective, help me see this as you see it. Help me have that frame of reference of experiencing the reality of the Flame of Mercy and the unreality of the human condition."

> O Kuan Yin, your sanity,
> now sets me free from vanity.
> For truly, what is that to me;
> I just let go and follow thee.
>
> **In Kuan Yin's sweet melody,**
> **I am set free my Self to be.**
> **In Kuan Yin's vitality,**
> **I claim my immortality.**

9. Kuan Yin, help me go into a neutral frame of mind and commune with you directly in my own heart. I will meet you with a new view. I set you free, and I set myself free. I meet you anew and I experience your Presence with me.

> O Kuan Yin, so sweet the sound,
> that emanates from holy ground.

As I let go of ego's chore,
I find myself on farther shore.

**In Kuan Yin's sweet melody,
I am set free my Self to be.
In Kuan Yin's vitality,
I claim my immortality.**

Sealing

In the name of the Divine Mother, I call to Mother Mary for the sealing of myself and all people in my circle of influence in the creative flow of the Divine Mother, the River of Life. I call for the multiplication of my calls by all representatives of the Divine Mother, so that we form the perfect figure-eight flow of "As Above, so below." Thus, I accept that this is fully manifest, because the mouth of the Lord, the Divine Mother that I AM, has spoken it. Amen.

16 | YOU ARE NOT A SLAVE OF TIME

I AM the Ascended Master Gautama Buddha. What I desire to expound upon in this discourse is a certain variety of topics that may seem unrelated but are not. Let me begin by talking about the fact that it is absolutely necessary on the path to Christhood, on the path to Buddhahood, that you understand that the self that you had when you first found the teachings and awakened to the existence of a spiritual path, that self cannot bring you to Christhood or Buddhahood.

Now, you have been giving this latest invocation on the primal self where you have learned that the primal self must die and you are reborn into a new self [From the book *Healing Your Spiritual Traumas*]. This is, of course, a perfectly valid process, but do not put yourself into a state where you think that even if you feel that your primal self has died, that the new self you are born into is the self that you will carry with you until you ascend. Certainly, do not fall into the illusion of thinking that it is this self that will ascend.

Ascending with all karma balanced

We have in this dispensation given you some teachings on the process of the ascension on what we might call "the psychology of the ascension" that are far beyond what we have given in any previous dispensation. This is not to say that the teachings given previously were invalid or could not take people to the ascension. There were some people who in past lives had come so close to the ascension point that the teachings given previously could take them those last steps until they were ready to ascend, but there were not so many people in that category. You will know that in the last dispensation it was said that you could ascend with just 51% of your karma balanced. I will say that there are very, very few people who could take the teachings we have given previously and come to the point where they had balanced 100% of their karma (which also means resolving your psychology) and therefore ascend from earth, being, so to speak, "clear," clear of all encumbrances and therefore becoming immediately an ascended master.

However, our goal with the teachings we have given now, that go so much deeper into the psychology, is to enable a larger group of people to balance their karma, resolve their psychology and then have some time in this state before they take leave of the physical body and ascend from the planet. You need to recognize that progressive revelation is *progressive*. This has, of course, many ramifications but one of them is that certain things that were said previously were correct enough but they were not the full story, they were a limited view, a simplified view of the topic.

So many people from previous dispensations have not asked the question: "If an ascended master is a being who has balanced all karma and if a person ascends (so to speak) with 51% of the karma balanced, does that mean that this person now becomes an ascended master after 'ascending?'" It was not asked: "If a person has balanced more than 51 percent of their karma and therefore does not have to come back into physical embodiment, has that person truly ascended and become an ascended master?" The obvious answer to the question is "No!" How do you become an ascended master if you still have unbalanced karma and unresolved psychology from earth? It simply is not logical, my beloved, that this can happen. Therefore, it needs to be recognized, by some of you at least, that this was a simplified teaching, not the full understanding of the topic. Naturally my beloved, you need to have resolved everything you need to resolve on earth before you can actually ascend and become an ascended master. There are, of course, some people who have only the karma left they (as Mother Mary has explained) have with themselves, which basically means that what they have left is unresolved psychology and they can resolve this without being in physical embodiment.

Why was the dispensation given that you can ascend with 51% of your karma? It was precisely because there were so few people ascending. It was so difficult, given the density of the collective consciousness, to ascend with 100% of your karma balanced, your psychology resolved. In order to speed up the process of raising the collective consciousness, the dispensation was given that if you have balanced (resolved) 51%, you do not have to come back into physical embodiment. You can go into a special program in the etheric realm where you are given help to resolve whatever you have that is unresolved. This can more quickly bring you to the point where you can fully ascend than if you had to go through the process of being born in a physical body, growing to adulthood before you were able to embrace the spiritual path and follow it more consciously. This sped up the process whereby some could resolve whatever was unresolved and then ascend more quickly than taking embodiment again.

We have moved into a new cycle and we now aim to help a much larger group of people go through the process of resolving all of their psychology while you are still in embodiment. This is, first of all, directed at avatars, but it is a teaching that is perfectly valid and useful for the original inhabitants of the earth who have reached a certain level of spiritual growth. It is useful for those who are not technically avatars but may have come from other planets that ascended and they were not able to ascend with their planet or with the rest of the lifestreams on their planet.

The essence of the path is letting selves die

This, of course, is the challenge we have put before you. You need to recognize here that when you go through a certain phase, for example, you uncover your primal self as an avatar and you let that self die, then you are born into a new sense of self. There were certainly selves that you created after you created the primal self. You still have a certain view of yourself, a certain view of earth, and that means that when you create a new self after you overcome the primal self, then that new self is not necessarily the highest possible. Or rather, it is *not* the highest possible. As you go up to higher and higher levels of consciousness, there will come points where you need to step back, look at your current sense of self and again let it die so that you can be reborn again. You can be reborn in Christ, you can be reborn in Buddha. Perhaps you are beginning to recognize that the essence of the spiritual path is to come to see that you have a certain sense of self that is limited and you let it die. Now, we have so far talked about specific selves, we have talked about these reactionary selves that are created in reaction to a specific situation on earth. When you find the spiritual path, for example, you find an ascended master teaching (you start to study it, you start to practice it, you perhaps come into an organization that has a certain organizational culture), you are actually creating a new self and you do this all the time, not only in this lifetime but in past lifetimes. You create certain selves that are not, strictly speaking, in a reaction to a particular traumatic situation. There are actually selves created in reaction to the understanding, the awareness that you currently have. You are rising to a higher awareness, you create a new self based on that higher awareness. When you come to the higher levels of the path, you need to become conscious of this process. For a long time the process is unconscious. You are actually not realizing that you are creating a new self.

There comes a point where you need to become conscious of this and you need to see: "What have I gone through since I became consciously aware of the spiritual path? What are my experiences, what are the insights I have gained?" You can just take sort of a look at your path up until this point and you can see: "What have I gone through, what beliefs have I come to accept based on the teachings I have followed, the organizations I have been involved with? What kind of a self have I created as a result of this?" As Kuan Yin said, some people come into the teachings, they have a desire for a sense of superiority and they may never let go of the self they have built that feels superior because they are ascended master students. Now, most of you do not have this issue but you have built other selves.

Again, there is no blame here. It is a natural part of growth that you build these new selves based on your awareness and your desire, what to express, what to experience, what to do here on earth. We have all done the same thing. I am simply making you aware that many of you are at the point where you are ready to become conscious of this. Look at yourself and consider what kind of self you have built so far and whether that self is actually based on a limited view, a limited understanding. Some of you will find, when you do this, that you realize you actually have a self that is built on a certain view of the path, a certain view of yourself that you had years ago. Now, you have in some part of your mind actually attained a higher understanding, higher insights, a higher view, a higher perspective. Therefore, you need to come to see that the self that you built during a certain stage of your path is no longer helping you grow. It is actually in a way limiting your growth, it is holding you back because you have an outdated view, especially of your abilities.

Selves that limit your abilities

Now, we have talked in several ways about how you need to go through a phase where you overcome this compulsory need to do something on earth. It is, of course, perfectly necessary to go through this stage but there also comes a point where, when you have gone through that phase, then there will come that point where you realize that what you are really here for is to be yourself, to express yourself. Expressing yourself means that you are allowing your I AM Presence to express itself through you because you realize that being yourself actually means being in some state of oneness with your I AM Presence. Then, you can benefit from realizing that you have, going all the way back to your birth trauma, built certain selves that had a certain view of what you *can* do on earth, what you are *allowed* to do on earth, what you are *supposed* to do on earth and these selves could have been refined or reinforced by finding a spiritual path.

We have said before that when you find a spiritual path, you see yourself as a spiritual student. We have said that there is a long phase of growth where the concept of a spiritual path is helpful and constructive. If you, for the rest of your time in embodiment, continue to see yourself as a spiritual student, then there comes a point where this is no longer constructive because the concept of a path implies: "I am at a certain level, there is a higher level that is possible, but I have not yet reached it." You may say, for example: "I am at the 88th level of consciousness, there are 144 levels, I am not at the 144th level." This in itself is not really problematic because, obviously, it will take some time before you reach the 144th level and some of you may not reach it until shortly before you are ready to exit the planet. Nevertheless, between the 88th level and the 144th level, there are certain stages that we have named, for example, Christhood. There could come a point where you have in your mind an image that you are a spiritual student who is moving towards Christhood but you are not there yet. If you forever continue to hold on to that sense of self, then how will you ever be the Christ in embodiment?

Now my beloved, there are many examples of ascended master students who have heard about the path to Christhood and who have decided with their outer minds, with their outer ambitions: "Yes, I am already the Living Christ." Now, they go out and they think they have to do whatever they have to do: pronounce the judgement of the fallen beings or awaken other people or blue-ray them or whatever. This is not what I am talking about. I am talking about that there comes a point where you have used these tools that we have given you. You have sincerely striven to overcome the primal self and many other selves. Therefore, you have reached a certain level but you are still holding on to a sense of self that you created at a previous level. At that previous level it was valid to see that there was a goal of Christhood but you were not there. There comes a certain point where, now you have actually reached a certain level. Say for example, you are at the 110th level. There is a level of Christhood that corresponds to that. There is a level of Christhood that corresponds to each of the levels from the 97th and onwards, (although there comes a point where we might say that the levels of Christhood gradually blend into the levels of Buddhahood). If you have reached the 110th level but you are still holding on to an image you created at the 95th level, that image is holding you back.

Acknowledging your Christhood

There comes a point where you need to recognize, as this messenger was willing to recognize at some point, that he had reached a certain level of Christhood. This did not mean that he went into any delusion that he had reached the ultimate level, but he had reached some level and it was necessary to be realistic and acknowledge this and it is the same thing for many of you. You have actually reached a certain level on the spiritual path but you have not yet dared to acknowledge it because you are still holding on to the sense of self that you created several levels below where you are at right now.

Yes, of course, there is always the risk that you can do this too early where you are not quite ready, but we need to run that risk because it is actually more common that you do not acknowledge your progress. What I am saying here is (again, building on what Kuan Yin said) that some people build a sense of self when they first find the teachings and they think that they have to carry it with them. This is a complete and very dangerous illusion. There is nobody who has ever ascended who ascended with the self they had in the beginning of their last embodiment when they first found the spiritual path. There is nobody who has ever ascended with the sense of self you have when you reach the 144th level, because the last act before the ascension is that you let that last self die and overcome the last illusion.

The process of the ascension is actually a process of letting one self after another die and be willing to be reborn into a higher sense of self. In order to let a certain self die, you must be willing to question the very, we might say *illusion* but even the *awareness* that the self is based on. You might say that at the 88th level you have gained a certain insight that you did not have at the 87th level. It is a *valid* insight. It is just not the *final* insight. If you build a sense of self based on that insight, you cannot really say that the insight is an illusion but if you think that it is some ultimate insight, or some ultimate self that you have built, then that certainly *is* an illusion. In a sense, you can say that each time you step up to the next level of consciousness, there is a self that dies and another self that is born, but you do not necessarily have to be aware of this for every step. There does come certain points where you do need to step back, look at your sense of self and one of them is when you begin to acknowledge that you have achieved, you have attained, some level of Christhood. Obviously, the self you had was based on thinking that Christhood was somewhere out there in the future at a higher level and so that self has to die. In order to let it die, you have to see it and see the limitations of it.

Like Kuan Yin said, if there are people that have built this sense of superiority, it might be very difficult for them to question the self that they have. That is why we unfortunately see some ascended master students who get stuck in a certain sense of self and simply cannot move on for the rest of that lifetime. We would very much like to see that this did not happen to anyone who has found or heard about these teachings. Can this be guaranteed? Of course not, but at least it has been stated. The teaching has been given and we must, then, set the teaching free and set the people free to do with it as they like.

The "mini guru" syndrome

Now, another topic that I wish to touch upon here is the whole concept of time. I said some remarks yesterday about time [See the last chapter of this book] but I wish to say a little bit more about this topic. You can take many different views on a topic like time. You can describe it in different ways. What I will give you here is merely one way, not the absolute or the final or the only way.

What is time? Well, in a certain sense, we can say that time has no objective existence. If you take the *My Lives* book, there are many, many important elements of that book but from the viewpoint of what I am talking about here, the most important element is given right in the introduction where it is said: "All people on earth are having a subjective experience. All problems on earth are caused by some people wanting to extend their subjective experience so that it seemingly becomes universal because other people have accepted these people's subjective experience over their own subjective experience."

This is what you see over and over again throughout history, most obviously exemplified in religions where someone is converted to a certain religion and now goes on a crusade to convert everyone else or kill those who will not be converted (in extreme cases). You see the same in ascended master students. I am not here just talking about wanting to convert other people to follow an ascended master teaching. I am actually talking about the fact that we sometimes see our students use a certain element of our teaching that they have found very important, that they have found did something, meant something to them, and now they take this and they want to get other people to accept this view.

There was once a student of the ascended masters who called this the "mini guru" syndrome, where people have a tendency (when they have been in a teaching for some time, they have created a hierarchy, they might have created a clique where they feel they are advanced students), to set themselves up as some kind of "mini guru" who is seeking to gather other students as a following who follow their particular interpretation and view of the teachings.

There is no blame here. It is inevitable that this will happen in any spiritual, religious movement. It is natural that certain more advanced students start teaching others. What I am talking about here is that many of these people have gone into this state of mind that is really the same state of mind you see in all religious movements when they are seeking to convert others. You see it among scientific materialists who are seeking to convert others. You go into this state of mind where you have convinced yourself that the way you look at the teachings, at life, at God, at science or whatever, is the ultimate or the only true one. Therefore, it is for other people's own good that they come to accept your view. Now, with all of the teachings we have given you, you should be able (and you are all *able* if you are *willing*) to step back and realize that no matter what level of consciousness you are at, even if you were at the 144th level of consciousness, you are still having an experience that is not absolute. It is not universal in the sense that it should apply to all people.

Even if you are at the 144th level of consciousness, it is not valid that you seek to get other people to have or to live their lives based on your experience. Now, it says in the introduction to the book that you can come to a point where you are no longer having, in a lower sense, a *subjective* experience but you are still having an *individual* experience, and the reason for this is simple. At the lower stages of awareness you are experiencing life through the outer self, which is a conglomerate of all of these separate selves. At the lower levels you have no connection to your I AM Presence. As you go higher on the path, you shed some of these outer selves. Your experience of life becomes less and less subjective, less and less colored by the separate selves, the consciousness of separation, the consciousness of duality. You become more and more in tune with your I AM Presence but your I AM Presence is not a *universal* being, it is an *individual* being.

Your I AM Presence experiences the situation on earth through that individuality. *Your* I AM Presence has an experience of earth that is different from the I AM Presence of another person and this is perfectly valid, perfectly in order. What I am saying here is this: There comes a point on the path where you need to make a shift and recognize that other people are not meant to have the same experience that you are having. They are meant to have their own experience. This does not mean that you cannot talk to other people and seek to help them or inspire them or whatever, but it does mean that there comes that point where you step up to that absolute respect for free will where you are not any more seeking to push your individual experience upon others.

This does not mean that you need to "shut up," as the popular saying goes, and not say anything to other people. It means that instead of trying to change their experience of life, you are sharing your own. There is a fundamental (I know that at some point it seems like there is no difference or that it is too subtle), there is a fundamental difference between pushing your experience onto others and then sharing your experience. The first one has an element of force, the second one does not. This is a challenge you need to pass, a test you need to pass, and you *can* pass it with the teachings you have.

Not all people want to escape suffering

There will come a point where you simply shed the self that gives you the desire because it is a self that was a reaction to conditions on earth. We have said, for example, that you saw that people are suffering. Before you came as an avatar, you suspected, you expected, that if you told people how to overcome suffering, they would accept your words and set themselves free from suffering. The reason for this is that you, as an avatar (based on your experience), you are willing to overcome your limitations and your suffering. If somebody tells you how to do it, you would be willing to do it and you expect that everyone else is the same way. This is, again, based on your experience. The expectation that other people will want to be free of their suffering, is logical on a natural planet but it is not applicable at all on an unnatural planet.

Why are some people on earth suffering? Well, because they have not had enough of the experience of suffering. Telling them that they should not be suffering and here is how you can stop suffering, just is not relevant for them. It is an attempt to push your subjective experience (that they should not be suffering) upon them. There will come a point where you work on these selves, where you just come to see this self. You let it go, you let go of the desire to get other people to live according to your view. When you have let go of this self, you can actually step back a little bit and realize that any time you feel a certain compulsion about how you relate to other people, anytime you feel a tension, it is because there is a self there. That self springs from this very attitude, this very desire to push your subjective experience upon others, to get them to live their lives according to your subjective experience instead of simply accepting that *your* subjective experience is perfectly valid for you, but *their* subjective experience is perfectly valid for them—whatever that experience is at their present stage.

It is actually never necessary or valid that you say: "My subjective experience would be better for other people. It would be better for them if they had my experience, or at least if they lived their lives according to my experience, rather than their own." It is *never* better for somebody else to have somebody else's subjective experience. It is always better for the person to have the subjective experience they are having because it is the only way they can grow.

Time is a subjective experience

I started out talking about time (some time ago) and then it seems like I got distracted into talking about separate selves and your subjective experience and pushing it upon others, but what did I say? I said time is a subjective experience; it is a product of a subjective experience. Time, as it is viewed by human beings on earth, is not an objective reality. It is an entirely subjective experience, of course created collectively over a long period of time. People have put a lot of mental-emotional-identity energy into creating the current view of time that can be seen as a separate self, existing in the collective consciousness. They think time is very linear, that there is nothing you can do about time. You cannot go back in time, you cannot change the past. As we have said, the fallen beings want you to think that you cannot just escape the mistakes you have made in the past.

Now, there is a certain experience of time that has become very common on earth and why is that? It is actually because the fallen beings had a desire to take their subjective experience of time and export it, project it upon all people on earth and they have been largely successful in doing this. That is why there is actually some validity in the books and movies out there that challenge people's view of time. Even though you cannot build a physical time machine, even movies that portray someone building a physical time machine and going back in time, it helps somehow challenge this very rigid view of time that people have.

Now, the question is: Yes, there is that collective view of time but you are a mature spiritual student. You have done a lot of work. You have separated yourself from the collective consciousness to a large degree. There comes a point where you need to consider: "What is my subjective view of time, my personal view of time?" Of course, on a personal level you have that view that in the past you did something and this created certain consequences that can carry on into what you see as the future. You have a view that your present situation is to some degree affected by your past. You even have spiritual teachings that will reinforce this view in the sense that you have made karma in past lives and this is affecting your situation now. Many, many people have felt that if something bad happened to them: "Oh, it must be a result of my karma."

A higher view of karma

In many cases, my beloved, what happens to you as a spiritual student is not the result of your personal karma. It is the result of the fact that you are embodied on a very dense, unnatural planet that is very chaotic. There are many things that can happen that are perpetrated by other people, by their actions, by their state of consciousness, by a certain collective karma but it is not your individual, personal karma. That is why, as I said, there can actually come a point where you can benefit from stepping back and looking at the view of yourself you created based on the spiritual teachings, even based on the teaching on karma. You may have built a view that: "Yes, I have karma from past lives. If something bad happens to me, it is because of that karma and I need to give decrees and invocations or practice yoga or whatever, in order to transmute that karma so I no longer have it." What if you had been on the spiritual path for a certain amount of time and you have actually invoked enough violet flame to transmute the energy that makes up your karma? Does that mean you have balanced your karma? Well, you have transformed the energy. That is one aspect of karma but what have other masters told you about these images that you hold from the past?

If you have the image of yourself that you have not balanced your karma, then you have not actually become free of your karma. Perhaps there is a self that really does not want to acknowledge that you do not have karma anymore because the self is afraid that something bad could happen to you, and how would you explain it if you could not explain it as a result of your karma? You might be thrown into a crisis of thinking why would God allow something bad to happen to you if you do not have karma. You think that the reason bad things happen to you as a result of your karma is that you are being punished for the bad things you did in the past. Many people have this view.

You can step up, based on the teachings we have given you, my beloved, to realize that many of you have actually completed the process that is described by many spiritual movements, even eastern versions of karma, of balancing your karma. If something bad happens to you, it is not the result of your personal karma, it is not a result of a mistake you made, but the fact that you live on a planet that is unnatural, very dense, very chaotic. You cannot predict with certainty, as other masters have said, exactly what is happening. Take the analogy of the difference between a rifle bullet and a cloud of pellets fired by a shotgun. You cannot predict the exact trajectory of one pellet from before it was fired to when it hits the target. It is impossible because there are many pellets that interfere with each other, bounce against each other, deform each other and therefore change the trajectory.

The universe is not a machine

The same thing right now. You cannot take a person and say this person has balanced her karma, therefore nothing bad should ever happen to that person. Because you are still living in a physical body in a certain environment, there is a very, very complex pattern of energy waves created by other people, sustained by other people. It simply is not possible, even for an ascended master, to predict exactly what events might happen for the rest of your lifetime. Things are so chaotic, so unpredictable, there are so many of what scientists call "hidden variables." For an ascended master, the variables are not hidden. It is just, my beloved, that the universe is not a clockwork, is not a machine. You can have a situation where, as an ascended master, we can see all of the factors involved with a particular situation but we do not know exactly what a person is going to choose. We can, of course, see the probability that he is going to choose the same thing he has chosen for the past fifty embodiments. We cannot *know* and therefore we cannot predict exactly how the rest of your life is going to form. It depends on your choices and choices of many other people and how this very, very complex pattern of energy waves interacts, interferes, all of these interference patterns.

It is not possible to say on a planet like earth that if you have no karma, nothing bad can happen to you for the rest of this lifetime. It simply is not possible. Therefore, you need to let go of this self. You need to accept: "I have balanced my karma," and then you need to accept that: "Because I am living on a planet like earth, something may indeed happen to me that is not a result of my karma. But I will not blame God, I will not blame myself, I will not blame other people. I will accept it for what it is, make the best of it and move on."

This requires a certain shift and this is also part of coming to the point where you accept yourself as a Christed being. My beloved, when Jesus started in his last embodiment, he had a certain sense of self. He gradually built on to and refined that sense of self so that when he started his public mission, he did it with a certain sense of self. Based on that sense of self, he had certain expectations like he has talked about himself, about nothing bad should really happen to him. If nothing else, God could send angels to perform a miracle and save him from the fallen beings. He has explained that this was the self he had to allow to die when he was hanging on the cross.

You do not have to wait until the end of your time in embodiment to let go of these selves. You can begin to do this already now. You can come to a point where you actually accept that you have reached a certain level of Christhood and if something "bad" happens to you, it may be part of your path to Christhood to go through this experience, to demonstrate how you can deal with this in a higher, more non-attached manner. How you can deal with this experience without having the primal self or other selves that you have overcome.

Time is and is not

So, what is time? Why have I said that time is not? Well, because it does not have this objective existence, at least not the way people see it. Now, to illustrate this, let me talk about something we have hinted at before. Traditionally, geometry says there are three dimensions in space: length, width, height. You have the traditional coordinate system with three axis and you are talking about a three-dimensional world where you can move. You can walk here on the floor, back and forth, but you can also walk up to another floor, if there was one. You can walk down. You can move in these dimensions.

Now, traditionally scientists say that time is the fourth dimension but they also say that time is entirely linear so you cannot go backwards in time. Of course, you cannot skip ahead and go into the future. The reality is that from the ascended perspective, we see that time is just like the other dimensions in the sense that it is not linear. You can move back and forth in time. Imagine that you are standing on a large square, a large flat area, and you are now starting to walk in one direction. Now, imagine someone comes in and says: "You will never be able to walk backwards, you can only keep going in the same direction." Well, that is what has happened with time. Now, of course, it needs to be understood fully. As an example, go to a city. There is a central square in the city. You are standing right now in the center of that square. You start walking in a certain direction, so let us say you walk a hundred meters. You go around the corner and now the view that you had when you started is no longer there, it is different. You have moved your position in space so you have a different perspective, a different view than you had when you started. You are where you are in space.

You can move back to where you started but you cannot move back there in one jump. You have to go through several steps to get there. You can also move forward to somewhere else but again you cannot jump ahead. You have to take one step at a time. We could say that at any given moment in space, you have a certain perspective, a certain viewpoint even a certain sense of self. There is a self, a sense of self, based on where you are now and what you can see. It is essentially the same in time—essentially the same in time. At any given moment, you are at a specific position, you might call it, on a time line but it is truly in the space of time, in the dimension of time. You are in a specific position at any given moment and at that moment you have a certain sense of self.

Now, the difference in the dimension of time is this: Say you started in that central square. You had a camera that would take a picture of exactly what you are seeing with your eyes as you are facing, turning your head in one direction. You stand there, you take this picture. You take one more step, now you take the picture of how your perspective has changed. Obviously, there is not going to be much of a difference but now, for every step you take, you keep taking a picture and when you have gone, say a hundred meters and gone around the corner, the pictures have changed quite a bit. Now, let us say that you were bringing all of those pictures with you so that your view of where you are now in space was affected by all of the previous views you had in space.

This is essentially what you do in the dimension of time. There was a certain point in time when you formulated a certain self, say your primal self. Ever since then, you have carried that self with you and that self set the parameters for how you look at life on earth, how you look at yourself on earth. Instead of taking a new picture every moment, for every step, you have kept building onto that old picture. It sets the tone for how you see yourself and how you see life in the now, which essentially means that you have carried something with you from the past and this, my beloved, is what time means for you.

Your personal time machine

Your individual, subjective time is actually the images that were created in the past that you are still carrying with you. That is why, from the ascended perspective, we are seeing that time is just another dimension and you can move in that dimension. You can learn to move in that dimension. As Master MORE says, we have given you a time machine with our teachings. We have given you the ability to go back, reconnect to, for example, the image you created in your birth trauma or any image you created in a past life. You can become aware of that image, see that it created a separate self and let the self die without trying to fix the situation that you could not fix back then. You are not changing anything in the physical. You are simply letting the self die and, as the last process, you realize there was an image held by that self and you are erasing that image, erasing the memory.

This is a time machine. This is time travel. Now, of course, when you reach higher levels of awareness, even higher levels of Christhood, you will start to have glimpses of situations in the future. Many of you have already had a glimpse of a situation or you have had what they call déjà vu. You suddenly realize you are in a physical situation that you saw in a dream or in a vision some time ago. This is an example of how you can also move forward in time. There are some instances where it is useful and appropriate for a Christed being to look forward in time, but it is an ability that needs to be used with caution. There is really no legitimate reason why you would want to know everything that will happen to you for the rest of your time in embodiment because, as we have said, how do you grow from one level to another? You grow by responding to a situation based on your present level of consciousness but still using that situation to reach for a higher view, and *that* is how you grow.

Living in the now as a span of time

Now, the other reason it is an ability to be used with caution is that, let us say that you right now have a vision of what will happen ten years from now, a situation that will happen ten years from now. Take, for example, Jesus, who had a vision that he would be crucified in Jerusalem. Is that vision of the future set in stone? Have we not told you that the past is not set in stone because you can go back and change it? How can the future be set in stone? Between here and that event that happens ten years from now, you are going to go through a lot of experiences, a lot of steps. You are going to make a lot of decisions, other people are going to make a lot of decisions. Even though you can move in the dimension of time and glimpse the future, you cannot know that this will actually come to pass. That is why it can be somewhat non-constructive, even dangerous, if you see the future and you think this absolutely has to come to pass. It could very well be that you would make decisions and other people would make decisions that would shift the equation, this very complex interaction of energy waves, so that the situation you saw would not happen. In other words, if you see the future, this is what will happen if nothing changes.

It is a pretty safe bet on an unnatural planet that something *will* change and therefore your snapshot of the future really might not be accurate ten seconds from now. Why would you need it? Why would you want it? In fact, the higher you go on the path, the less you are even concerned about the future, the less desire you have to know what is happening in the future. There are many people who have reached a certain level of Christhood or Buddhahood where they are no longer concerned about the past, they are no longer concerned about the future. They are focused on the immediate situation, not necessarily the now as a single moment in time, but their present situation, which can extend over some time. For example, if you are seeking to attain a certain goal, such as build a house, then you cannot build a house in the now. You cannot build a house if you are living in the now, only focused in the now. Of course, you are not talking about the distant past or the distant future. You must make a decision that: "I am going to start the process that will lead me to build this house." Then, it might take you a year to build the house. Now, you have been going through this process for three months and you can still look back to the past and say: "This is how I planned it three months ago." You are operating with a time span of a year to build the house.

That is why I am saying you are not necessarily, as a more evolved being, living in the now as a single moment. You have a certain time span you are working with but you are not burdened by what happened to you two million years ago, or in your last lifetime or in your childhood. You are not still blaming your parents for what they did to you in childhood. You are not concerned about what is going to happen ten years from now. You realize something; you realize the essence of what we have been telling you. You are not here to accomplish a particular physical goal. The purpose of your life is *not* to build the house. The purpose of building the house is to give you a certain experience. It does not really matter if you build the house and two years later it is wiped out by an earthquake because you still had the experience of building the house. If the house is destroyed by an earthquake, you have *that* experience.

You see my beloved, there comes that point where you have overcome these selves that want to control every aspect of your life and therefore want to be able to control the future. There is a self that is very, very concerned about controlling the future because that self is designed, is programmed, to make sure that you never again have the bad experience you had in the past. Therefore, this self wants to control the future so that you can protect yourself from anything bad happening to you. When you let go of this and other selves, you see that you are on an unnatural planet. It gives no meaning to try to live the same kind of life on an *unnatural* planet that you used to live on a *natural* planet. On a natural planet you can build a house and it is going to be there indefinitely. There is no risk of earthquakes, fires, storms, floods or whatever might destroy your house, but that is not the case on an unnatural planet. Therefore, you can still decide: "I want to have the experience of building a house here on earth," but you then become open to realize that, should that house be destroyed (and I am not saying it *will*, of course), then that is just another type of experience you can have on earth. Therefore, you can say: "Oh, it is actually interesting to experience myself in this situation where my house was destroyed." This is just another experience, another opportunity to be yourself regardless of what conditions are on earth.

Being free to experience life

You see my beloved, there comes a point where you begin to flow with the River of Life. Flowing with the River of Life does not mean that nothing bad can ever happen to you: you could not get ill, you could not have your house destroyed, you could not lose money, you could not have this, you could not have that. It does actually mean that you will not have a bad experience because whatever happens, you are not experiencing it through that separate self that must judge everything as being good or bad. That is when you are free to flow with the River of Life where you have no preconceived idea of what *should* or *should not* happen. Take the situation where Jesus tells his disciples that he is going to go to Jerusalem and suffer and be persecuted and crucified. Peter says to him: "Be it far from thee Lord, this is not going to happen." Why does Peter say it? Because he has a separate self that has a very particular view, an idolatrous view, of what should happen to the Living Christ or what should not happen to the Living Christ. This is an entirely subjective view that Peter is attempting to project onto Jesus, and because Jesus has a higher level of Christhood than Peter, he refuses to conform to Peter's subjective image. In order to help Peter snap out of this subjective image, he says: "Get thee behind me, Satan."

In a sense, you could say that the Satanic consciousness is when you project a subjective image upon others and want them to deny their own subjective experience and either have your experience (which, of course, they can never truly have) or at least live their lives according to your subjective experience. There comes that point where you have overcome the self that must evaluate every experience, everything that happens to you, on a scale of good and bad, right or wrong and this should not have happened. You are no longer afraid of what should not have happened. You are willing to flow into whatever situation comes up that you realize cannot be avoided.

Now, if you look back to a previous ascended master organization, you had a messenger and it was seen by most people in the organization that this messenger had reached a very high level of consciousness. Many people did exactly to her what Peter did to Jesus. They projected a certain view upon her of what should or should not happen. Then, what did happen? She became ill and many people became so disturbed, so distraught, so angry because this happened. They had a view of how she should serve them for the rest of their lives and basically enable them to walk the path without taking responsibility for themselves because they would just follow the guru.

Then, when she was no longer able to do this, they became very angry, very judgmental. Some of them even used this as an excuse for denying the path, refusing to follow the path, going back into a party lifestyle, a hedonistic lifestyle, doing all the things that they had stopped themselves from doing for so long. My beloved, why did this happen? Well, it actually happened because, as we have hinted at before, there were so many students that were not willing to move on. Therefore, this was one way to force them to confront something in themselves that they had not been willing to confront up until that point.

Letting time collapse

Coming back full circle, your subjective experience of time is based on whatever selves you created in the past that you are still carrying with you because they are affecting how you look at yourself, look at life, in the present moment. They are also affecting what you think about the future. If you were to see your future right now, it would be a future based on the separate selves you have right now and how they would affect your future. The moment you start getting rid of these selves, you are changing the equation for your future. You are also changing your past. You are in a sense eradicating, wiping out, erasing your past.

We have actually said that you cannot ascend in the past. You cannot ascend in the future. You can only ascend in the now. What happens when you are at the 144th level and, as we have said before, you are standing there and one step further will take you into the ascended realm? Well, at that moment, you need to look at earth and you need to see if there is anything that pulls you back there. What can pull you back there is any attachment you have, any self, anything you feel is not resolved from your past. This will be your *past* pulling on you. On the other hand, if you have something on earth you have not done, you have not completed, something you want to do, something you want to experience, then this is your *future* pulling you back to earth.

You see, in order to ascend, you have to come to a point where you have no past on earth because there is nothing unresolved that you are dragging with you. At the same time, you have no future on earth because you have no vision of wanting to do anything on earth. When, we might call it, your time line for being on earth collapses (the waveform collapses, as they talk about in quantum physics) and when there is no extension of time anymore (no past, no future, time collapses into a single moment) *that* is the moment where you ascend. *That* is truly the ultimate meaning that time is not, time is no longer.

Making peace with being here

How can you use these teachings to make peace with being on earth? Well, the teachings themselves can help you shift your perspective. Let me, as an example, refer to an experience that this messenger had when he was young where he had an out-of-body experience. He went out of his body, into a tunnel, into a light and then came back into his body. He realized that although this had been a profound experience, he did not need to repeat it. The experience had demonstrated to him — not theoretically but on an experiential level — that there is something beyond the material world, which helped him realize that he is not going to be in the material world forever. Therefore, he gave up the need to attempt to have more spiritual experiences and he has never done anything since to have a spiritual experience. He has had some that happened spontaneously but he has never made an effort to have it, to force it. It is the same that you can do.

You can shift and you can realize that after you ascend, time as you see it on earth, no longer applies to you. You literally have what people call an eternity (but is not truly an eternity, as there is progress in the ascended realm as well). You have a time span that is almost infinitely greater than the time span you have on earth. Even if you look at the two million years you have been on earth, the time you have in the ascended realm is infinitely greater than that.

You could potentially make the shift of saying: "Why am I in such a hurry to get out of here? Well, perhaps I want to experience what it is like to be in the ascended realm." Well, yes but if you have an eternity to experience what it is like in the ascended realm and you only have a limited time on earth, why are you in such a hurry to get away from earth and experience what you have plenty of time to experience? Why are you not making peace with being on earth, knowing it is only for a limited time and then saying: "Well, since I only have a limited time on earth, why wouldn't I make the most of that time? Why wouldn't I seek to have the best possible experience I can have in the time I have left on earth, rather than all of the time feeling like I am behind, feeling that I just want to get out of here?"

My beloved, we have said it before. There are masters who have ascended (and they needed to ascend in a certain time scale), but they have looked back at earth from the ascended realm and thought: "Ah, I wish I had taken the time, I wish I had had the awareness to enjoy being on earth more fully, to enjoy whatever experiences I could have, to enjoy being myself in the situations that I encountered in the physical realm." I hope that some of you will be inspired by this to make the most of it so that you do not have that thought after you ascend.

I can also say that the more you are at peace with being on earth, the more you are making the most of the experience, the more powerful is the impact you have on the collective consciousness, the more you will pull up on the collective consciousness. Surely, you pull up on the collective consciousness by ascending. I can assure you that you pull up much more on the collective consciousness when you still have the anchor point of a physical body in the physical octave, yet have that higher level of awareness where you can fully embrace being here, being at peace, enjoying being you on earth.

I did, my beloved, after I had passed the initiation under the Bo tree with the demons of Mara, I did come to the point where I could fully enjoy being on earth. What was the temptation of Mara? It was to somehow react to them so I could not be fully at peace, I could not be fully myself. I could not fully enjoy being myself on earth because of all of these conditions. In my last years, when I did teach, I had a constant sense of enjoying experiencing the situations that were unfolding before me in the physical, enjoying interacting with the students, seeing the students grow or not grow, whatever the case may be. I had no intent. I had no regrets. I had no intention of what *should* happen. I just enjoyed being me in whatever situation I was witnessing in the physical realm. *That* my beloved, was a great joy. It also meant that I had, of course, no regrets about the past.

Not regretting the past or fearing the future

The last topic I want to touch upon (and I know I have stretched your patience already), but, you see, the purpose of giving this long dictation is to teach you patience. I cannot do this theoretically. You must *experience*. Are you enjoying the experience you are having, experiencing yourself listening to a dictation by the Buddha? Are you enjoying that experience? [audience: "Yes."] Well, I am certainly enjoying the experience I am having of giving you this discourse.

My last topic. So many students have found an ascended master teaching and have thought: "Oh, why did I not find this teaching earlier? I have wasted so much time. I have reached this age, I have only so many years left. Why did I not find the teachings earlier?" Then, they say: "Now that I found it, I need to use every waking moment to decree and to pursue my growth." They basically forget enjoying the present, enjoying their experience. My beloved, this goes on to a much wider topic that is when you start thinking in these long terms of the avatar, and maybe you have been here for two million years. You have gone through all kinds of experiences, how can you avoid having regrets about the past? How can you avoid touching upon your birth trauma and not having regrets that this happened or the way you reacted to it and what you have done in many past lifetimes and what you have done in this lifetime and so forth and so on? Well, the key to this is what we have already given you, namely to know that whatever happened in the past, you can erase it.

As we have said, there is no objective event that is still in some physical space in the past. The physical octave has moved on. All that is left is what is in your consciousness and you have the knowledge, you have the tools, to erase it. If you know you can erase anything that happened in the past, why would you have any regrets about the past? Well, *you* are not having those regrets. There is a separate self that is having those regrets. *You* can come to see that separate self and just let it go and say: "I have had you influencing me long enough. This is it. You are gone."

That is when you can start enjoying life because now you get to the point where you realize that if your past does not affect you, why do you need to have fears about the future? Why do you need to fear you could make a mistake in the future?

Some of you have reached a certain level on the spiritual path where you feel you have gotten rid of some of the things from the past that are painful to you, but there is still a certain fear of what could happen in the future. "What if I made a mistake? What if I did something that I should not have done?" You know, my beloved, whatever you might do in the future is just another choice. Given that you have a higher state of consciousness today, it is not likely to be as severe of a choice as you made in the past. If the past severe choices could be erased, as you have experienced, then anything that could happen in the future can surely be erased also. So why would you have any fear about the future?

If you have no regrets about the past, the flip side of the coin is to have no fears about the future. That is when you can start focusing on enjoying the present moment while in, as I said, this time span that you are operating with. The time span is not one fixed time span. It is flexible, depending on what you are doing. As I said, if you are focused on building a house, there is a certain time span that it takes to achieve this in the physical. If you are focused on brushing your teeth, then, obviously, that is not going to take a year and so forth and so on. You have this very flexible view of time and it goes in and out and it changes in different situations.

Do not be a slave of time

That is also one aspect of getting to the point where you are not a slave of time. Time is not ruling your experience on earth. You could say that for most people, they are slaves of time. Time is their master. You see how many people are always looking at the clock, having to be somewhere at a certain time. You come to that point where you are flowing with the River of Life.

Of course, there is time. There is a certain time scale. You are looking into the future. You are thinking back to the past of how you decided to implement a certain decision and so forth. But you are not ruled by time. Time is not your master. You are not a slave. Time is just a tool.

It is just like moving in space. If you move in space and you find yourself in a location where you do not want to be, then you move to some other position in space and it is the same in time. You erase something from the past. You move somewhere else. It is not a problem for you. You are not ruled by it.

Again, it has been my great joy to experience myself interacting with you. I have interacted with each and every one of you, as you have allowed me to do during this dictation. I can do so again when you play the dictation or when you read it, I can interact with you. Perhaps you have not noticed but you can come to notice in the future. You can come to have that experience of: "How do I actually experience myself in the Presence of Gautama Buddha?" You can have the same with any other ascended master that is close to your heart. This, my beloved, is the final thought that we wish to give you for this element, this block of teachings that we have given you, on how to start with this primal self and overcome it so you can be at peace with being on earth.

We are very grateful for you having been willing to organize these conferences, to participate in these conferences, leading to this one. We are, of course, looking forward to what we can give you in the future. Many, many other teachings we have that I will not give you a glimpse of because it is part of the experience that you experience a teaching without having any forewarning or expectation about it. You can experience it more with the mind of the child without having any filters that you are projecting upon it. That way, the teaching can have its greatest effect on you.

So, our deepest gratitude to you.

17 | INVOKING AN EXPERIENCE OF ONGOINGNESS

In the name I AM THAT I AM, Jesus Christ, I call to all representatives of the Divine Mother, especially Gautama Buddha, to help me overcome all selves that make me think I have reached an ultimate stage of the path and no longer need to step back and question my selves, including…

[Make personal calls.]

Part 1

1. The self that I had when I first found the teachings and awakened to the existence of a spiritual path, that self cannot bring me to Christhood or Buddhahood.

> Gautama, show my mental state
> that does give rise to love and hate,

your exposé I do endure,
so my perception will be pure.

**Gautama, Flame of Cosmic Peace,
unruly thoughts do hereby cease,
we radiate from you and me
the peace to still Samsara's Sea.**

2. Even when my primal self has died, the new self I am born into is not the self that I will carry with me until I ascend. This is not the self that will ascend.

Gautama, in your Flame of Peace,
the struggling self I now release,
the Buddha Nature I now see,
it is the core of you and me.

**Gautama, Flame of Cosmic Peace,
unruly thoughts do hereby cease,
we radiate from you and me
the peace to still Samsara's Sea.**

3. I need to have resolved everything I need to resolve on earth before I can ascend and become an ascended master.

Gautama, I am one with thee,
Mara's demons do now flee,
your Presence like a soothing balm,
my mind and senses ever calm.

**Gautama, Flame of Cosmic Peace,
unruly thoughts do hereby cease,
we radiate from you and me
the peace to still Samsara's Sea.**

4. When I go through a certain phase, and uncover my primal self and let that self die, then I am born into a new sense of self. There were selves that I created after I created the primal self.

17 | *Invoking an experience of ongoingness*

>Gautama, I now take the vow,
>to live in the eternal now,
>with you I do transcend all time,
>to live in present so sublime.
>
>**Gautama, Flame of Cosmic Peace,**
>**unruly thoughts do hereby cease,**
>**we radiate from you and me**
>**the peace to still Samsara's Sea.**

5. I still have a certain view of myself, a certain view of earth, and this means that when I create a new self after I overcome the primal self, then that new self is not the highest possible.

>Gautama, I have no desire,
>to nothing earthly I aspire,
>in non-attachment I now rest,
>passing Mara's subtle test.
>
>**Gautama, Flame of Cosmic Peace,**
>**unruly thoughts do hereby cease,**
>**we radiate from you and me**
>**the peace to still Samsara's Sea.**

6. As I go up to higher and higher levels of consciousness, there will come points where I need to step back, look at my current sense of self and again let it die so that I can be reborn again. I can be reborn in Christ, I can be reborn in Buddha.

>Gautama, I melt into you,
>my mind is one, no longer two,
>immersed in your resplendent glow,
>Nirvana is all that I know.
>
>**Gautama, Flame of Cosmic Peace,**
>**unruly thoughts do hereby cease,**
>**we radiate from you and me**
>**the peace to still Samsara's Sea.**

7. The essence of the spiritual path is to come to see that I have a certain sense of self that is limited and I let it die.

> Gautama, in your timeless space,
> I am immersed in Cosmic Grace,
> I know the God beyond all form,
> to world I will no more conform.

> **Gautama, Flame of Cosmic Peace,**
> **unruly thoughts do hereby cease,**
> **we radiate from you and me**
> **the peace to still Samsara's Sea.**

8. When I find the spiritual path, I am actually creating a new self and I do this all the time, not only in this lifetime but in past lifetimes. I create certain selves that are not in a reaction to a particular traumatic situation.

> Gautama, I am now awake,
> I clearly see what is at stake,
> and thus I claim my sacred right
> to be on earth the Buddhic Light.

> **Gautama, Flame of Cosmic Peace,**
> **unruly thoughts do hereby cease,**
> **we radiate from you and me**
> **the peace to still Samsara's Sea.**

9. There are selves created in reaction to the understanding and awareness that I currently have. I am rising to a higher awareness, I create a new self based on that higher awareness. When I come to the higher levels of the path, I need to become conscious of this process.

> Gautama, with your thunderbolt,
> we give the earth a mighty jolt,
> I know that some will understand,
> and join the Buddha's timeless band.

> **Gautama, Flame of Cosmic Peace,**
> **unruly thoughts do hereby cease,**

we radiate from you and me
the peace to still Samsara's Sea.

Part 2

1. Gautama, help me become conscious of this process and see: "What have I gone through since I became consciously aware of the spiritual path? What are my experiences, what are the insights I have gained?"

Gautama, show my mental state
that does give rise to love and hate,
your exposé I do endure,
so my perception will be pure.

**Gautama, Flame of Cosmic Peace,
unruly thoughts do hereby cease,
we radiate from you and me
the peace to still Samsara's Sea.**

2. Gautama, help me take a look at my path up until this point and see: "What have I gone through, what beliefs have I come to accept based on the teachings I have followed, the organizations I have been involved with? What kind of a self have I created as a result of this?"

Gautama, in your Flame of Peace,
the struggling self I now release,
the Buddha Nature I now see,
it is the core of you and me.

**Gautama, Flame of Cosmic Peace,
unruly thoughts do hereby cease,
we radiate from you and me
the peace to still Samsara's Sea.**

3. It is a natural part of growth that I build these new selves based on my awareness and my desire, what to express, what to experience, what to do here on earth. I am ready to become conscious of this.

> Gautama, I am one with thee,
> Mara's demons do now flee,
> your Presence like a soothing balm,
> my mind and senses ever calm.
>
> **Gautama, Flame of Cosmic Peace,**
> **unruly thoughts do hereby cease,**
> **we radiate from you and me**
> **the peace to still Samsara's Sea.**

4. Gautama, help me look at myself and consider what kind of self I have built and whether that self is based on a limited view, a limited understanding. Help me see if I have a self that is built on a certain view of the path, a certain view of myself that I had years ago.

> Gautama, I now take the vow,
> to live in the eternal now,
> with you I do transcend all time,
> to live in present so sublime.
>
> **Gautama, Flame of Cosmic Peace,**
> **unruly thoughts do hereby cease,**
> **we radiate from you and me**
> **the peace to still Samsara's Sea.**

5. Gautama, help me see if I have in some part of my mind attained a higher understanding. Help me see that the self that I built during a certain stage of my path is no longer helping me grow. It is limiting my growth, it is holding me back because I have an outdated view, especially of my abilities.

> Gautama, I have no desire,
> to nothing earthly I aspire,
> in non-attachment I now rest,
> passing Mara's subtle test.
>
> **Gautama, Flame of Cosmic Peace,**
> **unruly thoughts do hereby cease,**

> we radiate from you and me
> the peace to still Samsara's Sea.

6. What I am really here for is to be myself, to express myself. Expressing myself means that I am allowing my I AM Presence to express itself through me. Being myself means being in a state of oneness with my I AM Presence.

> Gautama, I melt into you,
> my mind is one, no longer two,
> immersed in your resplendent glow,
> Nirvana is all that I know.
>
> **Gautama, Flame of Cosmic Peace,**
> **unruly thoughts do hereby cease,**
> **we radiate from you and me**
> **the peace to still Samsara's Sea.**

7. Going back to my birth trauma, I built selves that had a certain view of what I *can* do on earth, what I am *allowed* to do on earth, what I am *supposed* to do on earth and these selves could have been refined or reinforced by finding a spiritual path.

> Gautama, in your timeless space,
> I am immersed in Cosmic Grace,
> I know the God beyond all form,
> to world I will no more conform.
>
> **Gautama, Flame of Cosmic Peace,**
> **unruly thoughts do hereby cease,**
> **we radiate from you and me**
> **the peace to still Samsara's Sea.**

8. When I find a spiritual path, I see myself as a spiritual student, which is constructive for a time. If I continue to see myself as a spiritual student, there comes a point where this is no longer constructive because the concept of a path implies: "I am at a certain level, there is a higher level that is possible, but I have not yet reached it."

Gautama, I am now awake,
I clearly see what is at stake,
and thus I claim my sacred right
to be on earth the Buddhic Light.

**Gautama, Flame of Cosmic Peace,
unruly thoughts do hereby cease,
we radiate from you and me
the peace to still Samsara's Sea.**

9. There can come a point where I have in my mind an image that I am a spiritual student who is moving towards Christhood but I am not there yet. If I forever continue to hold on to that sense of self, then how will I ever be the Christ in embodiment?

Gautama, with your thunderbolt,
we give the earth a mighty jolt,
I know that some will understand,
and join the Buddha's timeless band.

**Gautama, Flame of Cosmic Peace,
unruly thoughts do hereby cease,
we radiate from you and me
the peace to still Samsara's Sea.**

Part 3

1. Gautama, help me see if I have reached a certain level but I am still holding on to a sense of self that I created at a previous level. Help me see if that image is holding me back.

Gautama, show my mental state
that does give rise to love and hate,
your exposé I do endure,
so my perception will be pure.

> Gautama, Flame of Cosmic Peace,
> unruly thoughts do hereby cease,
> we radiate from you and me
> the peace to still Samsara's Sea.

2. There comes a point where I need to recognize that I have reached a certain level of Christhood. This does not mean that I have reached the ultimate level, but it is necessary to be realistic and acknowledge this.

> Gautama, in your Flame of Peace,
> the struggling self I now release,
> the Buddha Nature I now see,
> it is the core of you and me.

> **Gautama, Flame of Cosmic Peace,
> unruly thoughts do hereby cease,
> we radiate from you and me
> the peace to still Samsara's Sea.**

3. Gautama, help me see if I have reached a certain level on the spiritual path but I have not yet dared to acknowledge it because I am still holding on to the sense of self that I created several levels below where I am at right now.

> Gautama, I am one with thee,
> Mara's demons do now flee,
> your Presence like a soothing balm,
> my mind and senses ever calm.

> **Gautama, Flame of Cosmic Peace,
> unruly thoughts do hereby cease,
> we radiate from you and me
> the peace to still Samsara's Sea.**

4. There is nobody who has ever ascended with the self they had in the beginning of their last embodiment or when they first found the spiritual path. There is nobody who has ever ascended with the sense of self we have at the 144th level, because the last act before the ascension is that I let that last self die and overcome the last illusion.

Gautama, I now take the vow,
to live in the eternal now,
with you I do transcend all time,
to live in present so sublime.

**Gautama, Flame of Cosmic Peace,
unruly thoughts do hereby cease,
we radiate from you and me
the peace to still Samsara's Sea.**

5. The process of the ascension is a process of letting one self after another die and be willing to be reborn into a higher sense of self. In order to let a certain self die, I must be willing to question the *illusion* even the *awareness* that the self is based on.

Gautama, I have no desire,
to nothing earthly I aspire,
in non-attachment I now rest,
passing Mara's subtle test.

**Gautama, Flame of Cosmic Peace,
unruly thoughts do hereby cease,
we radiate from you and me
the peace to still Samsara's Sea.**

6. The self I have right now has gained a certain insight, and it is a *valid* insight. It is just not the *final* insight. The insight is not an illusion but if I think that the insight is ultimate, or that the self I have built is ultimate, then *that* is an illusion.

Gautama, I melt into you,
my mind is one, no longer two,
immersed in your resplendent glow,
Nirvana is all that I know.

**Gautama, Flame of Cosmic Peace,
unruly thoughts do hereby cease,
we radiate from you and me
the peace to still Samsara's Sea.**

17 | Invoking an experience of ongoingness

7. Each time I step up to the next level of consciousness, there is a self that dies and another self that is born, but I am not necessarily aware of this. There does come certain points where I need to step back and look at my sense of self. One of them is when I begin to acknowledge that I have attained some level of Christhood.

> Gautama, in your timeless space,
> I am immersed in Cosmic Grace,
> I know the God beyond all form,
> to world I will no more conform.

> **Gautama, Flame of Cosmic Peace,**
> **unruly thoughts do hereby cease,**
> **we radiate from you and me**
> **the peace to still Samsara's Sea.**

8. The self I had was based on thinking that Christhood was somewhere out there in the future at a higher level, and that self has to die. In order to let it die, I have to see it and see the limitations of it.

> Gautama, I am now awake,
> I clearly see what is at stake,
> and thus I claim my sacred right
> to be on earth the Buddhic Light.

> **Gautama, Flame of Cosmic Peace,**
> **unruly thoughts do hereby cease,**
> **we radiate from you and me**
> **the peace to still Samsara's Sea.**

9. Gautama, help me see my sense of self because I truly do not want to get stuck in a certain sense of self and be unable to move on for the rest of this lifetime. I want to fulfill the highest potential of my Divine plan, and I am willing to let any self die that stands in the way of this goal.

> Gautama, with your thunderbolt,
> we give the earth a mighty jolt,
> I know that some will understand,
> and join the Buddha's timeless band.

> Gautama, Flame of Cosmic Peace,
> unruly thoughts do hereby cease,
> we radiate from you and me
> the peace to still Samsara's Sea.

Part 4

1. Gautama, help me see if I have created a self that is attempting to extend my subjective experience so that it seemingly becomes universal because other people have accepted my subjective experience over their own subjective experience.

> Gautama, show my mental state
> that does give rise to love and hate,
> your exposé I do endure,
> so my perception will be pure.
>
> **Gautama, Flame of Cosmic Peace,
> unruly thoughts do hereby cease,
> we radiate from you and me
> the peace to still Samsara's Sea.**

2. Gautama, help me see if I have convinced myself that the way I look at the teachings is the ultimate or the only true one. Therefore, it is for other people's own good that they come to accept my view.

> Gautama, in your Flame of Peace,
> the struggling self I now release,
> the Buddha Nature I now see,
> it is the core of you and me.
>
> **Gautama, Flame of Cosmic Peace,
> unruly thoughts do hereby cease,
> we radiate from you and me
> the peace to still Samsara's Sea.**

17 | Invoking an experience of ongoingness

3. Gautama, help me step back and realize that no matter what level of consciousness I am at, I am still having an experience that is not absolute. It is not universal in the sense that it should apply to all people.

> Gautama, I am one with thee,
> Mara's demons do now flee,
> your Presence like a soothing balm,
> my mind and senses ever calm.
>
> **Gautama, Flame of Cosmic Peace,**
> **unruly thoughts do hereby cease,**
> **we radiate from you and me**
> **the peace to still Samsara's Sea.**

4. It is not valid that I seek to get other people to have or to live their lives based on my experience.

> Gautama, I now take the vow,
> to live in the eternal now,
> with you I do transcend all time,
> to live in present so sublime.
>
> **Gautama, Flame of Cosmic Peace,**
> **unruly thoughts do hereby cease,**
> **we radiate from you and me**
> **the peace to still Samsara's Sea.**

5. Gautama, help me come to a point where I am no longer having a subjective experience but I am still having an individual experience.

> Gautama, I have no desire,
> to nothing earthly I aspire,
> in non-attachment I now rest,
> passing Mara's subtle test.
>
> **Gautama, Flame of Cosmic Peace,**
> **unruly thoughts do hereby cease,**
> **we radiate from you and me**
> **the peace to still Samsara's Sea.**

6. At the lower stages of awareness I am experiencing life through the outer selves, and I have no connection to my I AM Presence. As I go higher on the path, I shed some of these outer selves. My experience of life becomes less and less subjective, less and less colored.

> Gautama, I melt into you,
> my mind is one, no longer two,
> immersed in your resplendent glow,
> Nirvana is all that I know.
>
> **Gautama, Flame of Cosmic Peace,**
> **unruly thoughts do hereby cease,**
> **we radiate from you and me**
> **the peace to still Samsara's Sea.**

7. I become more and more in tune with my I AM Presence but my I AM Presence is not a *universal* being, it is an *individual* being. My I AM Presence experiences the situation on earth through that individuality.

> Gautama, in your timeless space,
> I am immersed in Cosmic Grace,
> I know the God beyond all form,
> to world I will no more conform.
>
> **Gautama, Flame of Cosmic Peace,**
> **unruly thoughts do hereby cease,**
> **we radiate from you and me**
> **the peace to still Samsara's Sea.**

8. *My* I AM Presence has an experience of earth that is different from the I AM Presence of another person and this is perfectly valid, perfectly in order.

> Gautama, I am now awake,
> I clearly see what is at stake,
> and thus I claim my sacred right
> to be on earth the Buddhic Light.

> Gautama, Flame of Cosmic Peace,
> unruly thoughts do hereby cease,
> we radiate from you and me
> the peace to still Samsara's Sea.

9. Gautama, help me make a shift and recognize that other people are not meant to have the same experience that I am having. They are meant to have their own experience.

> Gautama, with your thunderbolt,
> we give the earth a mighty jolt,
> I know that some will understand,
> and join the Buddha's timeless band.

> Gautama, Flame of Cosmic Peace,
> unruly thoughts do hereby cease,
> we radiate from you and me
> the peace to still Samsara's Sea.

Part 5

1. This does not mean that I cannot talk to other people and seek to help them or inspire them, but it does mean that I need to step up to that absolute respect for free will, where I am not anymore seeking to push my individual experience upon others.

> Gautama, show my mental state
> that does give rise to love and hate,
> your exposé I do endure,
> so my perception will be pure.

> Gautama, Flame of Cosmic Peace,
> unruly thoughts do hereby cease,
> we radiate from you and me
> the peace to still Samsara's Sea.

2. This does not mean that I need to stop saying anything to other people. It means that instead of trying to change their experience of life, I am sharing my own.

> Gautama, in your Flame of Peace,
> the struggling self I now release,
> the Buddha Nature I now see,
> it is the core of you and me.
>
> **Gautama, Flame of Cosmic Peace,**
> **unruly thoughts do hereby cease,**
> **we radiate from you and me**
> **the peace to still Samsara's Sea.**

3. Gautama, help me see the fundamental difference between pushing my experience onto others and then sharing my experience. The first one has an element of force, the second one does not. Help me pass this test.

> Gautama, I am one with thee,
> Mara's demons do now flee,
> your Presence like a soothing balm,
> my mind and senses ever calm.
>
> **Gautama, Flame of Cosmic Peace,**
> **unruly thoughts do hereby cease,**
> **we radiate from you and me**
> **the peace to still Samsara's Sea.**

4. Gautama, help me shed the self that gives me the desire to change other people because it is a self that was a reaction to conditions on earth.

> Gautama, I now take the vow,
> to live in the eternal now,
> with you I do transcend all time,
> to live in present so sublime.
>
> **Gautama, Flame of Cosmic Peace,**
> **unruly thoughts do hereby cease,**

> we radiate from you and me
> the peace to still Samsara's Sea.

5. The self expects that if I tell people how to overcome suffering, they will accept my words and set themselves free from suffering. The expectation that other people will want to be free of their suffering is logical on a natural planet but it is not applicable at all on an unnatural planet.

> Gautama, I have no desire,
> to nothing earthly I aspire,
> in non-attachment I now rest,
> passing Mara's subtle test.
>
> **Gautama, Flame of Cosmic Peace,**
> **unruly thoughts do hereby cease,**
> **we radiate from you and me**
> **the peace to still Samsara's Sea.**

6. Some people on earth are suffering because they have not had enough of the experience of suffering. Telling them that they should not be suffering and how to stop suffering is not relevant for them. It is an attempt to push my subjective experience that they should not be suffering upon them.

> Gautama, I melt into you,
> my mind is one, no longer two,
> immersed in your resplendent glow,
> Nirvana is all that I know.
>
> **Gautama, Flame of Cosmic Peace,**
> **unruly thoughts do hereby cease,**
> **we radiate from you and me**
> **the peace to still Samsara's Sea.**

7. Gautama, help me work on these selves, help me come to see this self. I will let it go, let go of the desire to get other people to live according to my view.

Gautama, in your timeless space,
I am immersed in Cosmic Grace,
I know the God beyond all form,
to world I will no more conform.

**Gautama, Flame of Cosmic Peace,
unruly thoughts do hereby cease,
we radiate from you and me
the peace to still Samsara's Sea.**

8. Any time I feel a certain compulsion about how I relate to other people, anytime I feel a tension, it is because there is a self there. That self springs from this attitude, this desire, to push my subjective experience upon others, to get them to live their lives according to my subjective experience.

Gautama, I am now awake,
I clearly see what is at stake,
and thus I claim my sacred right
to be on earth the Buddhic Light.

**Gautama, Flame of Cosmic Peace,
unruly thoughts do hereby cease,
we radiate from you and me
the peace to still Samsara's Sea.**

9. Gautama, help me accept that *my* subjective experience is perfectly valid for me, but *their* subjective experience is perfectly valid for them. My subjective experience is *not* better for other people. It is *never* better for them that they have my experience or live their lives according to my experience rather than their own. It is always better for people to have the subjective experience they are having because it is the only way they can grow.

Gautama, with your thunderbolt,
we give the earth a mighty jolt,
I know that some will understand,
and join the Buddha's timeless band.

**Gautama, Flame of Cosmic Peace,
unruly thoughts do hereby cease,**

**we radiate from you and me
the peace to still Samsara's Sea.**

Sealing

In the name of the Divine Mother, I call to Mother Mary for the sealing of myself and all people in my circle of influence in the creative flow of the Divine Mother, the River of Life. I call for the multiplication of my calls by all representatives of the Divine Mother, so that we form the perfect figure-eight flow of "As Above, so below." Thus, I accept that this is fully manifest, because the mouth of the Lord, the Divine Mother that I AM, has spoken it. Amen.

18 | INVOKING FREEDOM FROM THE SLAVERY OF TIME

In the name I AM THAT I AM, Jesus Christ, I call to all representatives of the Divine Mother, especially Gautama Buddha, to help me overcome all illusions about time, including…

[Make personal calls.]

Part 1

1. Time is a subjective experience; it is a product of a subjective experience. Time, as it is viewed by human beings on earth, is not an objective reality. It is an entirely subjective experience, created collectively over a long period of time.

> Gautama, show my mental state
> that does give rise to love and hate,

your exposé I do endure,
so my perception will be pure.

**Gautama, Flame of Cosmic Peace,
unruly thoughts do hereby cease,
we radiate from you and me
the peace to still Samsara's Sea.**

2. People have put a lot of mental-emotional-identity energy into creating the current view of time. This can be seen as a separate self, existing in the collective consciousness. The self thinks time is linear, that there is nothing we can do about time. We cannot go back in time, we cannot change the past.

Gautama, in your Flame of Peace,
the struggling self I now release,
the Buddha Nature I now see,
it is the core of you and me.

**Gautama, Flame of Cosmic Peace,
unruly thoughts do hereby cease,
we radiate from you and me
the peace to still Samsara's Sea.**

3. The fallen beings had a desire to take their subjective experience of time and project it upon all people on earth and they have been largely successful in doing this.

Gautama, I am one with thee,
Mara's demons do now flee,
your Presence like a soothing balm,
my mind and senses ever calm.

**Gautama, Flame of Cosmic Peace,
unruly thoughts do hereby cease,
we radiate from you and me
the peace to still Samsara's Sea.**

4. There is that collective view of time but I am a mature spiritual student. I have done a lot of work and separated myself from the collective consciousness to a large degree. I am ready to consider: "What is my subjective view of time, my personal view of time?"

> Gautama, I now take the vow,
> to live in the eternal now,
> with you I do transcend all time,
> to live in present so sublime.
>
> **Gautama, Flame of Cosmic Peace,**
> **unruly thoughts do hereby cease,**
> **we radiate from you and me**
> **the peace to still Samsara's Sea.**

5. I have a view that in the past I did something and this created certain consequences that can carry on into what I see as the future. I have a view that my present situation is to some degree affected by my past, by my karma.

> Gautama, I have no desire,
> to nothing earthly I aspire,
> in non-attachment I now rest,
> passing Mara's subtle test.
>
> **Gautama, Flame of Cosmic Peace,**
> **unruly thoughts do hereby cease,**
> **we radiate from you and me**
> **the peace to still Samsara's Sea.**

6. In many cases, what happens to me is not the result of my personal karma. It is the result of the fact that I am embodied on a dense, unnatural planet that is very chaotic.

> Gautama, I melt into you,
> my mind is one, no longer two,
> immersed in your resplendent glow,
> Nirvana is all that I know.

> Gautama, Flame of Cosmic Peace,
> unruly thoughts do hereby cease,
> we radiate from you and me
> the peace to still Samsara's Sea.

7. There are many things that can happen that are perpetrated by other people, by their actions, by their state of consciousness, by a certain collective karma, but it is not my individual, personal karma.

> Gautama, in your timeless space,
> I am immersed in Cosmic Grace,
> I know the God beyond all form,
> to world I will no more conform.
>
> Gautama, Flame of Cosmic Peace,
> unruly thoughts do hereby cease,
> we radiate from you and me
> the peace to still Samsara's Sea.

8. Gautama, help me step back and look at the view of myself I created based on the spiritual teachings, especially the teaching that if something bad happens to me, it is because of my karma.

> Gautama, I am now awake,
> I clearly see what is at stake,
> and thus I claim my sacred right
> to be on earth the Buddhic Light.
>
> Gautama, Flame of Cosmic Peace,
> unruly thoughts do hereby cease,
> we radiate from you and me
> the peace to still Samsara's Sea.

9. Gautama, help me see if I have invoked enough violet flame to transmute the energy that makes up my karma. I have transformed the energy but if I have the image of myself that I have not balanced my karma, then I have not actually become free of my karma.

18 | Invoking freedom from the slavery of time

> Gautama, with your thunderbolt,
> we give the earth a mighty jolt,
> I know that some will understand,
> and join the Buddha's timeless band.
>
> **Gautama, Flame of Cosmic Peace,**
> **unruly thoughts do hereby cease,**
> **we radiate from you and me**
> **the peace to still Samsara's Sea.**

Part 2

1. Gautama, help me see if I have a self that does not want to acknowledge that I do not have karma anymore, because the self is afraid that if something bad happened to me, how would I explain it if I could not explain it as a result of my karma?

> Gautama, show my mental state
> that does give rise to love and hate,
> your exposé I do endure,
> so my perception will be pure.
>
> **Gautama, Flame of Cosmic Peace,**
> **unruly thoughts do hereby cease,**
> **we radiate from you and me**
> **the peace to still Samsara's Sea.**

2. Gautama, help me step up and realize if I have completed the process of balancing my karma. If something bad happens to me, it is not the result of my personal karma, it is not a result of a mistake I made, but the fact that I live on a planet that is unnatural, dense and very chaotic.

> Gautama, in your Flame of Peace,
> the struggling self I now release,
> the Buddha Nature I now see,
> it is the core of you and me.

> Gautama, Flame of Cosmic Peace,
> unruly thoughts do hereby cease,
> we radiate from you and me
> the peace to still Samsara's Sea.

3. I cannot predict with certainty exactly what is happening. I cannot say that if a person has balanced all karma, nothing bad should ever happen to that person.

> Gautama, I am one with thee,
> Mara's demons do now flee,
> your Presence like a soothing balm,
> my mind and senses ever calm.

> **Gautama, Flame of Cosmic Peace,
> unruly thoughts do hereby cease,
> we radiate from you and me
> the peace to still Samsara's Sea.**

4. Because I am still living in a physical body in a certain environment, there is a very complex pattern of energy waves created and sustained by other people. It is not possible to predict exactly what events might happen for the rest of my lifetime.

> Gautama, I now take the vow,
> to live in the eternal now,
> with you I do transcend all time,
> to live in present so sublime.

> **Gautama, Flame of Cosmic Peace,
> unruly thoughts do hereby cease,
> we radiate from you and me
> the peace to still Samsara's Sea.**

5. Things are so chaotic, so unpredictable. The universe is not a clockwork, is not a machine. It is impossible to predict exactly what a person is going to choose. I cannot *know* and therefore cannot *predict* exactly how the rest of my life is going to form. It depends on my choices and choices of many other people and how this very complex pattern of energy waves interacts.

18 | Invoking freedom from the slavery of time

> Gautama, I have no desire,
> to nothing earthly I aspire,
> in non-attachment I now rest,
> passing Mara's subtle test.
>
> **Gautama, Flame of Cosmic Peace,**
> **unruly thoughts do hereby cease,**
> **we radiate from you and me**
> **the peace to still Samsara's Sea.**

6. It is not possible to say that if I have no karma, nothing bad can happen to me for the rest of this lifetime. I let go of this self, and I accept: "I have balanced my karma."

> Gautama, I melt into you,
> my mind is one, no longer two,
> immersed in your resplendent glow,
> Nirvana is all that I know.
>
> **Gautama, Flame of Cosmic Peace,**
> **unruly thoughts do hereby cease,**
> **we radiate from you and me**
> **the peace to still Samsara's Sea.**

7. I also accept: "Because I am living on a planet like earth, something may indeed happen to me that is not a result of my karma. But I will not blame God, I will not blame myself, I will not blame other people. I will accept it for what it is, make the best of it and move on."

> Gautama, in your timeless space,
> I am immersed in Cosmic Grace,
> I know the God beyond all form,
> to world I will no more conform.
>
> **Gautama, Flame of Cosmic Peace,**
> **unruly thoughts do hereby cease,**
> **we radiate from you and me**
> **the peace to still Samsara's Sea.**

8. Gautama, help me let go of the selves that have built expectations about nothing bad happening to me, even thinking that some kind of miracle could save me.

> Gautama, I am now awake,
> I clearly see what is at stake,
> and thus I claim my sacred right
> to be on earth the Buddhic Light.

> **Gautama, Flame of Cosmic Peace,**
> **unruly thoughts do hereby cease,**
> **we radiate from you and me**
> **the peace to still Samsara's Sea.**

9. I accept that I have reached a certain level of Christhood and if something "bad" happens to me, it may be part of my path to Christhood to go through this experience, to demonstrate how I can deal with this in a higher, more non-attached manner. I can demonstrate how to deal with this experience without having the primal self or other selves that I have overcome.

> Gautama, with your thunderbolt,
> we give the earth a mighty jolt,
> I know that some will understand,
> and join the Buddha's timeless band.

> **Gautama, Flame of Cosmic Peace,**
> **unruly thoughts do hereby cease,**
> **we radiate from you and me**
> **the peace to still Samsara's Sea.**

Part 3

1. Time is not, because it does not have an objective existence the way people see it. Time is just like the other dimensions in the sense that it is not linear. I can move back and forth in time.

18 | Invoking freedom from the slavery of time

> Gautama, show my mental state
> that does give rise to love and hate,
> your exposé I do endure,
> so my perception will be pure.
>
> **Gautama, Flame of Cosmic Peace,**
> **unruly thoughts do hereby cease,**
> **we radiate from you and me**
> **the peace to still Samsara's Sea.**

2. In space I can go in any direction, and I can also go back, but only by taking one step at a time. At any given moment in space, I have a certain perspective, a certain viewpoint even a certain sense of self. There is a self, a sense of self, based on where I am now and what I can see.

> Gautama, in your Flame of Peace,
> the struggling self I now release,
> the Buddha Nature I now see,
> it is the core of you and me.
>
> **Gautama, Flame of Cosmic Peace,**
> **unruly thoughts do hereby cease,**
> **we radiate from you and me**
> **the peace to still Samsara's Sea.**

3. It is essentially the same in time. At any given moment, I am at a specific position in the space of time, in the dimension of time. I am in a specific position at any given moment and at that moment I have a certain sense of self.

> Gautama, I am one with thee,
> Mara's demons do now flee,
> your Presence like a soothing balm,
> my mind and senses ever calm.
>
> **Gautama, Flame of Cosmic Peace,**
> **unruly thoughts do hereby cease,**
> **we radiate from you and me**
> **the peace to still Samsara's Sea.**

4. There was a point in time when I formulated a certain self, such as my primal self. Ever since then, I have carried that self with me and that self set the parameters for how I look at life on earth, how I look at myself on earth.

> Gautama, I now take the vow,
> to live in the eternal now,
> with you I do transcend all time,
> to live in present so sublime.
>
> **Gautama, Flame of Cosmic Peace,**
> **unruly thoughts do hereby cease,**
> **we radiate from you and me**
> **the peace to still Samsara's Sea.**

5. Instead of taking a new picture every moment, I have kept building onto that old picture. It sets the tone for how I see myself and how I see life in the now, which essentially means that I have carried something with me from the past and this is what time means for me.

> Gautama, I have no desire,
> to nothing earthly I aspire,
> in non-attachment I now rest,
> passing Mara's subtle test.
>
> **Gautama, Flame of Cosmic Peace,**
> **unruly thoughts do hereby cease,**
> **we radiate from you and me**
> **the peace to still Samsara's Sea.**

6. My individual, subjective time is the images that were created in the past that I am still carrying with me. From the ascended perspective, time is just another dimension and I can learn to move in that dimension.

> Gautama, I melt into you,
> my mind is one, no longer two,
> immersed in your resplendent glow,
> Nirvana is all that I know.

18 | Invoking freedom from the slavery of time

> **Gautama, Flame of Cosmic Peace,**
> **unruly thoughts do hereby cease,**
> **we radiate from you and me**
> **the peace to still Samsara's Sea.**

7. The masters have given me a time machine with their teachings. I have the ability to go back, reconnect to the image I created in my birth trauma or any image I created in a past life. I can become aware of that image, see that it created a separate self and let the self die without trying to fix the situation that I could not fix back then.

> Gautama, in your timeless space,
> I am immersed in Cosmic Grace,
> I know the God beyond all form,
> to world I will no more conform.

> **Gautama, Flame of Cosmic Peace,**
> **unruly thoughts do hereby cease,**
> **we radiate from you and me**
> **the peace to still Samsara's Sea.**

8. I am not changing anything in the physical. I am simply letting the self die and as the last process, I realize there was an image held by that self and I am erasing that image, erasing the memory. This is a time machine. This is time travel.

> Gautama, I am now awake,
> I clearly see what is at stake,
> and thus I claim my sacred right
> to be on earth the Buddhic Light.

> **Gautama, Flame of Cosmic Peace,**
> **unruly thoughts do hereby cease,**
> **we radiate from you and me**
> **the peace to still Samsara's Sea.**

9. As I reach higher levels of awareness, I may start to have glimpses of situations in the future. Yet there is no legitimate reason why I would want to know everything that will happen to me for the rest of my life. I grow

by responding to a situation based on my present level of consciousness but still using that situation to reach for a higher view.

> Gautama, with your thunderbolt,
> we give the earth a mighty jolt,
> I know that some will understand,
> and join the Buddha's timeless band.
>
> **Gautama, Flame of Cosmic Peace,**
> **unruly thoughts do hereby cease,**
> **we radiate from you and me**
> **the peace to still Samsara's Sea.**

Part 4

1. Any vision I might have of the future is not set in stone. Between here and any event in the future, I am going to make a lot of decisions, other people are going to make a lot of decisions. It can dangerous to see the future and think this absolutely has to come to pass.

> Gautama, show my mental state
> that does give rise to love and hate,
> your exposé I do endure,
> so my perception will be pure.
>
> **Gautama, Flame of Cosmic Peace,**
> **unruly thoughts do hereby cease,**
> **we radiate from you and me**
> **the peace to still Samsara's Sea.**

2. Why would I want to know the future? The higher I go on the path, the less I am concerned about the future, the less desire I have to know what is happening in the future.

> Gautama, in your Flame of Peace,
> the struggling self I now release,

the Buddha Nature I now see,
it is the core of you and me.

**Gautama, Flame of Cosmic Peace,
unruly thoughts do hereby cease,
we radiate from you and me
the peace to still Samsara's Sea.**

3. At a certain level of Christhood or Buddhahood I am no longer concerned about the past, I am no longer concerned about the future. I am focused on the immediate situation, not necessarily the now as a single moment in time, but my present situation, which can extend over some time.

Gautama, I am one with thee,
Mara's demons do now flee,
your Presence like a soothing balm,
my mind and senses ever calm.

**Gautama, Flame of Cosmic Peace,
unruly thoughts do hereby cease,
we radiate from you and me
the peace to still Samsara's Sea.**

4. As a more evolved being, I am not necessarily living in the now as a single moment. I have a certain time span I am working with but I am not burdened by what happened to me in the past. I am not concerned about what is going to happen ten years from now.

Gautama, I now take the vow,
to live in the eternal now,
with you I do transcend all time,
to live in present so sublime.

**Gautama, Flame of Cosmic Peace,
unruly thoughts do hereby cease,
we radiate from you and me
the peace to still Samsara's Sea.**

5. I realize that I am not here to accomplish a particular physical goal. The purpose of my life is *not* to accomplish a specific task. The purpose of engaging in any activity is to give me a certain experience. It does not really matter what happens in the physical because it always gives me an experience.

> Gautama, I have no desire,
> to nothing earthly I aspire,
> in non-attachment I now rest,
> passing Mara's subtle test.

> **Gautama, Flame of Cosmic Peace,**
> **unruly thoughts do hereby cease,**
> **we radiate from you and me**
> **the peace to still Samsara's Sea.**

6. There is a self that is very concerned about controlling the future because that self is designed to make sure that I never again have the bad experience I had in the past. This self wants to control the future so that I can protect myself from anything bad happening to me.

> Gautama, I melt into you,
> my mind is one, no longer two,
> immersed in your resplendent glow,
> Nirvana is all that I know.

> **Gautama, Flame of Cosmic Peace,**
> **unruly thoughts do hereby cease,**
> **we radiate from you and me**
> **the peace to still Samsara's Sea.**

7. I am letting go of this and other selves. I see that I am on an unnatural planet. It gives no meaning to try to live the same kind of life on an *unnatural* planet that I can live on a *natural* planet.

> Gautama, in your timeless space,
> I am immersed in Cosmic Grace,
> I know the God beyond all form,
> to world I will no more conform.

> Gautama, Flame of Cosmic Peace,
> unruly thoughts do hereby cease,
> we radiate from you and me
> the peace to still Samsara's Sea.

8. I can still decide: "I want to have the experience of building a house here on earth," but I realize that, should that house be destroyed, then that is just another type of experience I can have on earth. Therefore, I can say: "Oh, it is actually interesting to experience myself in this situation where my house was destroyed." This is just another opportunity to be myself regardless of what conditions are on earth.

> Gautama, I am now awake,
> I clearly see what is at stake,
> and thus I claim my sacred right
> to be on earth the Buddhic Light.

> **Gautama, Flame of Cosmic Peace,**
> **unruly thoughts do hereby cease,**
> **we radiate from you and me**
> **the peace to still Samsara's Sea.**

9. Flowing with the River of Life does not mean that nothing bad can ever happen to me. It means that I will not have a bad experience because whatever happens, I am not experiencing it through the separate self that must judge everything as being good or bad. That is when I am free to flow with the River of Life where I have no preconceived idea of what should or should not happen.

> Gautama, with your thunderbolt,
> we give the earth a mighty jolt,
> I know that some will understand,
> and join the Buddha's timeless band.

> **Gautama, Flame of Cosmic Peace,**
> **unruly thoughts do hereby cease,**
> **we radiate from you and me**
> **the peace to still Samsara's Sea.**

Part 5

1. The Satanic consciousness is when I project a subjective image upon others and want them to deny their own subjective experience and either have my experience or at least live their lives according to my subjective experience.

> Gautama, show my mental state
> that does give rise to love and hate,
> your exposé I do endure,
> so my perception will be pure.

> **Gautama, Flame of Cosmic Peace,**
> **unruly thoughts do hereby cease,**
> **we radiate from you and me**
> **the peace to still Samsara's Sea.**

2. Gautama, help me overcome the self that must evaluate everything that happens to me on a scale of good and bad, right or wrong. Help me to no longer be afraid of what should not have happened. I am willing to flow into whatever situation comes up that cannot be avoided.

> Gautama, in your Flame of Peace,
> the struggling self I now release,
> the Buddha Nature I now see,
> it is the core of you and me.

> **Gautama, Flame of Cosmic Peace,**
> **unruly thoughts do hereby cease,**
> **we radiate from you and me**
> **the peace to still Samsara's Sea.**

3. My subjective experience of time is based on whatever selves I created in the past that I am still carrying with me, because they are affecting how I look at myself, look at life, in the present moment. They are also affecting what I think about the future.

18 | Invoking freedom from the slavery of time

> Gautama, I am one with thee,
> Mara's demons do now flee,
> your Presence like a soothing balm,
> my mind and senses ever calm.
>
> **Gautama, Flame of Cosmic Peace,**
> **unruly thoughts do hereby cease,**
> **we radiate from you and me**
> **the peace to still Samsara's Sea.**

4. Right now, my future is based on the separate selves I have and how they will affect my future. The moment I start getting rid of these selves, I am changing the equation for my future. I am also changing my past. I am eradicating, wiping out, erasing my past.

> Gautama, I now take the vow,
> to live in the eternal now,
> with you I do transcend all time,
> to live in present so sublime.
>
> **Gautama, Flame of Cosmic Peace,**
> **unruly thoughts do hereby cease,**
> **we radiate from you and me**
> **the peace to still Samsara's Sea.**

5. I cannot ascend in the past. I cannot ascend in the future. I can only ascend in the now. When I face the ascension, I need to look at earth and see if there is anything that pulls me back there.

> Gautama, I have no desire,
> to nothing earthly I aspire,
> in non-attachment I now rest,
> passing Mara's subtle test.
>
> **Gautama, Flame of Cosmic Peace,**
> **unruly thoughts do hereby cease,**
> **we radiate from you and me**
> **the peace to still Samsara's Sea.**

6. What can pull me back is any attachment I have, any self, anything I feel is not resolved from my past. This will be my past pulling on me. If I have something on earth I have not done, I have not completed, something I want to do, something I want to experience, then this is my future pulling me back to earth.

> Gautama, I melt into you,
> my mind is one, no longer two,
> immersed in your resplendent glow,
> Nirvana is all that I know.
>
> **Gautama, Flame of Cosmic Peace,**
> **unruly thoughts do hereby cease,**
> **we radiate from you and me**
> **the peace to still Samsara's Sea.**

7. In order to ascend, I have to come to a point where I have no past on earth because there is nothing unresolved that I am dragging with me. At the same time, I have no future on earth because I have no vision of wanting to do anything on earth.

> Gautama, in your timeless space,
> I am immersed in Cosmic Grace,
> I know the God beyond all form,
> to world I will no more conform.
>
> **Gautama, Flame of Cosmic Peace,**
> **unruly thoughts do hereby cease,**
> **we radiate from you and me**
> **the peace to still Samsara's Sea.**

8. When my time line for being on earth collapses and when there is no extension of time anymore (no past, no future, time collapses into a single moment) *that* is the moment where I ascend. *That* is truly the ultimate meaning that time is not, time is no longer.

> Gautama, I am now awake,
> I clearly see what is at stake,

and thus I claim my sacred right
to be on earth the Buddhic Light.

**Gautama, Flame of Cosmic Peace,
unruly thoughts do hereby cease,
we radiate from you and me
the peace to still Samsara's Sea.**

9. After I ascend, time as I see it on earth, no longer applies to me. I have what people call an eternity, I have a time span that is almost infinitely greater than the time span I have on earth.

Gautama, with your thunderbolt,
we give the earth a mighty jolt,
I know that some will understand,
and join the Buddha's timeless band.

**Gautama, Flame of Cosmic Peace,
unruly thoughts do hereby cease,
we radiate from you and me
the peace to still Samsara's Sea.**

Part 6

1. I now make the shift of saying: "Why am I in such a hurry to get out of here? Well, perhaps I want to experience what it is like to be in the ascended realm. Yes, but if I have an eternity to experience what it is like in the ascended realm and I only have a limited time on earth, why am I in such a hurry to get away from earth and experience what I have plenty of time to experience?"

Gautama, show my mental state
that does give rise to love and hate,
your exposé I do endure,
so my perception will be pure.

> Gautama, Flame of Cosmic Peace,
> unruly thoughts do hereby cease,
> we radiate from you and me
> the peace to still Samsara's Sea.

2. Why am I not making peace with being on earth, knowing it is only for a limited time and then saying: "Well, since I only have a limited time on earth, why wouldn't I make the most of that time? Why wouldn't I seek to have the best possible experience I can have in the time I have left on earth, rather than all of the time feeling like I am behind, feeling that I just want to get out of here?"

> Gautama, in your Flame of Peace,
> the struggling self I now release,
> the Buddha Nature I now see,
> it is the core of you and me.

> Gautama, Flame of Cosmic Peace,
> unruly thoughts do hereby cease,
> we radiate from you and me
> the peace to still Samsara's Sea.

3. The more I am at peace with being on earth and the more I am making the most of the experience, the more powerful is the impact I have on the collective consciousness, the more I will pull up on the collective consciousness.

> Gautama, I am one with thee,
> Mara's demons do now flee,
> your Presence like a soothing balm,
> my mind and senses ever calm.

> Gautama, Flame of Cosmic Peace,
> unruly thoughts do hereby cease,
> we radiate from you and me
> the peace to still Samsara's Sea.

4. I pull up on the collective consciousness by ascending. I pull up much more on the collective consciousness when I still have the anchor point of

a physical body, yet I have that higher level of awareness where I can fully embrace being here, being at peace, enjoying being me on earth.

> Gautama, I now take the vow,
> to live in the eternal now,
> with you I do transcend all time,
> to live in present so sublime.

> **Gautama, Flame of Cosmic Peace,**
> **unruly thoughts do hereby cease,**
> **we radiate from you and me**
> **the peace to still Samsara's Sea.**

5. After Gautama passed the initiation under the Bo tree with the demons of Mara, he did come to the point where he could fully enjoy being on earth. The temptation of Mara is to somehow react to them so I cannot be fully at peace, I cannot be fully myself. I cannot fully enjoy being myself on earth because of all of these conditions.

> Gautama, I have no desire,
> to nothing earthly I aspire,
> in non-attachment I now rest,
> passing Mara's subtle test.

> **Gautama, Flame of Cosmic Peace,**
> **unruly thoughts do hereby cease,**
> **we radiate from you and me**
> **the peace to still Samsara's Sea.**

6. Gautama, help me have a constant sense of enjoying experiencing the situations that are unfolding before me in the physical. I have no intent. I have no regrets. I have no intention of what *should* happen. I just enjoy being me in whatever situation I am witnessing in the physical realm.

> Gautama, I melt into you,
> my mind is one, no longer two,
> immersed in your resplendent glow,
> Nirvana is all that I know.

> Gautama, Flame of Cosmic Peace,
> unruly thoughts do hereby cease,
> we radiate from you and me
> the peace to still Samsara's Sea.

7. How can I avoid having regrets about the past? How can I avoid touching upon my birth trauma and not having regrets that this happened or about the way I reacted to it and what I have done in many past lifetimes and what I have done in this lifetime?

> Gautama, in your timeless space,
> I am immersed in Cosmic Grace,
> I know the God beyond all form,
> to world I will no more conform.

> **Gautama, Flame of Cosmic Peace,**
> **unruly thoughts do hereby cease,**
> **we radiate from you and me**
> **the peace to still Samsara's Sea.**

8. Gautama, help me truly accept that whatever happened in the past, I can erase it. There is no objective event that is still in some physical space in the past. The physical octave has moved on. All that is left is what is in my consciousness and I have the knowledge, I have the tools to erase it.

> Gautama, I am now awake,
> I clearly see what is at stake,
> and thus I claim my sacred right
> to be on earth the Buddhic Light.

> **Gautama, Flame of Cosmic Peace,**
> **unruly thoughts do hereby cease,**
> **we radiate from you and me**
> **the peace to still Samsara's Sea.**

9. If I know I can erase anything that happened in the past, why would I have any regrets about the past? *I* am not having those regrets. There is a separate self that is having those regrets. *I* can come to see that separate

self and just let it go and say: "I have had you influencing me long enough. This is it. You are gone."

> Gautama, with your thunderbolt,
> we give the earth a mighty jolt,
> I know that some will understand,
> and join the Buddha's timeless band.
>
> **Gautama, Flame of Cosmic Peace,**
> **unruly thoughts do hereby cease,**
> **we radiate from you and me**
> **the peace to still Samsara's Sea.**

Part 7

1. If my past does not affect me, why do I need to have fears about the future? Why do I need to fear I could make a mistake in the future?

> Gautama, show my mental state
> that does give rise to love and hate,
> your exposé I do endure,
> so my perception will be pure.
>
> **Gautama, Flame of Cosmic Peace,**
> **unruly thoughts do hereby cease,**
> **we radiate from you and me**
> **the peace to still Samsara's Sea.**

2. Whatever I might do in the future is just another choice. Given that I have a higher state of consciousness today, it is not likely to be as severe of a choice as I made in the past.

> Gautama, in your Flame of Peace,
> the struggling self I now release,
> the Buddha Nature I now see,
> it is the core of you and me.

> **Gautama, Flame of Cosmic Peace,**
> **unruly thoughts do hereby cease,**
> **we radiate from you and me**
> **the peace to still Samsara's Sea.**

3. If the past severe choices can be erased, then anything that could happen in the future can surely be erased also. So why would I have any fear about the future?

> Gautama, I am one with thee,
> Mara's demons do now flee,
> your Presence like a soothing balm,
> my mind and senses ever calm.

> **Gautama, Flame of Cosmic Peace,**
> **unruly thoughts do hereby cease,**
> **we radiate from you and me**
> **the peace to still Samsara's Sea.**

4. If I have no regrets about the past, the flip side of the coin is to have no fears about the future. I am focusing on enjoying the present moment while in this time span that I am operating with.

> Gautama, I now take the vow,
> to live in the eternal now,
> with you I do transcend all time,
> to live in present so sublime.

> **Gautama, Flame of Cosmic Peace,**
> **unruly thoughts do hereby cease,**
> **we radiate from you and me**
> **the peace to still Samsara's Sea.**

5. Gautama, help me get to the point where I am not a slave of time. Time is not ruling my experience on earth. I am flowing with the River of Life.

> Gautama, I have no desire,
> to nothing earthly I aspire,

in non-attachment I now rest,
passing Mara's subtle test.

**Gautama, Flame of Cosmic Peace,
unruly thoughts do hereby cease,
we radiate from you and me
the peace to still Samsara's Sea.**

6. Of course, there is time. There is a certain time scale. I am looking into the future, I am looking to the past of how I decided to implement a certain decision. But I am not ruled by time. Time is not my master. I am not a slave.

Gautama, I melt into you,
my mind is one, no longer two,
immersed in your resplendent glow,
Nirvana is all that I know.

**Gautama, Flame of Cosmic Peace,
unruly thoughts do hereby cease,
we radiate from you and me
the peace to still Samsara's Sea.**

7. Time is just a tool. It is just like moving in space. If I move in space and I find myself in a location where I do not want to be, then I move to some other position in space and it is the same in time. I erase something from the past. I move somewhere else. It is not a problem for me. I am not ruled by it.

Gautama, in your timeless space,
I am immersed in Cosmic Grace,
I know the God beyond all form,
to world I will no more conform.

**Gautama, Flame of Cosmic Peace,
unruly thoughts do hereby cease,
we radiate from you and me
the peace to still Samsara's Sea.**

8. Gautama, I want to interact with you. I want to have the experience of how I experience myself in the Presence of Gautama Buddha.

> Gautama, I am now awake,
> I clearly see what is at stake,
> and thus I claim my sacred right
> to be on earth the Buddhic Light.

> **Gautama, Flame of Cosmic Peace,**
> **unruly thoughts do hereby cease,**
> **we radiate from you and me**
> **the peace to still Samsara's Sea.**

9. Gautama, help me experience life without having any expectation about it. I experience it with the mind of the child without having any filters that I am projecting upon it. Gautama, help me experience life as you experienced it as the Buddha in embodiment.

> Gautama, with your thunderbolt,
> we give the earth a mighty jolt,
> I know that some will understand,
> and join the Buddha's timeless band.

> **Gautama, Flame of Cosmic Peace,**
> **unruly thoughts do hereby cease,**
> **we radiate from you and me**
> **the peace to still Samsara's Sea.**

Sealing

In the name of the Divine Mother, I call to Mother Mary for the sealing of myself and all people in my circle of influence in the creative flow of the Divine Mother, the River of Life. I call for the multiplication of my calls by all representatives of the Divine Mother, so that we form the perfect figure-eight flow of "As Above, so below." Thus, I accept that this is fully manifest, because the mouth of the Lord, the Divine Mother that I AM, has spoken it. Amen.

19 | A QUESTION ABOUT TIME

Question: Could the masters give a deeper teaching about the non-existence of time and spiritual reality. We know that certain things happen chronologically, for example filling the newly created sphere with light. If time does not exist and everything is happening at the same time, how can we relate it to free will, which has the opportunity to realize the path to Christ consciousness or is it an opposite direction? From our terrestrial perspective this happens in particular time. How do the beings in the spiritual world feel the time that flows on earth?

Answer by Gautama Buddha: My beloved, I am the one who has said: "Time is not," which of course is a Koan. Surely, time exists at some level. Surely, the world is to some degree linear. There is a progression from one stage to the next. You might say that the entire world view we have given you is that the Creator starts by creating a void and then it creates a process whereby co-creators fill that void—and that is an entirely linear process. From that perspective, you could say that you can look at time as a progression from one stage to the next where one stage creates a certain manifestation that sets the foundation for further development, which then happens at the next stage. If you look at time this way, then certainly time exists. What I wanted you or people in general to contemplate with the statement that: "Time is not," is that time is not necessarily exactly the way that you currently see it with the consciousness that is "normal" on earth. It is not quite as linear, as set in stone, as unavoidable, as unchangeable as you normally perceive it.

One aspect of this is the entire teaching we have given you on how to get rid of these separate selves and therefore heal your four lower bodies. We might say that at some point in the distant past, you experienced a birth trauma and that moment is no longer there, that moment has moved on. You are now in a different time but you are carrying the birth trauma with you. You are still affected by it because the later moments, the moments that came after that birth trauma, were given a certain direction by the birth trauma. Everything that came after, builds on the birth trauma.

If you could not change time, if you could not change the past, if you did not have a time machine (where you could go back in the past where you could resolve that birth trauma), how could you ever be free of it? You see that at the very moment that the Creator gave co-creators free will, in order to exercise their free will, there had to be a linear progression, which is what you call time. That way, co-creators could see that when they project a certain image onto the Ma-ter Light, after some time the Ma-ter Light outpictures it as physical circumstances. Those physical circumstances do not just disappear after a split second but can exist for a period of what you call time.

In order to exercise free will, there has to be time so that certain manifestations can be maintained. However, in order to make sure that free will does not become a self-limiting system (where you gradually create consequences for yourselves that you carry with you over time and they become so severe that pretty soon you have no options left, you have no free will), in order to avoid this scenario, time cannot go in just one direction. There has to be a way for you to go back and change the past. Two million years ago there might have been a physical situation where you were exposed to the birth trauma, but the positive aspect of time is that time has moved on. That physical situation is no longer there.

That is a grace because (contrary to what science fiction writers want you to believe), you cannot build a physical machine that goes back to a physical situation that happened two million years ago and now you are physically back there and can make physical changes. This cannot be done. This will never be possible but what you *can* do is that you can create a time machine in your mind. Mother Mary, (in her exercise where she takes you through the seven gardens back to the theatre where your birth trauma happened), she actually gave you such a time machine so you can go back to the situation where the situation still exists. The situation does not exist in the physical but it does exist in your emotional, mental and identity bodies. [This exercise is in the book *Healing Your Spiritual Traumas*.]

You can go back in a time machine through those bodies, dissolve the traces that are left there, the matrices, the limitations, the selves, whatever you want to call it. You dissolve that and now you have changed your past even though time has moved on. You have changed your past. By getting rid of your primal self, you are no longer the same person as you were when your very sense of identity and the way you thought about life and the way you felt about life was colored by that primal self. You have become a new being in Christ. That is at least one level of why I say that time is not. Time is not something that is a fixed quantity.

Now, in terms of free will, there has always been a discussion, both amongst spiritual people and among philosophers. For example, religious people will say: "If God is all-knowing, then God must know the end from the beginning. God must know what is going to be the ultimate outcome of the universe before he even started the process of creating the universe. And if God knows everything that's going to happen, how can a human being have free will?"

The answer to that is that this is a flawed vision of God, a flawed image of God, created by the fallen beings precisely to create this kind of confusion. God is not all-knowing in the sense that God knew exactly how everything was going to unfold. God knew certain overall things but not all of the details. God has actually said, the Creator has said: "I am giving you free will. I am giving you the ability to surprise me." So from a traditional viewpoint, God is not all-knowing.

You can even take materialists who say that everything is determined by laws of nature. You had the old image that the world is like a big clock and if you knew everything about the initial conditions of how the world started, then you could, by knowing the laws of nature, determine exactly where the world will be at any point in the future. You could predict the future if you knew the initial conditions and the laws of nature. This is also completely incorrect because a materialistic view does not incorporate free will and does not incorporate the fact that the physical universe is just the effects of what is happening in the three higher bodies. Physical manifestation is a product of what is happening at the level of consciousness.

Consciousness comes before the physical manifestation, as we have said. These views are simply incorrect. You *do* have free will.

What you do one minute from now is not known by God, is not determined by God, is not limited by God, nor is it limited by the laws of nature. You can look at a certain person, his psychological state, look at the separate selves he has and you can with very high probability predict what that person is going to do one minute from now. Nevertheless, over time you cannot know if that person chooses to change. Even if people do not know anything about ascended master teachings, they can still make the choice: "I've had enough of this kind of experience. Why am I doing this over and over again? I'm going to choose to change. I'm going to stop this."

Throughout history, people have made these kinds of choices and it is what has bought them forward personally and what has bought civilization forward. Once you understand the separate selves, you can remove those selves, you can let them die and then, for each self you let die, you can have a more free will. You *have* free will, but you can only choose the options you can see. The options you can see right now depends on your entire four lower bodies, the separate selves, the colorings you have. Some of these separate selves will block out many options so you simply cannot see them, and if you cannot see an option, you cannot choose it. Ultimately, free will and awareness are very much tied together. You could say you always have free will to choose the options you can see at your present level of consciousness. You only have a will that is as free as what you can see.

Definitely, free will is a reality and any philosophy, any thought system, that denies free will or seeks to restrict free will by some factor over which you have no potential to take control, any such system springs from the minds of the fallen beings. We are not saying that all people who promote such systems are fallen beings, but the original ideas sprang from the minds of the fallen beings. Their primary concern is not to limit the size of the population but to limit the choices that the population can make or rather that individuals can make. They want to limit your free will.

www.ingramcontent.com/pod-product-compliance
Lightning Source LLC
Chambersburg PA
CBHW030519230426
43665CB00010B/686